Wisps of Violence

Wisps of Violence

Producing Public and Private Politics in the Turn-of-the-Century British Novel

EILEEN SYPHER

VERSO
London · New York

First published by Verso 1993

Verso
UK: 6 Meard Street, London W1V 3HR
USA: 29 West 35th Street, New York, NY 10001-2291

Verso is the imprint of New Left Books

ISBN 0-86091-436-4

British Library Cataloguing in Publication Data
A catalogue record for this book is available from the British Library

Library of Congress Cataloging-in-Publication Data
A catalogue record for this book is available from the Library of Congress

Printed and bound in Great Britain by Bookcraft (Bath) Ltd

To my mother and the memory of my father

Contents

Acknowledgements

Like every book, this one was not a solitary undertaking, however much it may have felt so for much of the time. My gratitude goes to my friends and colleagues at George Mason University who supported me in numerous, often subtle ways throughout this process. I thank Devon Hodges, Michelle Massé, John Radner, Patrick Story, and Jan Cohn for their always helpful comments on particular chapters. Many conversations with Hans Bergmann, Terry Comito, and Lorna Irvine subtly shaped the final product. Roy Rosenzweig both suggested invaluable contacts and helped me comprehend the preparation of camera-ready copy. The university provided me with grant money to acquire copies of the Margaret Harkness material, made available a wonderful computer support services center and Mary Blackwell, Sandy Slater, and Anne Bonanno in particular, and funded much needed research time.

I would also like to thank Margaret Mikesell, Epifanio San Juan, and Anthony Ugolnik for the large insight, encouragement, and practical criticism they have offered of my work over the years; Susan Gibson (Sharpe) for sharing with me her ideas and dissertation on women's suffrage and the novel; and Joyce Bellamy and Deborah Nord for helping me track down information on Margaret Harkness.

Without the support of three people in particular, however, this book would not be at all. I will always be especially indebted to my friend and colleague Deborah Kaplan. Over the years she has spent countless hours not only discussing larger concepts with me, but reading and weighing with me every word of many drafts. Her generous patience, warm encouragement, and just criticisms thoroughly inform this undertaking.

I am also deeply indebted to Michael Sprinker, who encouraged this project from the very first piece of it that he read, an earlier version of the chapter on William Morris's *News from Nowhere* which he accepted for *the minnesota review*. Subsequently, over the years, he offered substantive suggestions for revisions, often engaging me on my interpretations of what an Althusserian/Machereyan critical reading could look like, and then staunchly championed the finished manuscript through its final stages.

Above all, I thank my husband John Yrchik for not only sustaining my will to finish, but also devoting incalculable hours to discussing ideas with me, reading my drafts, polishing my style, and patiently teaching me the ways of the computer.

To my first family, my grandparents, my brother, and my mother and father to whom I dedicate this book, I will always be grateful for all they have given.

Earlier versions of these chapters have appeared as essays in *the minnesota review*, *Turn-of-the-Century Women*, *The Henry James Review*, and *Literature and History* and I thank the editors for their permission to include the revisions here.

1

Producing "Politics" in the Turn-of-the-Century Novel

"I should hate it more if I didn't also find it interesting," Henry James wrote to Thomas Sargeant Perry in 1883–84. "The air is full of events, of changes, of movement" (Edel 1962, 84). James was referring to the rumblings of social unrest he heard all around him as he wandered through London. A short time later, fueled by an economic depression during the period 1884–87 that was more prolonged and widespread than previous slumps (Jones, 281), these rumblings erupted. A series of public events shocked, terrified, even fascinated a broad spectrum of the middle and upper classes, and created an audience for a fiction that would let them release their complex feelings by offering them ways of managing them. For these events made visible both the vast size of the impoverished, restive "underclass" and the emergence of new powerful collectivist political ideologies, such as socialism. Not only were traditional middle-class strategies for dealing with the problem of poverty—namely blaming the individual's morality and recommending charity for the worthy—unworkable,[1] but more terrifying, or for some compelling, a radically new social organization was being proposed. Revolution, the possibility of both destroying and cleansing, was in the air.

To recall some of the more public events: in a highly publicized incident that illuminated the newly emerging socialism, supported by a number of leading British figures, William Morris was scandalously arrested in September of 1885 and brought before the dock. He was accused of disorderly conduct at a trial in which several of his Socialist League colleagues were given fines and hard labor for "obstruction," or demonstrating in public. In early 1886, during an exceptionally severe winter, violence openly erupted in what Morris later called the "first skirmish of the Revolution" (Jones, 294). Another, larger socialist group (from which Morris's League had recently split off), the Social Democratic Federation, or SDF, interrupted a demonstration of the unemployed in Trafalgar Square. As the SDF led the crowd out of the square with the intention of dispersal, rioting broke out. The crowd smashed windows, looted shops, and overturned carriages (Jones, 291–2). The West End feared that "the East End was marching through the fog" towards it (Thompson, 406). The rioting of early 1886 and the general hysteria it provoked abated after a time. Nevertheless, British workers and the unemployed became even more organized, demonstrating and striking. Socialist ideas were more frequently bandied about in public, if not seriously adopted.

As the depression worsened during the fall of 1887, tensions again peaked and police brutality against the demonstrating unemployed escalated. On November 13, as thousands turned out to demonstrate in Trafalgar Square, three were killed and two hundred injured in what came to be known as "Bloody Sunday." This event disabused many socialists of any naive ideas that a revolution could be quickly and painlessly won, although it did not stop labor on its march nor quiet middle-class fears. What Gareth Stedman Jones terms the "cathartic release" (315) from such tensions of the mid 1880s was the great dock strike of 1889, which, in E. P. Thompson's words, "set the movement of the unskilled aflame throughout the country" (528). The union to emerge from this strike also eventually worked to divide the British poor into "respectable workers" and a "casual residuum," allaying middle-class fears of revolution and drawing, in fact, their support of the trade union movement as preferable to revolution (Jones, 319–21). As the union movement became institutionalized in British society it also drew much of the steam from a socialist movement which had, throughout, largely failed to support the union movement from within (Thompson, 530) and which was in any case already weakened seriously by internal divisions.

During the 1880s and 1890s, "respectable" London was also terrified by the activities of foreign-born anarchists, who had sought refuge in England following the failed revolutions on the Continent. The popular press magnified and distorted anarchist activities, although anarchists committed no terrorist acts and although anarchism was very much more on the "fringe" of British radical politics than was socialism. Many people at the time, however, including Henry James and Joseph Conrad, could not or would not either see through the press's distortion or make any distinction between anarchism and socialism. Two of the more salient examples of reported anarchist activities engaged James's and Conrad's imaginations. The first event, extensively reported in magazines in 1884, was the discovery of an alleged plot by two conspirators to assassinate the German emperor on his visit to England. One of the conspirators, a youth of twenty-one, apparently had a change of heart. This incident was the likely occasion for James's *The Princess Casamassima*, although James's protagonist, bookbinder Hyacinth Robinson, seems also drawn from the leading anarchist figure at this time, bookbinder Johann Most. The other event, the only one that resulted in a death, involved Marcel Bourdin, a Frenchman, who in 1894 blew himself up in Greenwich Park—on his way, the press argued, to blow up the Greenwich Observatory. Conrad himself acknowledges that this latter story was the kernel for *The Secret Agent*.[2]

While the 1880s and 1890s were marked by the increased visibility of public political activities associated with socialism and anarchism, trouble surfaced on another front in the early decades of the twentieth century. Among political radicals throughout the nineteenth century were a number of people vocal in their criticism of the position of women (Rowbotham 1973, 39). By the 1880s socialists were violently split in their view of "the woman question." On the one hand the leadership of the SDF and some other non-Marxist socialists argued for postponing "the woman question" as a secondary concern, or even for leaving the family just as it was. On the other hand, a number of socialists, among them Friedrich Engels and Eleanor Marx, argued both for elaborating the connection between the oppression of women in the family and the exploitation of workers and for actively supporting women's emancipation. Many middle-class feminists became militant through their connection with, first, the mid-century radical and, later, the turn-of-the-century socialist movements. Sheila Rowbotham argues that even in the early years of the twentieth century the connection between feminism and socialism remained close. But the "divorce between the two [which began during this period] was long, painful, and protracted" (1973, 79). Some feminists were not always willing to trust the socialists to emancipate them. Others were not willing to go as far as socialists in their analysis of the origin or cure for women's oppression—revolution. Separate political groups of women, both socialist and nonsocialist, began to emerge. In 1904, facing yet another defeat of their attempts to secure the vote, which many believed would open the door to other legal and economic reforms, women took to the streets. For the next decade, until the movement was eventually forced underground because of its increasing militancy, large numbers of middle-class women were, for the first time in history, to receive jail sentences and endure brutal, life-threatening forced feedings for demonstrating, breaking windows, wrecking letter boxes, and starting fires. Though the disagreements among women, as among socialists, over goals and strategies widened before World War I, the women's movement at the turn of the century had, Rowbotham argues, a subtle and wide-ranging effect on developing "interest in a new consciousness among men and women" (1973, 103).

Twentieth-century historians of turn-of-the-century Britain, the years roughly spanning 1880 to World War I with which this book is concerned, typically sum up this period as one of extreme turbulence. Eric Hobsbawm hauntingly sketches these years as ones of "uneasiness, of disorientation, of tension . . . years of political breakdown . . . years when wisps of violence hung in the English air," wisps which persisted right up to the moment the war came "as a respite from crisis, a diversion, perhaps even as some sort of solution" (193). Jones calls the political crisis precipitated in the 1880s more "deep-rooted and more comprehensive" than the crisis provoked by the Reform Bills of mid century (281). And Raymond Williams characterizes this period as being an "identifiable . . . new phase of our history" (121), in which being "English," sharing any sense of a national identity, became problematic. The traditional English collective sense of "self" was disrupted both by the breaking down of class and gender lines and by the dissolution of identifiable inside/outside boundaries as more "outsiders" came to England and as England went "out" to become a colonizer.

This book is not, however, concerned with exploring in any detail such late-twentieth-century interpretations of this period, interpretations produced from within the discourse of history. This discourse certainly must be acknowledged, for it subtly influences the reader of literature who is curious about literature's relationship to history; the discourse operates as a kind of filter, foregrounding certain issues and, more pervasively, offering particular structuring paradigms that the reader inevitably brings to the interpretation of the literary text. But the task of this book is the very different one of trying to study literature historically by beginning "at the other end" from the study of the reigning historical discourse (insofar as such an "other end" exists). Using the critical theory of Pierre Macherey as a stimulus, this book "begins" historical interpretation with the literary text. Accordingly, the book does not extensively foreground either the historiography (and the period's political history has been amply studied[3]) or the reigning paradigms which could affect readers (and the latter would be a particularly innovative and important study). Instead, this book focuses on the period's own complex consciousness (and unconsciousness) of political agitation as it is produced within the discourse of the novel—that largely middle-class literary genre which attempts to negotiate social contradictions at the level of what Henry James called "felt" life.

Non-literary discourse of this period, such as newspapers and magazines, both foregrounds its middle-class readers' terror—and fascination—with the unstable political situation, and then seeks to control these feelings. The reader is routinely positioned in these documents as voyeur of an invoked "other" (the poor, the political activist), who is copiously described. Then the threat of that other is defused through varying strategies. An example of this is Charles Booth's monumental and influential detailed study of London's urban poor, *Life and Labour of the People in London*, a study undertaken between 1885 and the late 1890s. Booth, a politically conservative businessman, set out to disprove growing reports in leftist newspapers such as the *Pall Mall Gazette* that one of four Londoners lived in abject poverty—statistics which, if true, augured ill for the quelling of revolutionary sentiments. Booth's exhaustive study of London poverty, an enterprise in which he was helped by his young cousin Beatrice Webb, revealed that the leftists had, if anything, underestimated the situation. Closer to 35 percent of the population lived below the "poverty line" (a concept he developed). Booth's statistics clearly alarmed his readership, who could now no longer either dismiss poverty as the consequence of an individual's lack of initiative or hope to alleviate poverty in any significant way through charity. Yet Booth's statistical method and objective reporting serve to position as "other" the very poor whose humanity he occasionally recognizes. His text even goes beyond this in attempting to contain the frightening material it has made visible: Booth interrupts his report periodically to urge his readers not to be alarmed.[4]

A more ephemeral yet similarly typical example of obsessive scrutinizing (and then distancing), this time of political disturbances, is London's conservative newspaper *The Times*' series of articles, beginning on February 16, 1894, on the alleged attempt to bomb the Greenwich

Observatory. Finding a blown-up body of a man on a path leading to the observatory, reporters claimed to have "discovered" an anarchist conspiracy. In response to the incident, *The Times*, a relatively short paper by modern standards (with only four or so pages devoted to news reports), ran a two-week long series of articles on anarchism. The first few articles go into almost tabloid-like detail about the blown-up body. The articles first urge the reader to gaze closely at the man's wounds, reports of which are contested by various examiners. Then the shock is amplified: the articles tour the immediate periphery of the scene: who saw him? What were their reactions? Why didn't the gardener react more visibly? What did the surgeon say? Following this evocation of shock, the articles move to control the event, to assign blame, even to situate the problem outside of England. The brother is interviewed: what could have been the victim's motives? Reporters then root out the man's friends, who they allege belong to an anarchist club. The final strategy *The Times* uses to manage this event, now magnified in discourse with the reader positioned as outsider, as voyeur, is to shift the blame from England to France, generally perceived to be the seedbed of anarchist activity. After covering the response from abroad, the articles end with a series of detailed reports on various individuals on trial for disruptive and criminal acts in Paris. The state has, *The Times* assures the reader, remained intact and in control. Yet, at the same time, the newspaper has inadvertently met, even perhaps magnified, the public's need for horrid details of an event that has terrified it—an event so disturbing that Joseph Conrad over a decade later was to make some version of it the centerpiece for *The Secret Agent*.

But what of novelistic discourse at this time? One would expect, from the above examples of nonliterary discourse, numerous powerful novels that foreground what Yeats, ambivalent like James about political agitation, called a "terrible beauty" ("Easter 1916"). One would expect a number of British *Germinal*s, novels thick with representations of the clashes on the streets and discussions of various political strategies, even as the mid-century industrial, "condition-of-England" novels examined the new factory life and proposed solutions for its improvement. One would expect, in other words, an overt acknowledgement in this fiction of the enormity of this even more serious crisis—a crisis in the very viability of the entire British economic, political, social, and domestic order. One looks to find powerful examples of the kinds of novels often marginalized in literary criticism: "political" novels.

* * *

The "political" novel is a slippery generic category. Often the term is used to designate tendentious novels, novels which argue overtly for a particular political perspective (such as Richard Wright's *Native Son* or Upton Sinclair's *The Jungle*). Sometimes, however, the term is used to designate more broadly all novels which foreground a public political arena (such as Turgenev's *On the Eve*). In addition to these problems concerning the term's shifting referent, however, there are even more serious problems concerning the very labeling of some and not other novels as "political." Fredric Jameson argues against making such a generic distinction of "political" novel because, he says, all texts are "'in the last analysis' political" (20). In separating public from private, the distinction reinforces "the reification and privatization of contemporary life" (20). All novels, he argues, can be made to reveal a narrative of history which always involves political conflict. From a specifically feminist vantage point, one can go further to argue that isolating a group of novels as political, which usually means novels about the public and so usually masculine sphere of activity, could imply that novels which are primarily about the private, domestic, and feminine sphere are not then really about "politics," and so are not really about important, socially constructed arrangements. Nancy Armstrong argues that novels which foreground the domestic sphere only *appear* apolitical to us because the novel itself worked to *make* this division between the personal and the political. The middle-class project for the novel was to define first the female and later the home as an ahistorical, apolitical, and so stable emblem of timeless middle-class values. The novel, in other words, strenuously worked to "suppress other oppositions" than those of gender; it "translated the complex and competing ways of representing human identity into a single binary opposition represented by male versus female" (253).

Granted that all novels must be designated "political" in this largest sense, in that all are implicated in the power struggle that informs every area of human life, it can, nonetheless, be extremely revealing to isolate novels written during the same period which allude to public sphere politics, however topical, however superficial the novels' imagination of "politics" may be. The critic can then interpret these novels' historical limits of signification. What and how much do such novels allow to be spoken about the discourse and practice of public sphere politics? What clarifications, resolutions, or even exacerbations to yet unsolved public issues do the novels produce? What is not or cannot be spoken? What happens when one reads intertextually a number of such novels, drawn from any one time period and locale? How do the resulting resonances affect the reading of any single novel?

Even more importantly for the present project, how do such novels imagine the relations between the "public" and "private" arenas? How are "woman," "the home," and "sexuality" defined in these novels? What function do they have within the novels' projects? For example, does the domestic arena mirror the public arena? Is it contiguous with it? Or is it, as it was in mid century, a refuge from the public arena? Such questions are particularly significant because the novels considered in this book, in variously condemning or advocating the new radical politics, occupy the "ideological frontier" in that they probe a character or characters who question at least some dimensions of the reigning ideology. What happens in the most intimate space in these novels, that of men's and women's domestic relations, can be read as a kind of index of the novels' radicalness, since the private sphere has by the turn of the century already had a long history of being represented as an ahistorical, apolitical space. Have private, intimate relations in these novels, in other words, been radically interrogated as well as public ones? Do these novels, in other words, reveal in their political unconscious, if not on their politically conscious level, that the private arena and the figure of woman, who has for some years brooded over it, is as political, as socially constructed, and as changeable as the ownership of the means of production?

Turn-of-the-century Britain, however, produced no *Germinal* nor even any novel like Elizabeth Gaskell's *Mary Barton* or *North and South*, no novel which begins to detail in any large and sustained manner the political strife that characterized the period, no novel thick with topical allusions to current history. In the handful of novels written at the turn of the century that do represent characters engaged in public political activity, many of which will be interpreted in the chapters to come, such "politics" are represented far out toward the margins, decentered from the main plot which usually foregrounds the private relations between men and women in domestic life. If the violence on the streets can be accurately characterized as "wisps," the "political" as it is produced in these novels is one step removed from this—a snapshot, an embarrassed aside, even more of a "wisp." Although the novels are occasionally sprinkled with historically specific signifiers (such as the names of the socialist factions), the signifiers aren't elaborated. Characters, such as

James's Hyacinth in *The Princess Casamassima*, usually go offstage to political meetings. If they stay onstage, then the political character is not always the "real thing"; the central anarchist in Conrad's *The Secret Agent*, for example, is an agent provocateur and the rest of his anarchists are inept, impotent has-beens. Characters, like James's Hyacinth or Bernard Shaw's Sidney Trefusis in one of his early novels, *An Unsocial Socialist*, do profess belief in their different causes, but the novels focus on the anxiety or embarrassment the character feels—a far cry from, say, Turgenev's respectful if distanced handling of Insarov's beliefs in *On the Eve*. Labor conflicts are rarely, if ever, plotted or even hinted at. They occur offstage in both Shaw's novel and in George Gissing's *Demos*, which was a novel the middle class welcomed as a source of information about contemporary politics. Strikes are represented in some novels, such as in the now forgotten novel by Margaret Harkness, *George Eastmont: Wanderer*, but never in detail, and they never structure the narrative as in *Germinal*. The plots, in fact, typically avoid extensive reporting of violent public confrontations and instead foreground the individual's story. The crowd's jeering and taunting of Gissing's protagonist, Richard Mutimer, in *Demos* pales beside Zola's description of the mob scene in *Germinal*. Even Elizabeth Robins's novel, *The Convert*, which sustains a focus on open-air meetings about women's suffrage, represents none of the movement's violence. Though one such violent moment does emerge in H. G. Wells's *Ann Veronica*, it is quickly swept offstage, situated as a mere phase in Ann's recognition that she is not a feminist after all. The only novel which provides a sustained narrative of political events, in this case of the 1880s, is William Morris's utopian novel, *News from Nowhere*. But this narrative is pushed to the background, situated as part of the "history" of the old world that no one in utopia cares to listen to.[5]

Novels produced by middle-class writers in this moment in British history, in short, do not, like some nonliterary discourse, invoke (through overt representation) in order to attempt to manage the public's fear of disturbance and revolution. The oddity of this comparative "underrepresentation" in turn-of-the-century fiction of public sphere politics appears more forcefully if we briefly consider the example of mid-century industrial fiction. Two recent studies of this fiction, Rosemarie Bodenheimer's *The Politics of Story in Victorian Social Fiction* and Catherine Gallagher's *The Industrial Reformation of English Fiction: Social Discourse and Narrative Form, 1832–1867*, trace the close links between the fictional and nonfictional discourse of industrialism. Gallagher argues that the very form of the novel changed in response to the condition-of-England debate because some of the issues raised unsettled assumptions upon which earlier novels were based. The industrial novel both reflected the issues in this debate and simultaneously held them up for critical scrutiny, revealing their various paradoxes. Bodenheimer observes that mid-century narratives are

> full of description and dialogue about the factory system, industrial and rural poverty, working-class politics, and the plight of women; they link themselves directly with the condition-of-England debate that preoccupied so many public-minded Victorians during that critical period. (4)

Bodenheimer is not thereby claiming that these novels are necessarily "realistic" in their representation of the mid-century crisis; in fact a number of them might appear to the realist critic as deflections. Rather, what Bodenheimer is arguing is that the mid-century novel is "directly linked" with the debates, that the novels, however "inaccurate," are visibly part of the mid-century discourse on industrialism.[6]

The question that vexes the present inquiry is *why* the even greater deflection from public political issues in the middle-class turn-of-the-century novel. Why don't the novels more overtly feature the conflicts and attempt to control them? This is a question whose answer I can only begin to sketch here.

Such a question, of course, can be tackled from a number of vantage points. One of these is the vantage point of the general social and political ideology at the turn of the century, those large and subtle ways in which people conceive of the world. Georg Lukács's broad conception of this historical moment is one of the most cogent: toward the end of the nineteenth century, at the beginnings of modern capitalism, the institutions of society seem no longer "up for grabs." They have become "reified" in Lukács's terms, seemingly outside of human agency. In their apparent naturalness, the institutions have become, thus, more *invisible*, and so not readily identifiable as a problem. Fiction is affected: whereas Dickens could attack Chancery or the schools or the poor laws in mid century, such "institutions" all but disappear from the fictional horizon by the end of the century. Raymond Williams, studying the British novel in *From Dickens to Lawrence*, explains this phenomenon of disappearance in a somewhat different but related way. He argues that because the social canvas had become larger because "war," "imperialism," "poverty," and "revolution"— the events and terms of this era—cannot be known directly and particularly, an unfortunate split in consciousness develops between the "social" and the "personal." The "social" then becomes a pejorative adjective when applied to the novel because it signals the concept of art as a vehicle. The "personal," on the other hand, comes to be defined as all that is good and human—and the appropriate focus of an autonomous art.

Another related feature of this general ideology, one which helps explain why even those novels sympathetic to the notion of a radical change don't openly describe and attack social institutions, is the prevalence of theories of determinism. These theories were codified by Darwin and appear, nascently, in certain interpretations of Marx. Socialists, too, believed in the inevitability of change, and specifically in the "natural" decay of capitalism. Social institutions, like other organisms, were subject to the inexorable laws of dissolution. Socialists at this time generally believed that once these institutions had become unfit, one need only wait the process out, since it had become patently obvious that capitalism was "unfit" to manage the present crisis. Furthermore, the millennium seemed at hand. Applauding revolution in the abstract or producing utopian visions of life under socialism, both of which are routes taken by those sympathetic to change, is more to the point, therefore, than cataloging numerous social ills or criticizing specific social institutions in the hope that they might be reformed at this late date. While of all the socialist groups the Fabians (to which Shaw belonged) took the "longest view" (a position which, as we shall see when we read Shaw, affects the entire structure of his novel), the other groups were also optimistic about the inevitability of the coming of socialism. They quarreled only over the means of helping or possibly even hastening the process. It is only when novelists also know poverty that their novels represent social conditions more fully and urge more immediate action. For Margaret Harkness, who worked in and wrote about the East End, the Salvation Army at times seemed more attractive than the socialist movement because it at least tried to help the poor.

A consideration of the period's general ideology begins to help answer the question "why" this underrepresentation at the turn of the century. Yet considering the particular pressures exerted by novelistic convention also helps account for the underrepresentation. Armstrong argues that in the early years of the nineteenth century the novel began to be targeted by the middle class as the place where "apolitical truths could be told" (21). And the site of this "truth" was the private, domestic sphere, the terrain of sexuality. At the turn of the century, what the novel "should be" is highly contested, as a full-blown discourse on the theory of the novel begins to emerge. This time the desirable novel is defined somewhat differently, although it is still ahistorical and private rather than historical and public.

In the 1880s and 1890s public debates were waged in the magazines and courtrooms over naturalism. In the early decades of the twentieth century James and H. G. Wells were to go at the same issue (an issue to be recapitulated in somewhat different terms later in Virginia Woolf's argument with Arnold Bennett). These debates reveal not only dissension over the representation of public politics in any large-scale way in the novel but, considering the temper of the debate, also reveal that both "sides" were anxious about the question. The debate is not directly focused on the question, "to what extent should public political disruption be represented in the novel?" I think however that a plausible argument can be made that this issue was at least one of the subtexts of a debate whose major terms, as Gallagher has described them, were (historical) "fact" versus (timeless) "value."

Between 1885 and 1895, large segments of the British literary and reading public attacked French naturalism (though the sales of Zola and Flaubert, then appearing in translation, continued to be brisk). What critics attacked (as revealed in various magazine articles on the issue) was twofold: (1) naturalism's absorption in "fact," which was seen as implying that human action had its roots in social and organic forces rather than in human will; and, (2) naturalism's frankness about sexual details. Both tendencies, the British critics argued, destroyed faith in the power of human will and corrupted ideals of manhood and womanhood.[7] Another way of interpreting this issue is that the real concern was the detailed representation of the lives of a large number of people from the "underworld," of the poor, of prostitutes, miners, and the like, people whose representation in fiction challenged prevailing assumptions about the source of social unrest—what if it were the social system itself?—as well as bourgeois ideals of gender roles. The issue was so sensitive that it was fought out in the courts as well as the press. A "National Vigilance Association" launched a crusade against Henry Vizetelly, publisher of the French translations (as well as Margaret Harkness's publisher), with the result that Vizetelly first had to edit out large portions of Zola's novels and then, after a subsequent attack by the Association, was jailed for three months. Ironically, a number of British novelists, among them James, Gissing, and George Moore, the latter two of whom were popular, adopted some of the tendencies of naturalism, particularly its rejection of sentimentality (though never its sexual frankness). James, for example, says in his 1884 essay, "The Art of Fiction," that the novel should be inclusive of *all* life, including the ugly and the sad. One cannot proscribe any "raw materials" for a novel. He then, however, goes on to qualify this by saying that the novelist should, on the other hand, show "taste," that some "données" are "richer" than others and that one shouldn't read or discuss novels whose subject one doesn't like. Such anxieties about appropriate "facts" for fiction were so widespread and persistent that even twenty-five years later Conrad, in his preface to *The Secret Agent*, tried to defend himself from those who would read in his very representation of sordid characters and situations his approval of them.

James's argument with Wells over the next two decades continues the debate over "absorption in fact" and develops another line of argument: whether there should be a particular form for the novel. The discussion of both of these issues, fact and form, occurs within a larger discussion of what the function of the novel is.

Wells argues that the novel's function is to discuss "the great majority of the problems which are being raised in such bristling multitude by our contemporary social development." The novel must discuss these issues, argues Wells, because the novel is the only "medium" available. If the discussion does not take place in this medium, there will be less "sympathy," less "cooperation" among individuals and classes—a sympathy necessary if we are to get beyond the "confused discomforts and uneasiness of today." The novel for Wells, in short, is

> to be the social mediator, the vehicle of understanding, the instrument of self-examination, the parade of morals and the exchange of manners, the factory of customs, the criticism of laws and institutions and of social dogmas and ideas.

This does not mean that the novelist will teach. Rather "he . . . will discuss, point out, plead, and display" (Edel 1959, 148–55). Wells here implicitly argues that the novel should be as inclusive as possible in representing details about others' lives, so that the reader can become sympathetically connected. And he says that the form of this novel should be absolutely "free," unprescribed. David Lodge attempts to rescue one of Wells's novels, *Tono Bungay*, from the kinds of criticisms James would make of it, i.e. that "it is picaresque, full of apparent digressions in the form both of episodes, and of expository comment on politics, economics, history, and society. It is told in the first person. . . . Its characters are largely . . . 'flat'" (215). Lodge argues that it is precisely Wells's "free" form for this novel which prevents both its story line and its characters from becoming the center (as James prefers), and which, rather, allows the "frame"—the whole of the British social organism—to come to the foreground (215–18).

James, on the other hand, argues that Wells (and Bennett) are too "saturated" in the actual so that the novel loses its coherent center of interest. He claims he does not want to "undervalue the particular acquainted state, that of saturation and possession," but rather that such acquaintance constitutes only one half of the novelist's "authority." The other half rests in the quality of what the novelist does with this saturation. For James the "actual" is not really what is of interest. The novel should not be in thrall to the facts. Rather, novels need to create coherent, defined centers of interest. The reader needs the novelist to select so that the "general or inferential meaning" is "marked." For James this selection and marking does not mean, say, that the writer takes a particular political stand, but rather that he "sets" his light somewhere from which he can see the more general, more universal aspects of the situation (Edel 1959, 183–213).

James, in short, privileges a perceiving consciousness, whereas Wells privileges the wealth of facts drawn from the social world. For James the novel helps the reader "just" to "see" life, which means, for him, more the individual life than the life of the body politic. The perceiving consciousness, the author/narrator, or, later, one of James's centers of consciousness, the human making meaning, perceiving, or establishing coherence, is what is central. For Wells, the novel helps one understand specific social problems and stimulates at least the extension of human sympathy, if not also actually stimulating one to act politically. Stephen Spender, in *The Struggle of the Modern* (1963), contrasts the two writers in this somewhat oversimplified if cogent way: some, like Wells (along with Shaw, Bennett, and Orwell), believe in the possibility of social change and view the novel as an instrument in this struggle. Others, like James (along with Woolf, Eliot, and Joyce), despair of social change and view the novel as a vehicle for probing and sustaining the primacy of the inner, individual life (Lodge, 243–4).

It was Wells, and not James, who was popular at this time, a situation to be shortly reversed at least among academics, for whom both James's writings and his views about the novel were to become canonized. Yet the very public staging of such debates about fiction had effects not only on Wells and James's friendship, which was to cease, but more importantly on their fiction itself. Each was, to some extent, affected by the other's criticisms. Wells couldn't pull off a large-scale representation of public politics in all of his novels because he was attracted to foregrounding a character who "organizes" the story (as in, say, *Ann Veronica*). On the other hand, James could not confidently maintain the integrity of the perceiving consciousness in the face of a public politics which disrupted such integrity (as in, say, *The Princess Casamassima*). Each, to some extent, became the other's mirror—and brake.

The underrepresentation of the public sphere in turn-of-the-century fiction can be partly explained by the general ideology in the period and by these debates over the nature of the novel. Yet I think there is another, perhaps even more cogent explanation that can be offered, one that is suggested by Bodenheimer's way of interpreting plotting in the mid-nineteenth-century novel. Broadly influenced by Fredric Jameson's concept of the novel as a discourse which enacts strategies that attempt to manage social contradictions, Bodenheimer's book implies that the confrontation with industrialism in the middle-class mid-century novel goes hand in hand with particular strategies which attempt to control what was threatening about industrialism for that novel's middle-class reader. Put another way, without the strategies, the industrial novel might not have existed.

These strategies, however, are not chosen by the individual writer; they are not to be had for the asking. They are, rather, socially available ways of thinking, seeing, and feeling which work to maintain stability. In short, they are ideology. Uncomfortable with the broad term "ideology," Jameson, however, invents a new word to denote the "minimal 'units'" of a "larger class discourse": "ideologemes." One can speak, then, of a particular narrative paradigm as an ideologeme, as emitting "ideological message[s] in its own right without the mediation of authorial intervention" (87–8).

Carrying this argument to turn-of-the-century novels, I would suggest that perhaps the reason these later novels do not so openly confront public politics is that there were no workable ideologemes with which to manage either its threat or its promise, depending on one's position. There were no strategies, I would suggest, because this period was so turbulent on a number of fronts that there was not yet time for ideological management. The most familiar strategy for containing the threat of political disruption—a particular concept of woman—was now in disarray. On the other hand, the modernist strategy, described by James, of investing an integrated, "personal" organizing consciousness with stability, had not yet fully evolved.

Bodenheimer identifies at least two managing strategies mid-century fiction employs, strategies which turn-of-the-century novelists attempt, unsuccessfully, to resurrect. One is the concept of paternalism. Paternalism, as both Bodenheimer and David Roberts describe it, celebrates an older, allegedly humane hierarchical social arrangement in which the poor and the weak are "protected," rather than merely used, by those above them. Brontë's *Shirley* invokes this concept of a better kind of hierarchical relationship to criticize the evils of current utilitarian industrial employer–worker relations. The other socially available strategy is to invoke the pastoral, a pre-industrial refuge from the evils of urban capitalism. Dickens's *Oliver Twist*, for example, contrasts a pastoral haven with the evils of the urban system of social exchange symbolized by Fagin and his gang. The pastoral represents the realm of freedom, contrasted with the deterministic world of the city. Bodenheimer observes that invoking the pastoral in mid-century fiction works either to erase or transform the urban industrial landscape.

What is crucial about Bodenheimer's study of these strategies, however, is that both are activated by women. It is women who teach forgotten paternalist values to industrial men, as in Gaskell's *North and South*. It is women who typically invoke the pastoral haven. Women, Bodenheimer argues, are able to occupy this position of rescuer in the novels because of their position within the economy. Ideologically, and in the case of middle-class women economically as well, positioned "outside" of the industrial world, women occupied the social position of guardian of what had now become the "other," "private" world of the home.[8] And this "home," "traditional" in nature, connected readily with both the paternalist and pastoral ideologies. This unique position of women (as opposed to, say, the working class) as outsiders meant, however, that they could propose change *without at the same time* seriously threatening the status quo. Similarly, though connected with the working class through a shared oppression, women also connected with the upper class: they could both condemn inequity and marry the boss, so mediating between the classes. In other words, though women are the empowering agents in the mid-century novel, they do not fundamentally, at least at the level of the plot, which Bodenheimer focuses on, threaten either existing gender roles or the class system. They act as mediators, allowing the difficult issues both to be raised and simultaneously contained. This, explains Bodenheimer, is why the novels connect industrialism and male–female relationships. Gallagher, however, observes that this connection is always fraught with tension. Since the now separate worlds of public and private are constituted by contradictory values, the novels move continually to associate and dissociate the two arenas.

What will emerge from this study of turn-of-the-century novels is that although the novels (whether conservatively or radically imagined) still sometimes invoke these two ideologemes of paternalism and pastoralism in order to ensure some social stability, the ideologemes are confused, even lifeless. The ideologeme of paternalism is more important in turn-of-the-century fiction than that of pastoralism. For example, if the novel attacks radical politics as does Gissing's *Demos*, it tries to resuscitate an aristocrat who could right the wrongs inflicted by an industry now in the hands of a ruthless utilitarian socialist. The aristocrat, however, is given only a very limited vision. His desires are only ecological (to restore the countryside), not social (to help the community). Worse, he is somewhat dissipated: he has problems with women. At the novel's end he turns out to be uninterested in anything but his own private pursuit of art and the proper education of his new wife. If the novels support socialism, they often invoke a benign paternalistic figure, in the form of a "saviour of the masses." This character is usually a gentleman who has given up his class to become a "man of the people," but he still maintains his individuality and authority over other characters, including other socialists. Such a figure, often likened to Jesus, is designed to quiet middle-class fears that socialism will mean anarchy. Yet this protective figure is also problematic, often ineffective, largely also because of his relation to women. For unlike paternalists in mid-century novels who have to learn through women, the modern paternalist reverses the role and attempts to *teach* women, either about socialism or, in Eldon's case, about art. The male character thus denies the woman much power at all. The novels, however, are extremely uneasy about this relationship. Women's repressed power erupts to discredit the paternalist's authority, an eruption which works against the novel's political project.

The ideologeme of the pastoral, as either escape or transforming agent of the diseased body politic, is invoked less frequently in turn-of-the-century novels, signalling the reification Lukács speaks of: an "outside" to present economic relations can less readily be imagined. The pastoral does, however, put in an appearance in the conservative novels such as James's *The Princess*, where the Princess's country house serves as an emblem of the culture that anarchism threatens to destroy, and in Gissing's *Demos*, where the rural valley of Wanley is an emblem of the old green England that a socialist experiment is already destroying. But neither novel seriously considers the pastoral as a refuge or potentially transforming agent. In *The Princess*, the working-class protagonist can only be an infrequent guest at the house, and the Princess herself gives it up to move to the working-class suburbs. In *Demos*, the paternalist Eldon, who could restore Wanley to its pre-industrial past after he gains the factory back from the socialist Mutimer, decides to leave the job to someone else and move to the Continent. The most extensive use of the pastoral in the novels studied here occurs in the pro-socialist novel, Morris's *News from Nowhere*, where, now itself radically transformed, cleansed of all gentry associations, Eden is premised on the destruction of capitalism and indeed all class relations. Echoes of the pastoral are also heard in Shaw's *An Unsocial Socialist*, most of which takes place in an aristocratic country house. Yet the novel deconstructs this arena: the gentry are as implicated in capitalism as is any factory owner.

Turn-of-the-century representations of the social crisis, in other words, whether conservatively or radically inflected, gesture toward these earlier ideologemes to secure some stability. As close reading of the novels will reveal in more detail, however, the novels are seriously troubled in this attempt. The older ideologemes of paternalism and pastoralism are, it seems, no longer available in any efficacious way in the present social crisis. The reasons behind their untenability are the same: both ideologemes are premised on social relationships which have been so radically disrupted that the old ones cannot even be nostalgically resurrected in any convincing way. For both women and the working class are no longer in their old "place." They have been heard from, in history as well as in fiction. The old hierarchy based on masculine privilege, in the home, in the shop, was in the process of being destabilized. In new schools of fiction, accordingly, both women and working-class characters gain a voice. New kinds of working-class and women characters and plots appear. Working-class characters are less sentimentalized and idealized. Writers in the Cockney School, for example, attempt to present the working class in a realistic light, including the use of working-class dialect.[9] Concurrently, during the 1880s and 1890s a "new woman" fiction emerges. Hallmarks of this fiction are a thematic insistence that women will become organized and a narrative focus on female consciousness. This fiction, in addition, foregrounds heretofore marginalized subjects: prostitution, rape, divorce, adultery. Plots feature women characters making their own independent way in the world.[10] Although marginal as "schools" of fiction, these new representations of working-class and women characters made their mark on the mainstream literature of the period. Working-class and women characters invariably draw some coloring from these new forms of representation, a coloring which works to release them from their traditional place and which creates the promise of a very new place. Yet these new forms of representation cannot themselves function as stabilizing forces; there is too much in these new social arrangements that threatens both writer and implied reader alike.

The general ideology of this time (reification, determinism), the theory of the novel, and the absence of effective managing strategies—these are potential, related ways of accounting for the underrepresentation of the public political sphere in turn-of-the-century fiction. They also help account for the seemingly paradoxical overrepresentation of the private, domestic sphere in turn-of-the-century fiction. For the drift is toward the smaller social unit, toward the familial, toward the personal—the only social scale that at this point seems knowable and hence controllable. And yet the idea that even this smaller social unit can be managed is illusory. At the heart of the novels studied here is a sense of profound confusion: about what was valuable in the past, about present actions, about what changing class and gender relations will mean for the future.

The novelists studied here seem particularly to focus on what changing gender, rather than changing class, relations mean, and so the following readings focus more on gender than class. This focus is partly explainable because both these writers and their implied readers were middle class. To this group, gender, rather than class, changes seemed more immediately imaginable and more immediately threatening, and so more in need of working out. But also, these novels focus on working out gender relations because such is the history of the British novel. As Armstrong observes, the nineteenth-century novel implied that resolutions in the private, domestic sphere would bring about resolutions in the public one, that a stable hearth meant a stable world. Yeats interrupts his *Autobiography* at one point with a statement which, underneath, both sounds the note of deep sorrow that those of the old order felt at the change in woman's place and signals the critical importance of a certain concept of "woman" to the very notion of a settled and artistic life. Speaking of the years at the end of the century, he says:

> Woman herself was still in our eyes . . . romantic and mysterious, still the priestess of her shrine. . . . Johnson's favourite phrase, that life is ritual, expressed something that was in some degree in all our thoughts, and how could life be ritual if woman had not her symbolical place? (201)

But what happens if the confidence in this causality of home transforming society is disturbed as it was at the turn of the century, when the private sphere could no longer be confidently maintained as "private," as outside of history, as a stable bastion of middle-class order? What happens when there are only shells of strategies to manage what is threatening? One of the things that happens to the novel is that it itself becomes fragmented, fragmented so that its power is only latent, undeveloped, felt only in portions rather than throughout the whole. Bodenheimer defines an "unsuccessful" novel in this way: it "refus[es] to credit the stubbornness of the issues [it has] raised" (10). This could be said of a number of the novels studied here. But, as the foregoing discussion should imply, it is not accidental, a mere matter of the lack of enough "personal geniuses," that most of the political fiction produced in this era is not as powerful as it could be. Rather, this fiction on the whole is not as "successful" as it could be because it had not the wherewithal ideologically to squarely face the issues it raises. It is not surprising that the most powerful novels of the period, namely James's *The Princess*, Conrad's *Secret Agent,* and Morris's *News from Nowhere*, are either conservative (which means they rely the most confidently upon the older ideologemes), or are written in the utopian genre (which discourages the foregrounding of a private arena that is now chaotic). And it is not surprising that some of the least successful novels, studied here in juxtaposition with these better-known texts, are produced by women writers who are struggling to represent what is still historically almost unthinkable: women remaking the public political sphere.

The following chapters focus on a variety of those novels produced at the turn of the century which are ostensibly engaged with radical public politics. The book is structured around close readings which interpret the complex and different ways each novel struggles to produce an image of the new politics. By studying individual instances of the way the turn-of-the-century novel stages its problem, we are able to probe its ideological ensemble—particularly the ways "public" and "private" spill over into one another on both the conscious and unconscious levels of the text.

But how to get at the "unconscious" of the text? And how to interpret the text's unconscious, as well as its consciousness, historically? Such have been the implicitly expressed aims of this book throughout the foregoing discussion. The following close readings are produced from within a particular theoretical framework, one which at this point needs to be made more explicit.

This framework was first articulated in Pierre Macherey's seminal work, *Pour une théorie de la production littéraire* (1966), translated into English in 1978 as *A Theory of Literary Production*. In this work, Macherey begins to construct a literary theory and criticism based on Louis Althusser's revolutionary reinterpretation of Marx, a reinterpretation so profound in its effect on literary theory that it has altered the designation of "Marxist literary criticism" to "neo-Marxist literary criticism." Macherey's methodology is becoming increasingly known in the field of literary studies, largely because it has had a major influence on theoretical works such as Terry Eagleton's *Criticism and Ideology* (1976), Catherine Belsey's *Critical Practice* (1980), and, to a lesser extent, Fredric Jameson's *The Political Unconscious* (1981). In addition, Macherey's and Althusser's names are invoked in many contemporary works of criticism, although their framework is not as closely applied in interpretation as it is here. For this reason, a brief synopsis of this theory and methodology follows.

The critic's job, for Macherey, is not the formalist one of imitating, describing, or "explicating" the literary text. Macherey, like others influenced by poststructuralist assumptions about language, does not see texts as coherent and self-sufficient totalities that need only "transposition" (15) by a critic who, as the text's "accomplice" (17), prepares the text for consumption. While a text manifestly *gestures* toward coherence and self-sufficiency (and in this way produces "ideology"), since ideology is always both apparently free of contradiction and ahistorical, the text is also its other, what it does "not say" (85). The text is, in other words, latently incoherent, fragmented, and uneven, and so is not organized around a "single meaning" (76), nor is it fully autonomous, since it participates in language. In this way the text, always revealing the "gaps in ideology" (60), makes ideology's presence visible.

Macherey also does not see the critic's job as the normative one of "judging" the text against some model of "history" assumed to be a "fixed and independent entity which exists alongside the work" (19). This is the assumption of the mimetic critic. The text is not an epiphenomenal mirror of history, a document to be compared to some other model of history assumed to be true. Rather, for Macherey the text is fully, *constitutively* historical. It is one of many cameras that produces an image of history, as it stages, or produces, its own particular conflict between its "said" and its "not said," as it lays bare ideology.

For Macherey, the job of the critic is to "explain" the text. Although the text "gives an implicit critique of its ideological content," although in this sense the text "knows" the limits of ideology, the text cannot *explicitly* "critique its ideological content" (64). The critic's job is to "go beyond the work and explain it . . . say what it does not and could not say" (77), a process very different from the formalist one of paraphrasing the text in "explication." According to Macherey,

> we should speak of the work by moving it beyond itself, by establishing it in the knowledge of its limits. The question is then no longer one of commentary, of reconstitution or unification, but one of explanation—explanation which dislodges the work internally, just as it was obliged to deviate from its intentions in order to realise them . . . . Thus we are proposing a very different question: What is the principle of the work's *disparity*? . . . It is this differential relation which will define the area of the problematic: and it is this which will enable us to present the work simultaneously in its reality and in its limits, taking into account the conditions of possibility and impossibility which make it visible. (161–2)

What Macherey is proposing in the last sentence is the "last step" of the explanatory process: to read the work symptomatically for, in Jameson's paraphrase, its "formal and logical and, most particularly . . . *semantic* conditions of possibility" (57). Macherey here insists, in other words, unlike others influenced by poststructuralism, on theorizing the history which could have produced a particular text.

Macherey elaborates a methodology and offers several model readings in order to demonstrate what "explanation" of a text involves. The critic first interrogates the text for the evidence it leaves of its *project*. "Able to be read all through it like a programme" (165), this evidence indicates what the text "means" to say. Second, however, the critic must confront that which has been actually produced over and above, outside of, sometimes in spite of, the text's intention: the *product* itself. By considering the particular combination of project and product in a text, the critic can take the final step of beginning to theorize the historical "conditions of possibility and impossibility."

The project, which may itself be compound (as Macherey illustrates in his reading of Balzac's *Les Paysans*), is the text's "ideological theme," that which it "wishes" to say. (For Macherey, the author is not a "creator" but a producer who is but one element in a system (67); Macherey therefore does not speak of "authorial" intention.) In his definition of "ideological theme" he relies upon Althusser's interpretation of ideology as "a matter of the lived relation between men and their world," "a relation that expresses a will . . . a hope or a nostalgia, rather than describing a reality" (233–4). Ideology, Althusser argues, is not a matter of some "false" consciousness that a different (i.e. communist) social order could eliminate. Ideology is produced from within the discourses and institutions of every society, "if men are to be formed, transformed and equipped to respond to the demands of their conditions of existence" (235). In other terms, Althusser says that ideology "interpellates" subjects for every social formation. An "ideological theme," then, is one which works to conserve the existing social formation by producing subjects for that formation.

A principal indicator of the text's general intention, its ideological theme, is its genre. Genre is the medium through which the general intention can be translated into a narrative form. Macherey also calls this narrative form the *representation*. Macherey observes that the very act of writing in a form is an ideological act, an attempt to locate formal solutions for contradictions that are unresolvable. Genre offers the producer a subject, "one that implies a total vision of the world, an ideology" (172), and "the general shape of a representation" (172). For example, the comic courtship novel implies marriage as the fulfillment of women's desire specifically, and its shape (its plotting and characterization) involves the removal of internal or external blocks. Genre, in short, provides the closure ideology requires.

The real work, for Macherey, is not, however, the text's project, its ideological theme. After discovering the text's project, the critic turns to what has actually been produced: the product, or what Macherey sometimes calls the *figuration*. When the "author" goes to write the text, the product "backlights" the project, in Macherey's terms. The very act of figuring the themes (collecting the signs) distances and so objectifies ideology. Although ideology claims itself to be a totality, it is a "false totality," one that is unaware of its limits. When ideology is figured, its limits are revealed. "Perhaps no ideology is sufficiently consistent to survive the test of figuration," Macherey explains (195). Figuration invariably throws up to view the inconsistencies, the insufficiencies, the inadequacies of ideology. These "silences" and "absences" are not only what the text "refuses to say" but what the text "cannot say" (87) (since ideology exists "because there are certain things which must not be spoken of" [Eagleton, 90]). It is the critic's challenge to attend to all of these troubled textual moments, to hear what is "not said," perhaps what cannot be said.

* * *

From the exemplary readings that Macherey gives of Verne and Balzac, it is not taking a large step within his methodology to focus on the public political sphere in turn-of-the-century novels. For although Macherey does not focus specifically on public sphere politics since the novels he studies are not primarily about these, his essays are concerned with the social and historical dimensions of the public sphere. It is, however, taking a large step to focus on the "private" sphere and specifically on gender. For Macherey's essays are *not* at all concerned with the private and domestic, or women's, sphere. Macherey's work is blind to the social implications of domestic life in particular and about gender in general. Macherey's model, in other words, needs to be radically supplemented by feminist concerns, which is an underlying theoretical ambition of this book.

The possibilities of such a radical supplementation have been mentioned and exemplified in several articles. Toril Moi, for example, in *Sexual/Textual Politics* (1985) has recognized the potential of such a feminist/Machereyan criticism to avoid both the kind of author-centered readings produced by American feminism and the often ahistorical readings produced by the French feminists (95). She sees a feminist/Machereyan criticism "opening up a productive field of enquiry for feminist critics" (94).

Two short pieces written during the last decade are richly suggestive of the power of this approach. One of these is an article written by the Marxist-Feminist Literature Collective in 1978, "Women's Writing: *Jane Eyre*, *Shirley*, *Villette*, *Aurora Leigh*." Using the ideas of Lacan, Macherey, and others, this essay examines, for example, some inconsistencies in *Jane Eyre*. It discovers that although *Jane Eyre*'s project is "to install [Jane] as a full subject within a male dominated culture" (33), in its "not-said" the novel "inscribe[s] women as sexual subjects within this system" (35), so threatening male dominance.

The other compelling example of a feminist/Machereyan criticism appears in a chapter of Belsey's *Critical Practice* on the Sherlock Holmes stories. Belsey argues that the project of the Holmes stories is "to dispel magic and mystery, to make everything explicit, accountable, subject to scientific analysis" (111). The project, in short, is to celebrate a limitless positivistic science. Yet this project is undermined by women. Women in these stories, Belsey observes, are surrounded by uneasy silences and always hover mysteriously on the margins of Doyle's stories. Their positioning exposes the stories' scientific project as ideological. The texts "know" that there is at least one area such a "science" cannot "explain": women's sexuality.[11]

However provocative these individual instances of a nascent feminist/ Machereyan criticism, I felt a need to make a claim on a larger canvas for the power of a feminist/Machereyan criticism. These readings are that canvas.

2

Anarchism and Women: *The Princess Casamassima* and *The Secret Agent*

Disruptive forces preoccupy the often compared and best known of the novels alluding to radical public politics that were produced at the turn of the century: Henry James's *The Princess Casamassima* (1886) and Joseph Conrad's *The Secret Agent* (1907). The novels' similarly conservative projects are to contain the threat that turn-of-the-century anarchism seemed to pose for the British middle and upper classes. For although British anarchism was always a fringe movement, it captivated the public imagination. Not only did distorted press accounts of allegedly anarchist acts terrify respectable British society. But also, British anarchism had a particular fascination for those who loved art, for they saw in anarchism a way to guarantee the freedom for the individual that many believed was a precondition for the flowering of art.[1] Anarchism, in its terror and fascination, was a subject that many people wanted to read about, and yet control.

The accent, however, falls somewhat differently in each of the two most famous novels the anarchist threat occasioned. James, who found the charged political climate of the 1880s "interesting," writes his novel less to condemn than to contain the threat. *The Princess* probes the questions: who becomes an anarchist and why, and what is the cost of such a political commitment both to the individual and to the larger society? Conrad's novel's project, on the other hand, seems to be to condemn anarchism, to dismiss it absolutely as wantonly violent in its methods. Yet despite these differences in their specific projects, both novels are alike in showing no deep understanding of anarchist political theory; in using as the basis of their plots allegedly anarchist-inspired, terrorist incidents that were sensationally misrepresented in the newspapers of the time; and in being somewhat anomalous within each writer's career. What these similarities between the novels tentatively suggest is that the desire to contain implies not only the desire to distance (since neither novel probes the theory nor the veracity of the incidents), but also the opposing desire to look at the spectacular and forbidden.

As Macherey observes, however, the products, the actual novels themselves, always undermine their projects. When the novel is produced, when the project is figured, contradictions, gaps, silences inevitably emerge. These gaps reveal the project as ideology, as a limited, habitual, ahistorical way of feeling and thinking, and one which, by evading its contradictions and historicity, helps reproduce the existing social order.

This implies that the strategies each novel employs to fulfill its project of containing the threat of anarchism do not all work. One of the key strategies James's and Conrad's novels share is to telescope the spectre of upheaval onto, at best, marginal anarchists[2] whose main stories are really domestic ones. Using the conventions of the domestic novel, where gender relations are offered as the cause of all social behavior, the two novels attempt to contain the threat of individual male anarchists, and so, they hope, of anarchism itself, by blaming inappropriate domestic arrangements which created them. The novels, thus, attempt to invoke the mid-Victorian ideologeme of "home," with specifically the woman as a metonym for affection, social stability, and culture, in order to gauge (and so denounce) the destructiveness of the male characters. Yet the project of each novel founders: the invocation is feeble, the strategy empty. "Home" is blown apart and, instead, an uncontrollably disruptive feminine force hovers in the wings. For there must be, even in novels which blame "bad" women for destructive men, some image of home and woman as the serene other, as the anchor of a stable political order. "Bad" women must be, in short, contained if the old ideologeme is to work; yet in these two novels there is no such anchor. Images of women taking charge, acting out of line, abandoning their old roles, are powerful undercurrents in these novels. Winnie evokes the sexual femme fatale, the terrible mother,[3] and the aggressively angry wife. The Princess evokes the unfaithful wife and the priestess abandoning her shrine of high culture. The products, not surprisingly, punish such bad women with a punishment that is at times excessive, even misogynistic, in order to try to contain what becomes as disruptive a force as that of anarchism itself. Both novels, in short, have a double containment problem: containing anarchism, by using outdated traditional ideologemes, and then containing that which the use of the outdated ideologemes inadvertently opens up, woman's power. Both products reveal that their common project of containing the twin disruptive forces of anarchism and women is ideological. Neither force can be contained in these predictable, typical plots which do not position anarchist or proto-feminist actions on any broader historical map.

This shared problematic of *The Princess Casamassima* and *The Secret Agent*, whose workings this chapter will explore, suggests a number of aspects of particularly turn-of-the-century ideology concerning women. First and least surprisingly, the mid-Victorian angel of the house, celebrated in Coventry Patmore's poem, has not yet been entirely killed, a murder Virginia Woolf was to claim several decades later that she had accomplished. The representation of woman as angel still haunts the projects specifically of novels with a conservative viewpoint on social change. Yet these novels' inability to perpetuate this representation of woman reveals that even among conservative writers the breakdown in the patriarchy is being felt. For writers such as James and Conrad, the image of the new woman, who undermines their attempts to hold onto a traditional image, understandably is a ready vehicle for collecting their terror of radical social change. Anarchist and proto-feminist threats are, not surprisingly, inextricably linked in these novels. But James's and Conrad's novels do more than reveal how intimate the connection is between public and private politics. Their novels also suggest that the attraction implied in a decision to gaze at anarchist politics, whether as writer or reader, may also be an attraction to the new woman herself.

Although some critics, particularly of *The Secret Agent*, have observed the centrality of the female characters, few critics have read either novel as an attempt to manage a troublesome anarchist threat, never mind a proto-feminist one. Critics grounded in mimesis have either defended these novels as fully truthful, securely authoritative portraits of British anarchist politics, a politics the novels condemn, or, on the other hand, criticized them for their historical inaccuracy.[4] Rarely have critics closely read the ways either novel reveals anxiety about anarchism and so a crisis in representing it.[5] By first probing particularly the ambivalent relationship of the male narrators to the principal male anarchist characters we can recognize the extent of the texts' profoundly anxious relationship not only to anarchism, but, eventually, to feminism as well.

Both novels in their contemporary form appear with a Preface (*The Princess*) or an Author's Note (*The Secret Agent*). Although each of these was written some years after the original texts, both authors' desire to append a preface suggests they wish to persuade the reader to approach the novel in a certain way. In other words, each preface is intended as a sort of "reader's guide" to the novel's project, although each is not the transparent guide each preface's narrator (whom we will call the "author" to distinguish him from the textual narrator) would like to think it is; this means each preface is also a product. Although these prefaces are to some extent different from the novels they introduce, they are important to study for, usually read first, they tell the reader how to interpret the novel. Each preface attempts to justify the novel's focus on anarchist material by explaining the novel's genesis as the product of merely casual experience. So the authors hope to position the reader as aloof from the anarchist material. The gaps and evasions in each preface also, however, unwittingly reveal the terrifyingly intimate relation the author has to the central anarchists or to the subject of anarchism. The subject matter is not, in other words, as managed as it may appear even here.

James's Preface reveals at once his profound anxiety in writing about a working-class character and his profound desire to make such a character "his own." James chafes under the popularity of the empirical, naturalistic method used by authors such as Walter Besant and sociologists such as Charles Booth. Knowing he has no claims to any such "scientific" study of the working class and their political movements (his knowledge was, he claims, gleaned only from his "nocturnal walks" about London), he needs to assure his authority before a reader who might otherwise challenge it. Against these imagined claims, as well as against anyone who would criticize the elitism of his role as social investigator, James advances the humanist argument that anyone whose "imagination" is receptive can penetrate to any level of society; one need not "apply" for "authentic information" (22). He affirms again the "principle of the note" (a principle elaborated in "The Art of Fiction" written immediately before he wrote *The Princess*). To complete the metaphor, the note, in this case the working class, is a part of the whole symphony of humanity.

Yet while avowing his ability to create a working-class character such as Hyacinth, James simultaneously worries in the Preface about how to represent him. He clearly *is* troubled about using a working-class protagonist: will he "fill too full any supposed and above all obviously limited vessel of consciousness"? (10) At the outset, then, Hyacinth is not like other humans; by virtue of his class difference he is an unknown "other" and so his "proper fusion with the fable" is difficult for James (15). In the course of writing the Preface, James's anxiety about his choice of Hyacinth for his center seems only to increase. His certainty about his ability to know Hyacinth falters: "I may wonder at my confidence now—given the extreme, the very particular truth and 'authority' required at so many points" (21). Acknowledging at the end of the Preface that his "propriety might be challenged . . . by readers of a knowledge greater than mine," he is forced to aver that "my vision . . . was, exactly, my knowledge." Seeming though to recognize immediately the subjective relativism implied in this position, he quickly slips into using the humanist "we": "the value I wished most to render and the effect I wished most to produce were precisely those of our not knowing, of society's not knowing, but only guessing . . . what 'goes on'" (22).

James tries to manage his crisis over representing Hyacinth in a most revealing way, suggesting the extent to which this choice of protagonist was not at all, as Eloise Hay claims it was, "a little frivolous" for him.[6] He imagines Hyacinth as a "lesser James"—what James would have been like had he been shut out from the world of upper-class culture, a sort of putative son, a Hyacinth to his Apollo.[7] Others also have observed that the subject matter of *The Princess* meant a great deal to James. He is probing a question of particular concern to him: what is the relation between popular movements and the old world of high culture? James recognizes in mass movements a chance for a fresh clearing away. Yet the prospect of an anarchic army of envious people also terrifies him. By making Hyacinth a lesser, partial alter ego who fails in his quest to find a noble anarchism, James could achieve a catharsis of his own desires for change. To sustain his own identification with Hyacinth, he must make him only a novitiate, a bare outsider to the movement. To maintain his distance from Hyacinth, he must make him not a writer of books but only a binder of them. James names the novel not after Hyacinth, but after the Princess, revealing Hyacinth's subordination in the "fable" itself.

This relation between author and character in the Preface is repeated in the novel proper. In the language of the text Hyacinth is tightly controlled and protected by the ever surveillant narrator. The "son" can never rival the father's accomplishments: "little Hyacinth" is the narrator's favorite epithet for him. When the narrator describes Hyacinth's vacillation he uses characteristically "Jamesian" language as Hyacinth's own:

> he was afraid the democracy wouldn't care for perfect bindings or for the finer sorts of conversation. . . . At the same time there was joy and exultation in the thought of surrendering one's self to the wash of the wave, of being carried higher on the sun-touched crests of wild billows than one could ever be by a dry lonely effort of one's own.

Immediately following this passage, however, the narrator intrudes more openly and the gap between Hyacinth and narrator widens.

> The reader will doubtless smile at his mental debates and oscillations, and not understand why a little bastard bookbinder should attach importance to his conclusions. They were not important for either case, but they were important for himself—if only because they would rescue him from the torment of his present life. (428–9)

Both the direct address to the reader and the epithet "little bastard bookbinder" signal the narrator's abrupt attempt to frame, and so distance, himself and the reader from Hyacinth. While Hyacinth may be, as Leon Edel says, a more fully drawn character than his counterpart in *The Bostonians*, Verena Tarrant, and while he is certainly more substantial than his earlier rival for Christina Light, Roderick Hudson, he is not a comfortably discrete character. Controlled and overshadowed by the narrator at many turns, he has not that largeness or separateness true of the fuller Jamesian character—an Isabel Archer, a Lambert Strether. Perhaps James's anxiety about becoming too entangled in the "actual" political material here, his fear of looking too closely into facts (what he accuses Wells of doing), prevented his creating Hyacinth as a powerful central organizing consciousness.

James, in both the Preface and through his textual narrator, attempts to manage his fears about representing anarchism by making the anarchist a lesser version of himself, so suggesting not only that he could not know such a figure but that he wanted to. Conrad's Author's Note, written in 1920, twelve years after the publication of the novel, subtly prepares the reader to observe in the novel itself his narrator's similarly ambivalent relationship to his subject matter, if not to his anarchist characters. What seems to give rise to Conrad's Note is the memory of some negative criticism he received, at the time of the novel's publication, concerning the tale's "sordid surroundings" and "moral squalor" (7). His project in the Note is to meet this criticism, in other words, to attempt to justify his choice of subject matter. His justification has two parts. First, he affirms that he "was under no necessity to deal with that subject" (8). He was "detached" from the "squalor and sordidness" which lie simply in the "outward circumstances of the setting" (8). Toward the deeper, inner issues he is not detached, for such would be acceptance. Rather he chooses an ironic tone to inspire "indignation and underlying pity and contempt." In other words, the subject and surroundings held no fatal attraction for him and he has assumed a moral vantage point. Then Conrad goes on to offer the second part of his justification: to explain the story's genesis. He affirms that although he may have felt he wanted a "change" after writing *Nostromo*, he was "certainly not thinking of going out of [his] way to look for anything ugly" (9). It was then that a "friend" uttered some words about this subject. In other words, he did not seek the story out; it interested someone else, someone who "may have gathered those illuminating facts at second or third hand" and so was probably in the know. Then Conrad "came upon a book," the recollections of an Assistant Commissioner of Police, of which "ten lines" about "some unexpected anarchist outrage" "arrested" his attention (10). As the story grows in Conrad's imagination, "as crystals will do by their bizarre and unexpected shapes" (11), he tells the reader that he feared "it would take years to find the right way" through the "endless vistas" of the "enormous" dark town. Slowly, however, "the dawning conviction of Mrs. Verloc's maternal passion grew up to a flame between me and that background" (11). Conrad, here, establishes Winnie, the mother, the sybil, as his guide through the labyrinth of the underworld, and of his own imagination which threatened chaos.

In spite of Conrad's seeming control and authority, the Note is not the easy, simple statement it appears to be. Its trouble subtly teaches the reader to approach the novel itself as similarly troubled. In averring his detachment, in claiming his lack of responsibility for the tale and in his explanation for his center, Winnie, Conrad reveals much that is unsettled. Right from the start of the Note Conrad himself suggests it is odd that he, many years later, is answering the rare few who at the time criticized his tale, a few whose "general argument" he remembers years later "perfectly" (7). Their perception of his complicity in squalor and scorn for people apparently haunted him still. Why, unless he is less detached than he claims? In fact, the relationship between "detachment" from the circumstances and "scorn" and "pity" for the actors is not an easy relationship to negotiate. Nor is his "detachment" even from the circumstances convincingly expressed. When he describes the way the tale grew in him he calls the "enormous town" "monstrous" "in its man-made might," as "indifferent to heaven's frowns and smiles, a cruel devourer of the world light" (11). Then, in recounting the tale of how the story came to him, Conrad inadvertently reveals that *he*, not the others, was its author. In fact, he receives very little information from others, just grains which ferment in his mind. At one point the Note dramatizes his own fanaticism. Talking with his "friend" casually, Conrad "remarks":

> on the criminal futility of the whole thing, doctrine, action, mentality; and on the contemptible aspect of the half-crazy pose as of a brazen cheat exploiting the poignant miseries and passionate credulities of a mankind always so tragically eager for self-destruction. That was what made for me its philosophical pretences so unpardonable.

Then they "pass to particular instances" and Conrad is off on his own rancorous attack again:

> the attempt to blow up the Greenwich Observatory, a blood-stained inanity of so fatuous a kind that it was impossible to fathom its origin by any reasonable or even unreasonable process of thought. For perverse unreason has its own logical processes. But that outrage could not be laid hold of mentally in any sort of way, so that one remained faced by the fact of a man blown to bits for nothing even most remotely resembling an idea, anarchistic or other. As to the outer wall of the Observatory it did not show as much as the faintest crack. (9)

Conrad's friend "remained silent for a while," possibly embarrassed by Conrad's own fanaticism. Then the friend remarks "in his characteristically casual and omniscient manner"—as if to shut off conversation—"Oh, that fellow was a half idiot; his sister committed suicide afterwards." This remark, finally, renders Conrad "dumb." Even Winnie's eruption in Conrad's troubled mind as the anchor for the tale is itself sudden. Although alerting the reader to her importance in making the novel coherent, this connection between chaos and women is not by any means explained. Finally, near the very end of the Note, a curious sentence erupts, one that possibly accounts for some of these slippages:

> I have no doubt, however, that there had been moments during the writing of the book when I was an extreme revolutionist, I won't say more convinced than they but certainly cherishing a more concentrated purpose than any of them had ever done in the whole course of his life. (12)

Conrad here openly expresses an affinity between anarchist and artist. Perhaps he is not as detached as he claims. Perhaps this situation and these characters are not radically other to him.

In the novel itself, Conrad's strategy for managing the anarchist is quite different from James's. While James tentatively and ambivalently projects himself in Hyacinth, Conrad's narrator keeps Verloc and the others at a precariously maintained great distance. Verloc, for example, "fair game for a caricatural presentation" (12), defies all notions of "central character," which the title at least suggests that he is. The narrator rarely addresses him by his first name, he shows us few thoughts, and, perhaps most remarkably, he imbues Verloc with no past, nothing to explain his personality. Verloc is "summed up" by his bowler hat and his corpulent body. Yet the narrator's scorn for Verloc at moments gets out of hand, his ironic detachment undermined.

An example of this occurs during one of the moments when the narrator does pause to gaze into Verloc's mind, in the scene in which he is going to bed following his meeting with Vladimir. The narrator says:

> Pausing in his intention to turn off the gas burning in the middle of the shop, Mr. Verloc descended into the abyss of moral reflections. With the insight of a kindred temperament [to other anarchists] he pronounced his verdict.

The narrator here positions the reader far above Verloc's reflections; the language is formal ("his intention," "pronounced his verdict") or a cliché ("descended into the abyss of moral reflections"). At this moment the narrator seems detached from Verloc, but his ironic tone is just beginning to undermine this detachment; key destabilizing words are the hyperbole of the cliché and the inflation in the phrase "pronounced his verdict." Is Verloc, we ask, capable of seeing the abyss? And does he have the right to pronounce a verdict, given he is a "kindred spirit"?

Verloc then "pronounces his verdict," sneering at the rest of his fellow anarchists, all of whom, "a lazy lot," feed off women Verloc equally despises ("blear-eyed old woman," "indomitable snarling old witch," "his [Michaelis's] wealthy old lady," "silly girls"). The narrator's seething rage at Verloc is barely contained in the mechanical language he uses to describe him.

> And Mr. Verloc, temperamentally identical with his associates, drew fine distinctions in his mind on the strength of insignificant differences. He drew them with a certain complacency, because the instinct of conventional respectability was strong within him, being only overcome by his dislike of all kinds of recognized labour . . .

Then, after a dash, the narrator's accumulated rage at Verloc's conventionality, blindness, and laziness builds: the narrator openly intrudes to express his loathing.

> —a temperamental defect which he shared with a large proportion of revolutionary reformers of a given social state. For obviously one does not revolt against the advantages and opportunities of that state, but against the price which must be paid for the same in the coin of accepted morality,

> self-restraint, and toil. The majority of revolutionists are the enemies of discipline and fatigue mostly.

Finally the string of adjectives reveals an enraged narrator.

> There are natures, too, to whose sense of justice the price exacted looms up monstrously enormous, odious, oppressive, worrying, humiliating, extortionate, intolerable. Those are the fanatics. The remaining portion of social rebels is accounted for by vanity, the mother of all noble and vile illusions, the companion of poets, reformers, charlatans, prophets, and incendiaries. (55)

The narrator has tried to obliterate Verloc. But at the same time Verloc has inadvertently been included on a whole spectrum of the disaffected, fanatics and rebels alike. What is unnerving is not only the narrator's excessive rage at Verloc, but also the reader's suspicion that the narrator is somehow part of this spectrum himself, a "fanatic" disgusted with the "monstrously enormous" "injustice" in the world.[8] Verloc and the narrator are closer than they at first may appear.

The evidence suggests that not only anarchism but the male anarchists are dangerous, even intimate territory for Conrad, James, and their narrative personae. Not surprisingly, the novels attempt to manage their trouble with anarchists by introducing a third term: woman.

Conrad's Note points directly to his principal strategy of containment. His project in *The Secret Agent* is to invoke the "maternal female" to help him out of a threatening underworld. His language is almost religious. Winnie's "maternal passion" is the light (the "flame") which helps him find the "right way" through the hellish labyrinth of the London underworld. The story is even "Winnie Verloc's story."

James's Preface, likewise, reveals that the figure of the Princess, while less desperately so, was crucial to making his story work. The woman invoked here is not the mother protecting her hearth but her twin in nineteenth-century ideology: the priestess of high culture in a commercial and vulgar world. James says of his project in the Preface that he needs a "social" as well as a "socialist" connection for Hyacinth in order to account for his internal conflict. The Princess begins as his social connection, though she becomes a socialist one as well. An American who has begun to remedy that greatest of deficiencies in Americans, gaining intimate access to European high culture, she is to be the one to open the "door" for Hyacinth into "that warmer glow of things he is precisely to undermine." She, his teacher, is the one who introduces Hyacinth to culture, to beautiful things and places, and so wakens his aesthetic sense. By awakening Hyacinth, she becomes his object of adoration. This developing relationship of homage, in turn, urges Hyacinth to cling to hierarchical social relations in which he, the less worthy one, can be a perpetual suppliant. The Princess, in a book which otherwise is inexplicably titled after her and not Hyacinth, is in other words the channel through which the projected conservative vision of the novel is articulated, even as Winnie is in *The Secret Agent*: anarchism will destroy too many precious things, the example set by the few cognoscenti, maternal affection.

The prefaces are not alone in suggesting that these novels share a similar project of employing the women to manage the narrators' troubled relationship to the male anarchists. The structures of the novels themselves reveal how central domestic gender relations are. In *The Princess* the narrator's attempts to explain the causes of anarchist activity, the spaces represented in the novel, and the plot axis all suggest the primacy of domestic gender relations. The narrator consistently identifies only one cause of Hyacinth's attraction to anarchist politics, one whose formulaic quality makes it unconvincing. The narrator positions Hyacinth within an oedipal conflict overlaid with an argument from heredity reminiscent of Zola. Hyacinth, the narrator continually reminds us, is a "bastard," born of a French peasant woman and a British aristocrat. Hyacinth's conflict is whether to identify with his mother or his father. Should he align himself with his mother and avenge the political wrong done her by the state (she died in prison where she was placed for stabbing his father)? This he might do by aligning himself with anti-state anarchists, whose theories he first learns of as a child when he meets refugees of the Paris Commune. Or, should he abandon his mother and the lower class in which he was brought up and cultivate the aristocratic sensibility of his father? Hyacinth's class confusion is similarly evident in his sexual attraction to the working-class Millicent and his aesthetic attraction to the seemingly upper-class Princess. (The Princess is only aristocratic by marriage; she is in reality illegitimate and middle class by origin, accounting for one dimension of Hyacinth's attraction to her, although he never knows about this part of her background.)

The novel's foregrounding of domestic space similarly reveals that these are the spaces in which the threat of anarchist public politics is to be managed. Only one chapter represents a political meeting, that at the Sun and Moon, which, it turns out, isn't where the real action is at all anyway. The narrator can do no more than bring us to the door of the "real thing," Hoffendahl's "innermost sanctuary" (293). It is Hyacinth, not the narrator, who tells the Princess of how he actually made his oath there to do whatever deed they command. While *The Princess* claims that a labyrinthian underworld exists, the reader never sees the labyrinth. Overwhelmingly, the space of the novel is taken up by the rooms of Pinnie, Mr. Vetch, the Poupins, the Muniments, the Princess and Lady Aurora. Even though the characters occasionally discuss political matters in these domestic spaces, the discussions are truncated.

Gender relations, finally, generate much of the dynamics of the plot of *The Princess*. The central political plot of the novel turns on Hyacinth's decision to make a pledge to commit an anarchist act, then his conflict over whether he can keep his word given his lost heart for the cause. Yet in spite of the potentially inherent interest in the relationship between pledges and actions, words and deeds,[9] the narrative nestles this story primarily within a failed suitor plot (so subordinating it) and secondarily within a familial plot. Hyacinth, the impoverished knight smiled upon by the lady, makes his political pledge in the hope that he will secure her favor (since she is curious about political men). Once her influence over him is secure, once she has successfully incited Hyacinth to make a pledge (because as a woman she cannot be included in this movement), she begins to lose interest in him. He in turn begins to lose his ardor for the cause. His developing skepticism is protracted. While this could suggest the seriousness of Hyacinth's political dilemma, James again subordinates this dilemma to Hyacinth's painful, and so slowly, growing knowledge of the Princess's developing indifference toward him. His recognition that "she had done with him forever" (528) comes as he stands on the street corner alongside the man she earlier abandoned, her husband the Prince, and watches her go off with a new man, Paul Muniment. He then turns to the only other female in his life, Millicent, who has long been sexually fascinating for him. "He made in truth no effort to drive it [her image] away; he held fast to it in return, and it murmured strange things in his ear" (530). Yet, as he stands in the shop waiting for Millicent, he sees another rival, Sholto, there, "looking at him very hard a few seconds" (532). She, too, has gone off with another man. It is in the course of experiencing these betrayals that Hyacinth begins to feel horror at the idea of committing his pledged deed because he now sees that such an act would be a "repetition," a "public reappearance, in her person, of the imbrued hands of his mother" (529). His suicide, perhaps the ultimate anarchist act, follows fast on the heels of these multiple recognitions.

It is women, *The Princess* suggests, whose needs, needs for male attention, needs for sexuality, and needs for revenge, breed anarchistic men. A stable home, good women, according to the project of *The Princess*, are the only guarantee of both political stability and culture, and women who are out of line—Hyacinth's mother's out-of-wedlock liaison, the Princess's and Millicent's promiscuity, and the Princess's desires to be in politics—violate the rules and should be blamed for public political disruption.

Unlike James's narrator, Conrad's does not attempt to explain an interest in anarchistic acts as the result of either an oedipal conflict or hereditary psychology. Conrad's only genuine anarchist, the Professor, has little history and barely even any representation in the novel. Neither the defunct anarchists who gather in Verloc's shop nor secret agent Verloc are likewise given histories. They are all caricatures. Yet there are hints that failures in personal life explain anarchists and that a solid, loving home would eliminate the impulse. As the narrator sums it up at one point, "the way of even the most justifiable revolutions is prepared by personal impulses disguised into creeds" (76–7). The Professor, of "humble" origins (76), had a father who was a righteous preacher. Now the Professor, alone, is miserable among people whom he cannot trust and seeks "the refuge of his room." He lives in a city of decay which the narrator characterizes, using domestic imagery again, as a "second-hand furniture" shop, where "an unhappy, homeless couch" stands "in the open" (77–8). Verloc similarly hates the "latent unfriendliness of all out of doors" (58) and seeks refuge in Winnie's arms, a refuge she won't give. Verloc has only one motive for obeying Vladimir: he does not wish to jeopardize his domestic comfort and his position as provider for his chief possession, his family. He wants to keep his own illusions of his "home" and of Winnie's devotion even as he sees through the other anarchists' similar illusions. In fact, similarly to James's *The Princess*, domestic spaces dominate the landscape of *The Secret Agent* (the Verlocs' house). Even when characters are out of doors as is the Professor in the scene quoted above, they think of friendly rooms.

Finally, the plot axis of *The Secret Agent* similarly turns on the familial relationship. Even as Verloc acts to save his home, Winnie, in her anxiety that Verloc believe Stevie is "a useful member of the family" (59), pushes Verloc and Stevie to act as father and son. This desire prompts her to throw Stevie in Verloc's way so that he becomes Verloc's ready accomplice on his bombing mission. The plot ends when the entire family is destroyed.

Like *The Princess*, then, *The Secret Agent* implies that the threat to stable public political relationships derives from a malfunctioning family. *The Secret Agent*, like *The Princess*, goes even further: it is more women's than men's inappropriate desires that are to blame. For it is a needy Winnie who has manipulated Verloc for her own selfish ends: to gain a home for herself and Stevie. It is Winnie who thus feeds Verloc's misapprehension that he has a "home" to protect and that Stevie is part of his family, a putative son who could help him out.

The projects of both *The Princess* and *The Secret Agent*, thus, find in women and a malfunctioning family primary explanations for the male's anarchistic acts. But although each novel attempts to invoke the mid-century ideologeme of a possible functioning family as the corrective, it cannot. For the projects of both novels do not establish either woman or the family as desirable, possible retreats. Women and families are at best empty places (*The Princess*), at worst seething with destructive attributes (*The Secret Agent*). Each novel is dominated, rather, by proto new women and broken families, women whom the plots quite predictably punish, sometimes in misogynistic ways.[10]

The Princess is the less negative of these two novels about the *possibility* of "family." There is, after all, at least one "good" home represented here: the Poupins, refugees from the Commune. And yet, this family is minimally represented. The rest of the families are broken in some way or the characters have left their homes. The two central characters in the novel are "homeless": Hyacinth is an orphan and the Princess has left her husband to live on her own. She refuses to preside over a hearth not only by leaving her husband and taking up with other men, but also by desiring to be involved in anarchist politics. Also, she abandons her place as protector of culture when she decides to move into a "vulgar" working-class suburb. James's novel does not punish the Princess for her proto-feminist treachery except to leave her kneeling beside the dead Hyacinth, "a strange low cry [coming] from her lips" (537).

"Family" is never entertained in *The Secret Agent* as a possibility. The only marriage, the only domestic space represented, is the Verlocs', and this marriage is hopelessly malfunctional. Winnie is for this reason a more obviously pivotal character than is the Princess since she is the only one through whom Verloc's thoughts and actions can be explained. A number of critics have already argued Winnie's centrality to Conrad's novel. Some see her as a positive figure. Jonathan Arac sees in her the vehicle of Benjamin's *Erfahrung*, the one through whom the reader connects what the city has destroyed. H. M. Daleski seeks to show the ways in which Winnie's loss of self is a synecdoche for the vacancy of all selves in the modern world. More to our point, Claire Rosenfield calls *The Secret Agent* "a domestic drama, a story of personal relations and lack of communication" (108), and so Winnie assumes importance.

Winnie, however, is even more central and more problematic than such readings suggest. She is more than Conrad's "flame," as the way for the reader to lay hold of the chaos the novel represents, as an illumination into the problems of modern society, or as Conrad's own defiance of Vladimir's taunt to Verloc that no "journalist" could find any personal explanation at all in the bombing of an observatory (41) (which is why Vladimir thinks this will be such a perfect crime). For Winnie is also the problem itself. Where *The Secret Agent* desired to project the mother at the hearth, it offers instead a demon, in the form of a proto new woman, a woman who does not really love her husband, a woman who knows her sexuality, and, worse, a woman who will take things into her own hands. She is "outside" the boundaries of home. She is identified with the darkness, the chaotic city, the destructiveness that cannot be explained. Winnie, far more than the Princess, is a large, terrible, unanchored force in the novel. Because, as Arac observes, *The Secret Agent* invites the reader to be a detective, Winnie herself is not above suspicion as the true inciter to anarchist acts, as the real agent provocateur of the novel—an agent provocateur more dangerous because no one recognizes her real power.

With Winnie the reader's relationship is far more complicated, far richer, than with the Princess. The narrator intermittently attempts to provoke the reader's sympathy toward a woman in difficult straits. He cites the cruelty of her father as a reason for her subsequent protective attitude toward Stevie and her mother, and so her choice of Verloc as provider for them all. Yet in the product Winnie strangely garners little sympathy for her acts. The critics, responding to the narrator's own extreme discomfort at Winnie's prostitution to Verloc, however much he tries to explain or ennoble it, often argue that her "calculating" quality makes her far worse than Verloc. She treats Verloc either as a child (she'll feed him, put out the lights) or as the husband she has a duty to seduce in exchange for his protection of Stevie. Though she, like Verloc, is blind ("things do not bear much looking into"), her blindness, unlike his, is willed. Verloc does not need this litany to prevent his self-consciousness. Not surprisingly then, the plot ultimately positions Winnie, with her covert zealousness, not the "rosy complexioned" (58) child Verloc or the misguided, hoodwinked husband Verloc, as the well-spring of the anarchist act. The narrator even takes Verloc's side. He often reminds the reader, after all, that Verloc had "no other idea than that of being loved for himself" (207). She, the femme fatale, always provoking Verloc (and the narrator) with her "full bust, in a tight bodice" (18) and her "big eyes gleam[ing] under the dark lids" (59), makes Verloc think she adores him. She makes Verloc notice how malleable Stevie is so Verloc will think he controls him too. As the terrible mother, she even, in her dogged plotting to make a secure place for her putative child, Stevie, encourages Verloc and Stevie to go off together so she can view them as "father and son," thinking such a relationship will assure Stevie's adequate protection. Refusing to consider the consequences of her acts as well as of her husband's in her "ardour of protecting compassion exalted morbidly in her childhood" (59), she sacrifices Stevie. Winnie is the revealed secret agent behind the apparent secret agent, the bad woman behind the bad man.

Winnie is severely punished in subtle as well as not so subtle ways for choosing her son over her husband—and an unnatural son at that, a vestige of her premarital family—and for ultimately giving them both over to destruction. *The Secret Agent*, in this way, is not merely preoccupied with Winnie: it is a misogynistic text. Momentarily the novel, following its project, does elevate Winnie as the flame illuminating the underworld. It occasionally attempts to explain her protectiveness of Stevie. It even praises her rare passion posthumously through Ossipon. She had "a vigour of vitality, a love of life that could resist the furious anguish which drives to murder" (250). Yet Winnie in the product also emerges as the most terrifying of females for the male: the murderer of men. The scene in which Ossipon discovers her murder registers this fear. Though Ossipon disgusts the narrator, at this moment in the text the narrator is barely separated from him. This cover barely works, the language is so out of control. Ossipon becomes sick at the murder only when he discovers that Winnie has killed Verloc precisely at the moment when he makes sexual overtures to her. From this point on in his life, Ossipon's fear of women's castrating power controls him: he, the womanizer, can no longer look at women. Winnie becomes the Medusa. "He positively saw snakes now; He saw the woman twined round him like a snake" (237).

The plot spells out Winnie's punishment. Winnie suffers psychological dismemberment when she hears of Stevie's death as no other character suffers it. And, though her inadvertent murder of Stevie and her calculated murder of her husband make her feel her "freedom" (207), she is allowed no freedom. The narrative can imagine no other self for the female than that of the devoted mother and wife. She is allowed little representation except as the blind, dependent, and hysterical mother and wife before she leaves home. Once she flees with Ossipon her end is suicide. The reader does not see her in her final moments. Winnie in this sense is not just a synecdoche for modern vacancy, for the loss of self. She is a sign of the utter impossibility, the utter unacceptability, of a female self separate from the male.

Winnie is also identified with the powers of chaos and darkness in subtler ways in the novel. As Rosenfield has observed, much of the archetypally resonant imagery of the novel identifies the lost, squalid city with the bad woman. Winnie is consistently described as of a piece with the city. Unlike the male characters, she has no pretense of movement through the labyrinth. When she tries to move out of her house at the end of the novel, she gets lost "at the bottom of a black abyss from which no unaided woman could hope to scramble out" (222) and is brought back to her home by her memory of the open door. But her "home" too is not the semi-protected space that home is for James. Her domestic dwelling is no refuge from the city. A parody of "home," Winnie's place is pornographic. Her husband rarely even takes off his hat. The tales told children there are not fairy tales but stories of bloodshed. The only family member who shows any "normality" is Winnie's mother ("she had never really understood why Winnie had married Mr. Verloc" (45)), but she exits from their home early in the novel, signalling its eventual destruction. This "home" is a dark labyrinth itself, structured by the same system of exchange and the same ideology of protectionism that structure the world outside the home. Stevie, who can never remember his address, is indeed the only one who shows any sense about "homes."

Such a reading of *The Princess Casamassima* and *The Secret Agent* suggests that their projects are to manage their crisis in representing anarchism by subordinating the political to the domestic. Particularly, both novels attempt to cover their difficulty with knowing and handling the political material by seeking to invoke the other, woman, as an image of stability. Yet these women are not images of stability, angels in the house, good mothers and wives, priestesses of culture. Both novels reveal women who are independent, sexual, even demonic new women. Though women are posed as the source of affection (Winnie) and aesthetic value (the Princess), underneath they are the source of destruction itself because they manipulate men for "selfish" reasons. The products thus backlight their invocation of the ideal woman, revealing it as an empty ideologeme. The products' framing of the project encourages the last question necessary within a Machereyan analysis: what might this dynamic of project/product imply about the history which could have enabled it: the history of the author and, more largely, that of the historical moment?

Most readers of Conrad's novels immediately remark on both *The Secret Agent*'s unusual urban setting and its atypical focus on the female. If Conrad's mythic ship is his controlling metaphor for desirable human solidarity, his characters always journey to the land to discover the unexplored continent, the impenetrable city, his controlling metaphors for chaos. In Conrad's other novels, however, the narrator has more of a "ground," a moral base, from which to view Kurtz's unnamed cannibalistic evil, Nostromo's secret acquisitive evil, all forms of anarchism as they reveal the exercise of individual power in defiance of law. Although Marlow does have to struggle "to keep himself from being overwhelmed by the dark forces" (Nettels, 145), Conrad, at least in *The Heart of Darkness*, aligns with his narrator to voice his insecurity. Such an anchor prevents him from looking too closely at horrors. The representation stops before we all know too much. Conrad's choice of an ironic omniscient narrator in *The Secret Agent*, which Conrad felt would give him a moral vantage point, prevents the narrator from voicing his difficulties and encourages him to look too far into things. The Conrad of the Author's Note knows that he is without a foothold himself. In spite of his decoy, Winnie, he cannot resist looking into things.

Conrad's need to look is intimately related to his choice of the family and his focus on woman. The novel seems so *unheimlich* to Conrad readers because it is so *heimlich*. It probes the female, the most repressed force in all of Conrad. In his other novels her appearance is always surprising, unnerving, enigmatic, the "Intended," Kurtz's dancer, Mrs. Gould. In *The Secret Agent* Conrad openly confronts the most powerful of females for the male: the mother. He discovers she is at once the source of all life and the source of all destruction. The mother, who seems to love her son but who denies the oedipal relation by turning him over to a cannibalistic father, is the true anarchist. Conrad's narrator, like Heat who can barely view Stevie's remains but who persists in the investigation, himself is irresistibly drawn in to the circle to gaze at this horrible discovered truth. The most intimate of human arenas, the family, is the nest of political unrest. The family that should have been the landlocked counterpart to the mythic ship, it turns out, is the very horror itself. Anarchism, families, mothers, are all of a piece.

Winnie's psychological dismemberment and suicide is the *only* possible resolution to the novel. Only this will satisfy the narrator. She is better dead than alive. Her example leaves behind for Ossipon (the narrator's thin cover here) a disaffection for women and for revolutionary politics. In its place emerges an inspiring memory of her passion that allows Ossipon to "drink with pleasure, with anticipation, with hope" (252). Men are better off, the political order is more stable, with only memories of passionate, sacrificed women, not their embodied, active forms.

James's use of the Princess does not resonate with the same near-hysteria, the same despair, as does Conrad's use of Winnie. James's narrator does not link his female as imaginatively or as emotionally with destruction. Compared to Winnie, the Princess is a more peripheral force in the novel, in spite of what we have seen of the novel's foregrounding of the domestic and of the Princess's structural importance in advancing the plot. The Princess, however, does have a more significant relation to James than we have yet explored. She takes her place in James's gallery beside other characters such as Gilbert Osmond and Isabel Archer as a type of collector. The Princess is not as powerful as Osmond. James shields her, even as he does Isabel, from the full negative consequences of being a collector; he protects the woman. Yet James uses her as he uses Osmond as a decoy figure, as an alter ego for his narrator. She distracts the reader from the narrator's own problems in representing characters who are foreign to him, in this novel working-class characters. James is painfully aware of—and wants to avoid—collecting, "portraitizing," objectifying such characters as the "people," as specimens. Selzer observes that

> if a relation between seeing and power becomes evident in the literature of the London underworld, it asserts itself not because the writer acknowledges the relation but, rather, because he works so carefully to disavow it. (29)

A closer look at the Princess's relation to James's narrator provides further evidence for Selzer's argument that James characteristically uses covers for his own patronizing relation to the working class.

In the Princess, and secondarily in her foil Lady Aurora, the narrator calls into question the kind of relation to the working class practiced by reformers, revolutionaries, and all who seek ultimately their own gratification and amusement. As such, both have complex, if underdeveloped, symbolic functions. They both reveal the world of beauty and grace Hyacinth would destroy should he follow through on his anarchist sympathies. Yet they also are not images of the selfless female tranquilly presiding over the realm of culture. They reveal the distasteful relation to the have-nots that anarchism is imputed to destroy, the relation of possession.

The narrator is more cautiously uncomfortable with Lady Aurora than he is with the Princess. Perhaps this is because she is a charity worker who does measurable work in the slums. Yet she is a shadowy figure, wistful, lonely, unhappy. The narrator never represents her real work and finds it difficult to explain what her motives might be. He hints at several. She finds working-class people are more "interesting" to her than those of her own class (yet James's working-class characters certainly do not convince us of this). Furthermore, her family situation has left her no alternative. She is the youngest in a large family, she is unattractive and so presumably unmarriageable, and she is bored by aristocratic social life. Slum work gives her "liberty" (185). Finally, she has come to love Muniment. All of these personal motives sully her image as the selfless slum worker.

The narrator is unambiguous about the Princess's relation to people in the working class. Unlike Lady Aurora, she does no real slum work. Unlike Hyacinth, she will not practice her politics. Furthermore, she actively manipulates men (Sholto, Hyacinth, Paul) and women (Lady Aurora) to get what she wants in the way of knowledge, novelty, and power. She is often sketched as one on the hunt for "really characteristic types" (153), as one who takes up her "curious animals," her "specimens" of the working class or of the charity worker (433) "simply for what [they] can show [her]" (270). Then she abuses them when they fail to live up to her model or when they begin to adore her as Hyacinth does. Hyacinth even likens himself to a "showman's poodle" (448). Mme Grandoni reveals her egotism, claiming "she [the Princess] wishes to throw herself into the revolution, to guide it, to enlighten it" (156). The Princess is like all possessors in her egotism, unable to do more than collect and discard, unable to see the separate individual life. She is dangerous. She infects all who come under her influence, so Hyacinth comes to feel superior to Pinnie and Millicent.

The narrator does at rare moments attempt to evince some sympathy for the Princess. He shows her caught in a patriarchal world. Her husband wishes to cage her. Paul uses her for her money and, with the other anarchists, excludes her from the movement because she is wealthy and female. Yet the narrator's proto-feminist sympathies seem unconvincing (much as does Conrad's narrator's attempt to explain Winnie's duplicity). This is both because the narrator himself seems unconvinced by these excuses and because he never attempts to enter the Princess's consciousness. The Princess is only available to the reader "on stage," in dialogue with Hyacinth, the Prince, or Mme Grandoni (208). The only moment in the novel when her heart is visible is at Hyacinth's deathbed. This is one of the flattest moments in the novel.

It is significant that, like Conrad's, the narrator will not closely approach the central female pivots of his drama. While in Conrad's case the reason is horror at what he discovers in the female, in *The Princess* the narrator never gets to such a pitch regarding her, the mere vestige of the unfaithful wife. For "little" Hyacinth, his son, his double, occupies most of his attention. In the psychological drama the novel re-enacts between narrator and characters, the Princess is the female interloper, the wife, whose relation to the narrator's son, the double, does not assume frightening importance. As such, *The Princess*, with its structure displacing the Princess and its highly visible narrator, foregrounds a male bonding within which woman is less of a threat than she is to male relationships in Conrad's novel.

These novels' similar employment of an image of "woman" and "home" to control the threat of anarchism can thus be interpreted as the production of the individual authors' characteristic strategies, characteristic ways of thinking (as well as certainly of life circumstances, which could also be considered here). Yet these textual productions of "woman" must also be interpreted as the production of a particular historical moment and a particular ideological configuration, however much the general concept of women as other has a long history. These particular invocations of woman and home in conjunction with anarchist politics—the most far-fetched, the most "foreign," the most terrifying of all late-nineteenth-century British politics—suggest at the very least that an ambivalence toward anarchism, the desire to condemn and yet look, even identify, is more intimately linked with a similar ambivalence toward changing gender relations than at first meets the eye. Anarchists and proto-new women were both, in short, terrifying, compelling, unknown, feared, yet somewhere desired too. They reflected the profound disturbances in "the family, long regarded as a microcosm of the state, if not of the divine order [now] exposed as a nest of seething frustration, discontent, and deception" (Cunningham, 3). One 1890s reviewer of novels which represented the "new woman" even made the link between anarchism and new kinds of women explicit: they were "petticoat anarchists" (Cunningham, 18).

How we read this connection between private and public politics has important theoretical and political implications. While some might read the novels' compression of the political into the domestic as only a "cover," a strategy of displacement, I would argue that the novels through this compression uncannily reveal that domestic politics are of a piece with other, public ones. James's and Conrad's novels' foregrounding of woman in conjunction with the anarchist threat is remarkably astute. James and Conrad reveal that intimate gender relations are of a piece with "outside" politics. What is difficult about James's and Conrad's novels is that they do not merely connect the domestic with the political. In order to contain the politics, they had to try to contain the new woman herself.

3

Gissing's *Demos*: Managing Paternalism

George Gissing's third published novel, *Demos: A Story of English Socialism*, written during the turbulent winter of 1885–86, came out in 1886 while James was completing *The Princess Casamassima*. Gissing decided to publish the novel anonymously given the tense political atmosphere. *Demos* found a "respectable" number of readers, given its timely subject matter;[1] James himself probably read it since he admired Gissing, having known his work before he actually met him in 1901.[2] Like those of *The Princess Casamassima* and *The Secret Agent*, *Demos's* project is a conservative one of containing radical politics. And, like these other novels, *Demos* employs strategies which connect public and private sphere politics, strategies of containment which are similarly problematic in their reliance upon outdated ideologemes. *Demos*, in particular, relies not only upon the ideologeme of the domestic woman but also upon another, related, now empty ideologeme: that of paternalism.

Demos's project, is, however, inflected differently from these other two novels in a number of ways. Its narrator stands in a different relationship to radical politics. *Demos* chooses to attack "English" socialism, not a foreign-derived anarchism, and its narrator claims to be far more knowledgeable than either James's or Conrad's about these contemporary radical politics. This means that *Demos*'s narrator is defensive neither about his lack of knowledge nor about his choice of subject matter. How much Gissing himself actually knew about the contemporary socialist movement is in question. In the early 1880s he was interested in socialism and attended SDF meetings, although the socialism *Demos* attacks, curiously, has more in common with the image of a paternalistic socialism made popular by Robert Owen in the 1840s, than with the socialism of the 1880s. Although John Goode attributes the anachronistic quality of the novel to Gissing's ignorance, one can also interpret this choice both as a critique of tendencies Gissing may have seen in the contemporary socialist movement and as a convenient ideologeme for him to use in order to attack the new socialism. Whatever the actual extent of Gissing's knowledge, however, the central point is that he attacks an English socialism that he thinks he understands.

Demos's narrator is affected by the author's sense of certainty. *The Princess* features a voyeuristic, outsider narrator, one who wants to see the "underground" as his "little Hyacinth" does, before watching Hyacinth's growing anxiety over his revolutionary "pledge" and his subsequent suicide. *The Secret Agent*, on the other hand, offers an ironic, distant narrator, one who seems to wish he didn't have to consider such creatures at all but is nevertheless drawn to do so. Furthermore, both novels barely represent anarchists, never mind the philosophy of anarchism. Anarchism remains inscrutably "foreign," other. The narrator *Demos* features, on the other hand, is not an outsider. He is neither curious nor ironic. Rather, he seems, from the nature of his intrusions, actively and often distressingly involved in the many political scenes—the meetings and demonstrations—he represents. He looks across at his figures as they stand close to him, not down or from a far off vantage point. It is true that Gissing's narrator doesn't much *like* his central political figure, socialist Richard Mutimer, and he likes even less the world of London's East End where the socialists flourish and so he often deprecates them. But of Mutimer and even of socialist politics, nevertheless, the reader gets a much closer view than in James's and Conrad's novels. Whereas *The Princess* and *The Secret Agent* are produced by outsiders, *Demos* is produced by an implied author who feels trapped in this environment and so is resentful. This proximity of the implied author/narrator to the socialist ferment does not mean that *Demos* is thereby "objective" about socialism in the 1880s. It means only that the novel gives the *appearance* of being more authoritative about the movement.

In addition to Gissing's claims to knowledge about radical politics, there are also major differences between these three novels in what they fear these politics might bring about. *The Princess* fears anarchism spells the destruction of "culture" and aesthetic taste, as well as of misguided youths such as Hyacinth. *The Secret Agent* fears anarchism breeds social parasites, dangerously isolated individuals, and ultimately the wanton destruction of innocent victims. *Demos* is less afraid of any such disastrous consequences of radicalism. What it fears rather is the painful domestic and, less so, social upheaval it would create. *Demos*'s focus is on "non terroristic" socialist politics (the narrator in fact denounces its terrorist wing). The novel considers English socialism, which, in the mid 1880s, was dominated by the the Social Democratic Federation. This least visionary, most conservative of the socialist groups wanted to redistribute some of the wealth and to democratize the political arena. *Demos*'s project is to demonstrate, through the use of a representative figure, that the British lower classes haven't the vision to handle either more money or more power and so any thoughts of a new order are futile. For at root the people are a bestial mob, at best content with their simple old ways, at worst, in their passionate ignorance, a disgrace to the Greek ideal alluded to in the novel's title. *Demos* attempts to suggest that the consequences of any attempt at organizing society along socialist principles will be a pervasive breakdown of personal ties, a *social* anarchy more than any cultural impoverishment or terrorist incidents. Socialism would bring the usurpation of others' property and the continued despoliation of nature, a weakening of morality, and above all a loss of love and sympathy among individuals and families as they submerge themselves in divisive causes, in "isms."

Demos's vision derives more, generally, from the ideology of humanism than do James's or Conrad's novels; this is the ideology that individual good deeds will heal the body politic. His vision derives much specifically from Dickens's *Hard Times*, Dickens being the central literary influence on Gissing's work. In fact, *Demos* might be read as a sort of revision of *Hard Times* for the 1880s. Industrial capitalist social relations, with its nurturing of egotistical owners and polarized, unionized workers, is not *Demos*'s target, however, as it is for Dickens in *Hard Times*. Rather highlighted is *socialism*'s similarly authoritarian abuse of power and its perpetuation of divisions among people. What *Demos* recommends as the palliative to bridging the ever widening gulf between classes is similar to what *Hard Times* recommends: individual, not collectivized, expressions, within and across class lines, of love and respect. These expressions, however, both novels argue, are to be grounded in the existing hierarchy of class and gender roles—in short, in a patriarchy assumed to be benign. Even *Demos*'s authorial presence, the presence that selects the setting, writes the plot, and shapes the characters, is akin to Dickens's. The setting, when not in London as it is for a third of the novel, is a "new town," one that has blackened the once idyllic countryside. The plot of *Demos*, using all the stock items of Victorian narratives—melodramatic deaths, lost wills, chance meetings, and the like—is as contrived as is Dickens's to bring down the malefactors. What is missing in Gissing is both Dickens's sentimentality and his caricatures. *Demos*, instead, employs a highly intrusive, often sneering, narrator to pass judgments on characters and situations.[3]

Demos's project is, however, fundamentally "conservative" like those of James's and Conrad's novels, though with these distinguishing marks. All these novels attempt to confront the radical political acts they fear in order to demonstrate their destructiveness and futility and so purge them from the body politic. So cleansed, the societies of these novels can return to "normal." The plots therefore highlight political agitators who are destroyed. Yet, as with James's and Conrad's novels, *Demos*'s product, the novel that is actually produced, with all of its gaps, silences, indirections and misdirections, with all of that which occurs at its margins, shows that the "normal" it hopes to return to is not only ideological, a construct, but also highly flawed, even undesirable. The story *Demos* actually tells is that of the failed socialist endeavor, not the story of the "normal." The "normal" appears as corrupt, not a haven of individual inter- and intraclass connection ameliorating social ills. Instead there is class prejudice and male authoritarianism in the old order which prevents the possibility of real connection. In other words, *Demos*'s political unconscious reveals that the ideology of humanism (leaving the old hierarchies intact), as an alternative to class warfare, is not now historically viable, is in fact incapable of any extended representation. *Demos* is a nostalgic text, nostalgic for an old order, a golden age. But like all nostalgic texts, it simultaneously inscribes its subtle knowledge of its vision's outdatedness, impossibility, and even undesirability.

While many of the novels subsequently studied in this book inadvertently reveal various difficulties with paternalism, the rule of a benevolent father, as a social and political vision (its exorbitant demands on the individual hero to solve what are often social problems, its elitism, and, above all, its repression of the female in an era which began to hail the new woman), Gissing's *Demos* is the most uncomfortable with paternalism, can least serenely and confidently manage its contradictions. His narrator's vituperative reaction to what he sees as false (socialist) heroes and the narrative's ambivalence about what it gestures to as appropriate ones (aristocratic heroes), it can be argued, reveal the different class perspective from within which *Demos* is produced. Even without knowing the implied author's, Gissing's, biographical situation, the reader senses that he lacks, even as he desires, the ballast of a secure upper-class position from which he can confidently endorse paternalism. In other words, he looks upon the aristocracy as an uncomfortable outsider would, at once admiring and disdaining it.[4]

The genre of *Demos* reveals that the linchpin of its conservative project is solidifying the ideology of paternalism, of the public benevolent exercise of aristocratic male leadership. *Demos* is a variant of the *Bildungsroman*, a novel which attempts to portray the changing fortunes of an individual, in this case male, hero. In *Demos*, the hero's changing fortunes involve his relationship with an entire community, the village of Wanley, which is dependent upon his leadership to direct its fortunes. In other words, *Demos*'s very organization as a novel is predicated on the notion that a story about English socialism is best represented in the trajectory of the public career of a male individual. *Demos* at the outset offers two possible, opposing heroes for the reader's evaluation. One is the working-class socialist, Richard Mutimer, who wants to be a paternalistic hero, in this case a saviour figure to the masses, "the glorified representative of his class" (49). The other is the leisured aristocrat Hubert Eldon, who has no interest whatsoever in heroism or even social programs, but who does enjoy living the life of the individual wealthy patriarch (as the reader can see at the novel's end in Eldon's relationship with his wife). Eldon, the heir apparent to the New Wanley mill, is disinherited for Mutimer when Mutimer's uncle, who owned the mill but who had long ago parted company with Mutimer's working-class branch of the family, dies intestate. The issue of the lost-then-found will becomes a deus ex machina for moving along the plot; it also implies that power is arbitrarily given by fate, not won by individual effort. Not surprisingly, given the traffic in women, when Eldon is disinherited, he also loses the woman he loves, Adela Waltham, to Mutimer. Women's fortunes too, it seems, depend on the will. After the opening scenes in which the issue of the inheritance is temporarily solved in Mutimer's favor, Eldon exits, to return only infrequently. Mutimer, as the rising paternalist, then gets the spotlight for the duration of the novel.

Mutimer, however, it turns out, is the false hero, the inappropriate heir to the fortune both de facto and de jure. By discrediting Mutimer's ability to run his financial and political affairs, by having him fail as the appropriate husband for Adela (and indeed fail as a worthy individual for all but his family of origin), and even by attacking such things as his manners, the implied author hopes to sway the reader against Mutimer's socialist ideals. The *Bildungsroman* form is extremely useful for the novelist who wishes to use the negative fortunes of individuals to argue against their beliefs. *Demos*'s argument, in other words, borders on the ad hominem. In Mutimer's largely personal failures are to be read the inability of an entire class to expropriate and then manage the means of production. According to the structural logic of the novel, then, the reader's sympathies are pointed toward the other paternalist, the true hero, the aristocratic Eldon, with his pre-industrial sympathies of restoring the rural countryside. Not surprisingly, Eldon also "gets the woman," the newly widowed Adela, at the novel's end.

Gissing achieves his plot turns with a deft combination of stock Victorian devices on the one hand (wills, chance meetings) and the spare causality of Greek tragedy on the other. Mutimer's hubris is fanned when he inherits money and his uncle's factory at New Wanley. He conceives of a grand scheme, à la Robert Owen, of running his uncle's mill at New Wanley with well-fed, well-housed, and well-educated labor. Unlike Robert Owen's experiment, however, the profits from New Wanley will accrue to the socialist cause and not to Mutimer personally. Mutimer's overweening hubris, however, leads him to make one central mistake (harmatia) which swiftly reverses his fortunes (peripeteia). After he comes to some recognition, at least of the dignity of his wife, he dies as a direct result of his mistake.

Mutimer's tragic mistake, significantly, occurs in his relations with women. Unaware of the feelings of others, as well as of his own, and insufficiently reckoning with the importance of honor, his single critical mistake (according to *Demos*) is to overthrow his devoted lower-class fiancée, Emma Vine, to marry a "lady," Adela, whose higher class position will, he thinks, enhance his power. Like *The Princess*, *Demos*, similarly anxious about this particular breakdown in interpersonal relations, stresses the importance of keeping one's word. The narrative seeks to demonstrate dire consequences to the man who goes back on his personal commitments and abuses women who cannot recover so easily from the stigma of a broken engagement. Mutimer's old friends, his constituency of working-class socialists from Hoxton, interpret his jilting of Emma as a sign that he has similarly abandoned them. This act, for them, becomes the symbol of Mutimer's increasing egotism. The crowd's fury seethes, waiting for an opportunity to erupt which it eventually gets; Mutimer dies from their treatment of him. *Demos*'s handling of the consequences of

Mutimer's broken engagement is clearly an ideological maneuver (and not an attempt to portray working-class chivalry). It is a maneuver designed to focus and punish Mutimer's politics. For the novel does not portray the working-class crowd similarly punishing Rodman, who has abandoned another woman, Mutimer's sister Alice. It is not, then, that the working-class crowd is worth saving, is capable of high ideals; it is that Mutimer has failed in an area important to *Demos*'s narrator.

After Richard (wrongly) marries Adela his fortunes swiftly take a turn for the worse. His socialist enterprise starts failing financially and he contemplates abandoning his project. His birth family starts falling apart, corrupted by wealth. But most melodramatically, his wife, dissatisfied with her marriage and discovering that there are unpleasant secrets in her husband's past which suggest his moral inferiority, one Sunday removes her wedding ring while she is sitting in a church pew. The ring accidentally falls into a crevice. In searching for her ring, Adela stumbles upon the lost will, which old Mutimer had apparently taken with him to church and inadvertently dropped. Subsequently Richard and Adela give up their fortune and go back to live in London, amid the very people who have now become distrustful of them. When Mutimer poorly invests the workers' money, the crowd is primed to read in this another example of his perfidy. In a mob scene, someone throws a rock at Mutimer and he dies, melodramatically, in the arms of his jilted fiancée, Emma Vine, who happened to be there to rescue him from the mob. At this point, Adela is saved by Eldon, who plans to take her off to the Continent, cleansed of her fleeting socialist sympathies, her "English" socialism, to live a life of art.

Demos thereby suggests not only that appropriate interpersonal relations, especially class homogeneous male–female ones, are critical to the stability of the society, but also that violating these relationships can bring down the whole deck of cards, ruin political projects, end lives. The novel thus aims to argue that a failure in personal relationships is directly caused by Mutimer's being a zealot, lower class, and male. Mutimer, in other words, must appear as typical, not eccentric, else the novel's attack will not work.

Mutimer is offered as the only example in the novel of a zealot, of someone so committed to a cause, an "ism," his paternalistic socialism (with himself as father figure), that he does not have a fully developed heart. He lacks empathy, the ability to see the world through someone else's eyes, particularly women's (until, significantly, near the end as his fortunes wane). The narrator often intrudes with this interpretation of

Mutimer. For example, in the first scene in which we are introduced to Mutimer, his fiancée Emma Vine comes to his family's home with news of her ailing sister's health.

> "Jane's ill again, Richard," she said.
> Mutimer had to summon his thoughts from a great distance; his endeavour to look sympathetic was not very successful.
> "Not the fever again?"
> "Yes, it is," she replied sadly.
> "Going to work in the wet, I suppose?"
> He shrugged his shoulders; in his present mood the fact was not so much personally interesting to him as in the light of another case against capitalism. Emma's sister had to go a long way to her daily employment, and could not afford to ride; the fifth attack of rheumatic fever was the price she paid for being permitted to earn ten shillings a week. (35)

The kind of insensitivity Mutimer has to others' feelings, the novel suggests, is, furthermore, connected with the desires his inferior class position stimulates. Significantly, all the characters severely deficient in human sympathy are lower class, Richard's brother Harry, his sister Alice, and her husband Rodman being the other examples. Harry's, Alice's, and Rodman's hungers are more simple, for money, and for a man's love as well in Alice's case. Mutimer's desire is more complicated. When he inherits money and the possibility of respectability, his own hunger to advance his vision and be recognized as a leader is so great that an unbridled egotism emerges, one that will undermine his aims to be a model socialist paternalist. He becomes domineering in his family and with his fellow socialists and so is unable to listen to them. He fires a worker merely because he has insulted him. He feels overconfident in his ability to invest workers' money. Working-class leaders, *Demos* suggests, are bound to fail and so therefore are the political projects Gissing attributes to them. There can be no "progress," implies *Demos*, because the working class is ill-equipped to deal with power.

Nor could the working class ever be better equipped as a class. Their conditions of living do not favor any growth and so they are hopelessly caught. Adela is particularly important as a character not only because she is the one through whom the narrator often gazes at Mutimer's temper and spiritual emptiness, but also because she is the one who tries unsuccessfully to change him to be more sympathetic, more generous. Her failure is meant to demonstrate the impossibility of educating the entire working class.

Finally, *Demos* seems to suggest that Richard's maleness is partly to blame for his failures, insofar as his maleness urges him, as it does the other male characters in the novel, to focus on their own careers and less on sacrificing themselves for others as both Emma and Adela do. Richard's friend Daniel Dabbs becomes smug, self-satisfied, leaving his politics once he inherits a saloon. Rodman, the arch villain of the novel, goes so far as to desert his son and commit bigamy, all for money. All of the women, on the other hand, even selfish Alice, sacrifice themselves for love.

Although *Demos*'s principal strategy is one of attacking socialism by attacking the *person* of its advocates (a person who is at the same time affirmed to be a typical working-class male political type), the novel also attempts to deflate the power of Mutimer's vision of socialism by implying that it is irrelevant. The novel suggests that Mutimer's socialist schemes will not rectify any social problem except giving employment to a few workers. The novel projects an ambiguous reading of the nature of the social problem. For brief moments the novel, through the women characters, hints that material inequity is the problem. In one of the rare glimpses into Emma Vine's materially impoverished condition, the narrator warmly sympathizes with her inability to give her nieces and nephews all the food they ask for. Furthermore, Adela at moments argues abstractly that material inequity is the social problem, as for example when she pleads with Eldon to let the mill stay open when they quit the estate. But these voices are silenced, the moments of foregrounding material inequity brief. Little of the devastating depression of the 1880s, whose effects are represented in Margaret Harkness's novels, for example, is represented in this novel. Furthermore, *Demos* arranges for Emma's material conditions to improve (as a result of Adela's intercession to find her work) and it has Adela readily abandon her social goals under pressure from her new love Eldon. Adela's last words, and almost the last words in the novel, are these to Eldon: "There *was* a distance between us, and my ends were other than yours. That is the past; the present is mine to make myself what you would have me. I have no law but your desire—so much I love you" (477).

If anything, the novel points more to toil and lack of time among the poor rather than material want as the social problem. As the narrator, in another rare scene in which he evinces sympathy for the poor, surveys the "dull desolation" of the graveyards of the poor, he speaks of the relationship between toil and the lack of "aspirations," "hope of memory," "warmth, love" (221). Furthermore, this "toil" is affirmed to be relative;

the rich have their own burdens. The rector at Wanley, Wyvern, who was a socialist in his youth but has "outgrown it" (381) and who seems to have the narrator's approbation for his views, claims that everyone can be happy. If the poor have material suffering, the rich have mental suffering to compensate.

> The life of the very poorest is a struggle to support their bodies; the richest, relieved of that one anxiety, are overwhelmed with such a mass of artificial troubles that their few moments of genuine repose do not exceed those vouchsafed to their antipodes. (383)

Even if material want and toil are sometimes acknowledged as social problems, the fact of social inequity or exploitation itself is not projected as a serious issue—unless people start associating with others outside of their class as Mutimer does and begin to expect too much. It is *desire*, not inequity, that *Demos* attacks. Wyvern suggests this when he criticizes education for instilling "intellectual needs in ordinary people whilst refusing them the sustenance they are taught to crave" (384).

Because of this ambivalence in *Demos* about exactly what the social problem is, never mind who could solve it, Mutimer's paternalistic Owenite solution—a scheme whereby "his" factory, run at a profit, will provide jobs, decent working conditions, and "small houses, promising infinite ugliness in a little space" (68) for a few workers—is not presented as a convincing "solution" to any problem. The choice of Robert Owen as Mutimer's unacknowledged predecessor further works to marginalize his own politics for the reader: they seem anachronistic, quaint, backward looking. The narrative does not even bother to represent the workers' lives in New Wanley or their working conditions. From the behavior of the workers at New Wanley one would hardly know this was the 1880s, which saw the growth of the labor movement, demonstrations, and strikes. All the reader knows of the workers is their facelessness, their apparent docility, their acceptance of whatever kind of leader comes their way, again reinforcing the novel's acceptance of paternalism as the model for socio-political relations. Tellingly, although the workers grumble when Eldon, restored to his inheritance, closes the mill, they are not upset enough to organize or even protest (though a few stone the Manor House and inadvertently precipitate Mrs. Eldon's death, the reader later learns these were only a few drunks).

Through such strategies *Demos* attempts to dismiss Mutimer and all he stands for. At the center of this novel is opened up a question: who, then, can function well in this world? Who can restore the domestic peace and social harmony, a harmony in tune with nature, that socialists have disturbed?

One such positive signifier the novel gestures toward is the nineteenth-century ideologeme of the domestic woman. *Demos* offers, however, a less sentimentalized and longer-suffering Dickensian female at the hearth. Not surprisingly, it is the women, imprisoned in the domestic sphere, particularly Emma, who are filled with the constancy and sympathy Mutimer lacks. Emma patiently cares for her sister's children and continues to love Mutimer no matter what. Adela will honor her wedding vows to stay with Richard no matter how much she suffers. Since the novel marks Mutimer's errors as principally visible in, even derived from within his home life, the novel in this way, unlike *The Princess* and *The Secret Agent*, gestures toward the hearth run by faithful enduring women, rather than the alleviation of poverty or toil, as the solution to all the novel's problems. This argument is certainly supported by the sphere of representation of the novel: almost all of it concerns Adela's attempts to make a marriage with Mutimer. In fact, the first half of the novel is dominated by their courtship, not by the creation of New Wanley. This identification of domestic disharmony as the social problem might suggest then that the females, as keepers of the hearth, as capable of renunciation of their own egos, as sympathetic, could be the true "heroes" of the novel.

Yet these women, victimized by men, are largely impotent, are not powerful enough to silence the other voices of unrest and pain in the novel; the mid-century ideologeme of the intact, stable, restorative domestic sphere is impotent here. Emma and Adela provide a spectacle of martyrdom for the reader, a spectacle which is so protracted as to suggest even that the authorial presence takes a certain pleasure in their humiliation. The only potentially happy hearth (and it does not promise to be healthy given Adela's last comment to Hubert) seems to be Eldon and Adela's and this is unrepresented, a promised land at the end of the novel. While the narrative attempts to telescope social problems (and therefore their solutions) in the family, this strategy doesn't work. There is no imaginable intrafamilial sanctuary. Mutimer's money has torn him from Emma, and Adela's different class training makes any harmony and love between her and Mutimer impossible. The centrifugal pressures of the larger society, pressures against faithfulness to one's class, the only guarantor it seems of a harmonious marriage and a healthy society, have irreparably sundered the family.

The novel in these ways pulls the reader back toward the public sphere and to an individual male leader to heal the country (it never seriously considers the possibility of any collective leadership—the workers are always represented as emotional, mob-like, when they associate). The narrative may be sentimental about the hearth and sympathetic to women, but it more loudly calls for some individual, some man, to articulate a vision which will silence the rising of demos and its leaders such as Mutimer. The nineteenth-century ideologeme of paternalism dominates the project of the novel: individual solutions, masculine leadership for problems public in scope. The plot, by having the aristocrat Eldon finally receive the inheritance and by having Adela desire him, gestures toward Eldon as the hero of the novel, making *Demos*'s project a seemingly conservative one indeed. Eldon would, then, be the rightful Ruskinian paternalist, authoritative, denouncing radical politics and commerce, re-establishing the country house as a space free of the cash nexus, where the worlds of art and nature can be explored. In terms of the novel's positive (as opposed to its critical) project, Eldon as a character should be endowed with empathy, imaginative, unegotistical, and faithful to women. These qualities (the inverse of Mutimer's) would, according to the novel's logic, fit him to be the man to bring England "back" to some pre-industrial, rural golden age.

What the reader faces in Eldon and his cohort Wyvern are, however, at best almost empty signifiers, at worst unpalatable ones. Since the novel does not center on a particular definition of the social problem, even one that a return to pre-industrialism would solve, Eldon's role as would-be new head of a different Wanley is empty (signified by his letting the house and leaving for the Continent) and his role as the individual, solipsistic aesthete is uncomfortably out of place amidst the material suffering and public dissension the novel has represented. Something collapses at the point of *Demos*'s representation of Eldon as the appropriate paternalist. Eldon's inadequate representation deconstructs *Demos*'s project. The question then becomes: what does the inadequacy of Eldon's representation conceal? What does the novel thereby say that it did not "mean" to say? What, in Macherey's terms, is the "product," that which is latent, as distinct from the "project" of the novel, or its manifest intention?

The narrator does not speak much about Eldon, nor does the narrative give him much space. Although his social role is alleged to be more salutary than Mutimer's, it is not the one which preoccupies the narrative. Even conservative reviewers who applauded *Demos* when it was published noted Eldon's insubstantiality and were disturbed by it.[5] While some critics argue that the inadequate representation of Eldon is an indication of Gissing's lack of knowledge of the aristocracy, Eldon's shadowiness, as well as the narrator's venom toward Mutimer and his underrepresentation of Adela's sphere, can more largely be read as symptomatic of the political unconscious of this novel. Eldon's and Mutimer's characters suggest that the notion of authoritative, individual male privilege has an insecure, tenuous social role. The world of female sympathy is confined, impotent, in *Demos*, but the world of effective male leadership is similarly at a dead end.

Demos, however, conveys a particular desperateness in the face of the waning of this ideologeme of masculine leadership. In tracing its impossibility, in recording the limitations of Mutimer and the ineptness of Eldon, it yet seems to desire paternalism all the more, for without a paternalist vision of society the novel would be forced to acknowledge the necessity of demos organized, a specter which it fears. Nowhere is the novel's desperateness more visible than in the figure of its intrusive and omniscient narrator. *Demos*'s narrator has a highly emotional relationship with his characters. He is angry with both of his potential male leaders for they undermine his desire. Though the narrator's angry intrusions make it a less successful, irritating novel for many critics and readers, it is also the feature which most glaringly reveals the power of the attraction that the role of the paternalist had to have had for a writer in Gissing's class position. (For although one cannot always identify narrator and author, in Gissing's case the relationship is always close, the texts being so unself-conscious about their narrative vantage point.) The position of benevolent father, of leader, of seer, is seductive especially if one has been banished to the working class as Gissing was for a while. *Demos* is a particularly interesting novel because in magnifying this authorial desire, primarily through the figure of the narrator, for paternalism, the novel unwittingly magnifies also the unseemly underside of the ideologeme, namely its class bias and its subordination of women.

The narrator's sneeringly intrusive condescension toward Mutimer is evident throughout the novel. For example, he says things like, "Richard began to carve roast beef like a freeman, not by any means like the serf he had repeatedly declared himself in the course of the evening's oratory" (35). Or, as he explains to the reader Mutimer's ability to jilt Emma,

> Was there no sense of compassion in him? Very little. And in saying so I mean anything but to convey that Mutimer was conspicuously hard-hearted. The fatal defect in working people is absence of imagination, the power which may be solely a gift of nature and irrespective of circumstances, but which in most of us owes so much to intellectual training. Half the brutal cruelties perpetrated by uneducated men and women are directly traceable to lack of the imaginative spirit, which comes to mean lack of kindly sympathy. Mutimer, we know, had got for himself only the most profitless of educations, and in addition nature had scanted him on the emotional side. He could not enter into the position of Emma deserted and hopeless. (136)

Toward Eldon the narrator is perhaps less condescending. Yet everything the narrative projects about Eldon, his past, his tone in conversation with others, his thoughts, is such that the narrator has to qualify them. For example, the reader's first introduction to Eldon is through Adela's Radical brother's eyes ("he's a fellow who raises a great edifice of pretence on rotten foundations" [12]), and then a neighbor's gossip about Eldon's extravagance and his affair with an actress (15). The narrator sets Eldon up, in other words, so that the narrator has to be curiously defensive and protective toward Eldon if he is to salvage him. Only the narrator (not even the reader), his intrusions imply, can appreciate his noble mettle. Interpreted another way, the narrator, privileged, forgiving, condescends to Eldon. For example, in a rare long summary of Eldon in the middle of the novel, the narrator seeks to resurrect him. He tries to separate him from vulgar money-grubbers (167). In this way the narrator hopes to exonerate Eldon for not appearing at his potential benefactor's funeral (after all, he owned a mill). Then the narrator tries to explain the young Eldon's philandering as the mark of "no vulgar instinct of sensuality" (166), as an "expected" "exaggerated way" for his "fiery spirit of youth" to express itself (167). Little more is said about his past. The reader is asked to dismiss Eldon's sexual "flings" (though not Mutimer's breaking his engagement to Emma) as usual events in the life of an upper-class male. Such intrusions, though valiant, are, however, unconvincing. They come too late and are too fleeting. Also, their ideology (against money and excusing flings) is at odds with the novel's ideology expressed elsewhere that honest hard work and respect for women is laudable.

The narrator, furthermore, is inadequate in characterizing Eldon's imagination, an imagination upon which (in *Demos*'s eyes) lies Eldon's claim as the rightful heir to Wanley. The narrator, rather, only affirms that it exists. The parallel library scenes,in which both Mutimer and Eldon are shown before their books, are intended to elevate Eldon. Mutimer's books are outdated books of the "extreme" school. "English literature was to him a sealed volume." Mutimer's are, rather, books by Malthus, Robert Owen, Thomas Paine, and Voltaire, books which, the narrator says, "a bright youth of fair opportunities reads as a matter of course, rejoices in for a year or two, then throws aside forever." Mutimer, however, "treasured" them as "the guides of a lifetime" (42). The narrator, in contrast, describes Eldon in his library: a "large collection of superbly bound books" which reveal "strong intellectual tendencies" (17). Yet the irony of this scene, one of which the narrator seems unaware, is that Eldon's grandfather purchased the books and the narrator does not even suggest that young Hubert is acquainted with them. Later in the novel Eldon mentions Dante and the reader discovers that he has learned to appreciate art. The reader, however, never sees much evidence of Eldon's larger imagination. The narrator, rather, asks the reader to *trust* that Eldon is imaginative and will be kind to individuals, that he is Mutimer's "better."

This inadequate representation of Eldon coupled with a high degree of narrative intrusiveness tends to foreground the narrator. Given the narrator's aloofness from both Eldon and Mutimer, Eldon, not surprisingly, is more like Mutimer than at first meets the eye. Eldon is rarely given the stage on which to advance his social opinions. When he does, these are so lacking in vision, so devoid of human sympathy, and so arrogantly expressed that the narrative pairs him with the older, softer, wiser Wyvern and lets Wyvern do most of the talking. In fact, the narrator in these few scenes barely conceals Eldon's similar character flaws to Mutimer's. The narrator calls Eldon, like Mutimer, an "insurgent" (376). Like Mutimer, he cannot escape his class "instincts." Eldon says he grows "'arrogant, autocratic'" whenever he comes too close to the lower class. He even affirms some affinity to Mutimer's politics (though characteristically in a manner of one-upmanship, since he here implies that he would do more than Mutimer): "if I had been born one of them I should be the most savage anarchist" (376). Furthermore, Eldon's and Mutimer's strong mutual antipathy suggests the extent to which they are twins.

The larger question behind the narrator's shielding of Eldon (and the ultimately inferior positioning of Eldon to himself) is the same question we can ask of the rancorous relationship the narrator has to Mutimer: what is the narrator trying to repress or conceal in these near twins whose only real separation is one of their birth?

A persuasive answer is that the narrator thereby attempts to conceal his own drive for authority. The narrator, in other words, himself desires to be the male authority, a kind of paternalist vis-à-vis the reader, the one who knows best. *Demos* "knows" paternalism is ineffective as an ideologeme, as a social vision. Yet it tries to resuscitate this ideologeme through the figure of the narrator, who thereby becomes almost didactic at moments in his relationship with the reader and who certainly is always highly visible. Yet *Demos*'s narrator is also uncomfortable with this desire and so employs Mutimer and Eldon as decoys. In criticizing them, the novel displaces its own guilty desire for the greater authority of the "humanist" narrator.

Demos's political unconscious, its problematic desire for a return to paternalism, also, however, powerfully emerges in another area of the text than in its characterization of the male heroes: in its representation of women and particularly Adela. All the women characters, as Goode has observed, "hover questioningly on the edge of the novel's polemical narrative" (89). The narrative's positioning of them, and particularly Adela, "on the edge" reveals *Demos*'s desires for a submissive female, the unseemly underside of the paternalistic project. And, as is so often true in many such texts, the greater the spectacle of female effort and then suffering, the sweeter the victory of the patriarchal male.

On the surface, the narrative projects Adela as the calm spot in the novel and the median between the two opposing worlds of Mutimer's socialism and Eldon's aestheticism. On her the narrator lavishes the sweetness he denies Mutimer. "Adela," says the narrator, "did indeed embody in almost an ideal degree the fine essence of distinctly feminine qualities which appeal most strongly to the masculine mind" (134). Adela is like an "angel" (148). "Before all things" she was "feminine" (282). Hers, however, is a curious sweetness, an aloof sweetness; Adela, the reader feels, is only a distant ideal for the narrator. It is appropriate, then, that she finally be wrested from Mutimer, who, like a supplicant to Jesus, "was unworthy to touch her garment," and that she be paired with the more illusive Eldon. The narrator gives Eldon the same vision of Adela that he himself has: she is "a vision of purity," "a white rose" (169). She even reminds Eldon of Beatrice in *The Vita Nuova*.

But such adoration, as Gayatri Spivak points out in her article on male adoration of women and particularly Dante's of Beatrice, is really only a shield to hide male power, an excuse for further violence,[6] as is true in Adela's case in the way the novel treats her on the whole. Though the narrator does not handle her as roughly as he does Mutimer nor deny her representation as he does Eldon, *Demos* nonetheless represses her full story and features instead the spectacular moments of her suffering. The narrative focuses on her life with Mutimer, on his increasing attacks on her, and her escalating martyrdom.

And yet, *Demos* reveals that the narrator is not entirely comfortable with this spectacle of Adela as the dumb martyr. There are many moments when he seems uncomfortable with the female submission his ideology requires. There are moments when the narrator considers important questions about Adela, such as, how should she be educated? But, he seems highly ambivalent even about this. The narrator cannot decide whether Adela should be educated or not. As she is about to marry Mutimer, Eldon, one of the narrator's allies, explodes over her mis-education, which could have led her to take this step. Living with Mutimer she begins to get an education, though it is not the sort the narrator prefers: hers is a Gradgrindish education in socialism. When Stella Westlake introduces her to literature and teaches her that "there is a work in the cause of humanity other than that which goes on so clamorously in lecture halls . . . the work of those whose soul is taken captive of loveliness" (470), Adela finally seems to flourish with the narrator's approval.

But then the novel, through the shape of the plot, takes this back. Adela's tutelage under Stella is brief. In fact, the plot moves to discredit Stella when it has Eldon say of her that she lives in an "aesthetic reverie" and that her influence on her own husband has been "deplorable" (381). Furthermore, Adela is never represented as either producing or sustaining any clear idea as a result of her education. Adela's point of view, similar to Wyvern's in some ways, is so weakly expressed that Wyvern's more authoritative voice is needed. The narrator even praises Adela for this weakness. For the "feminine" Adela, "her true enthusiasms were personal" (282). And the narrator comments on her "coldness" and even "spiritual pride" (209) once she starts to learn. He gives to Letty some of these thoughts about Adela too: Adela's new "authority" brings with it a loss of a "lovable" "winning persuasiveness" (253). At one moment he reveals just how much a woman who does not think means to him: "from lips like Adela's it is delicious to hear such moral babbling. Oh, the gravity of conviction in a white-souled English girl of eighteen!" (82)

Just as the narrator is driven to educate her and simultaneously to deny her a mind, so too he is driven to make her rebel while at the same time confining her. For example, at the very moment when Adela takes her wedding band off in church, she is punished: she finds the will which disinherits them. When she privately meets Eldon to plead for his continuing the project at New Wanley (a brief interlude during which she is allowed to be a socialist), the secret meeting becomes a further source of Richard's antagonism to her. When she imagines escaping Mutimer or killing herself, the narrative prevents her. The language the narrator uses seems to ennoble her but also perversely diminishes her, its graphic imagery of self-flagellation suggesting even delight in her inner torture.

> She was deficient in the strength of character which will subdue all circumstances; her strength was of the kind that supports endurance rather than breaks a way to freedom. Every day, every hour, is some such tragedy played through; it is the inevitable result of our social state. Adela could have wept tears of blood; her shame was like a branding iron upon her flesh. (371)

The narrator's gratuitous, even punishing confinement of Adela is particularly evident in a completely unprepared-for set of episodes, episodes, as well, entirely absent from Gissing's other novels. Gissing strongly implies that Adela and Stella have a sexual relationship. While critics variously read this as evidence of Gissing titillating his audience (Goode) or as an "unnatural" expression of Adela's frustrated heterosexual love for Eldon (Sporn), one can find other, deeper explanations for his suggesting such a relationship.[7] For example, their passion can be interpreted as a sublimated *desire* of the narrator's. In this reading, Adela and Stella's relationship is an antidote to the paternalism of both the male characters and the narrator. In Adela and Stella's relationship briefly flourishes love free of possession, of domination. Yet even as this desire surfaces, it must be repressed. The melodramatic plot provides some evidence of the narrator's desire to punish Adela. After Adela's first visit with Stella, Mutimer is overcome by lust for Adela. After the second visit, the other male, Eldon, appears on the scene to deflect her attention from Stella. Eldon's appearance fans Mutimer's jealousy and he vows to keep her under lock and key, even striking her. Adela's ensuing long period of silent suffering can be read as her penance for loving Stella. Only at the end of the novel is their friendship rejuvenated, but now Eldon, in a fairy-tale ending, rescues her in marriage. Adela has been sacrificed to another domineering male. These narrative conjunctions strongly suggest the narrator's own need to punish Adela for her anti-male ventures.

The characterization of Mutimer and Eldon and the representation of the female, particularly of Adela, all point to the narrator's complicity in the ideology of paternalism, his desire to make it work. Yet at the same time *Demos* powerfully and uncomfortably reveals its discomfort with paternalism and its recognition of its insufficiency as a political strategy. Egotism, male privilege and heroism, female submission cannot serenely be represented in this text. These are now historically unconvincing as social solutions to the unrest the novel reveals. The political unconscious of this novel is one that reveals not the possibility of other, collective, feminized models, but at least the decay of now outmoded ones.

4

Shaw's *An Unsocial Socialist*: Mis/Educating Women

The publisher of Bernard Shaw's fifth novel, *An Unsocial Socialist* (1884), prophetically remarked to him,

> I still think it is as clever a novel as we have brought out. If you were to stick to novels or go in for plays (which are even more suited to you, in my opinion), I believe this book . . . would work into a good circulation. (quoted in Loewenstein, 14–15)

Shaw took this advice. Following a brief start on a sixth novel, he abandoned his unsuccessful career as a novelist and turned to writing plays.

While Shaw was approaching the end of his novel career, he was also becoming involved in the Fabian Society. The Fabians were the most middle class of the socialist groups and the least Marxist, in their rejection not only of the necessity of revolution but also of Marx's theory of surplus value, the concept upon which the idea of a working-class-led revolution rested. For if value were not produced by labor (but, as the Fabians argued, by utility, or the consumption of the object), the concept of exploitation itself and the working class's right to reappropriate their products was undermined. In place of a working-class-led revolution the Fabians argued for a collectivist, cooperative social structure to replace laissez-faire capitalism. This socialist society would come about gradually (since the notion of sharp class distinctions was abandoned), through the intervention of the enlightened in the parliamentary process—not through popular demonstrations and militancy.

Much has already been written about the Fabians (their gradual evolution as a group out of the Fellowship of the New Life Circle, their split with the SDF and later Morris's Socialist League, their philosophical roots in Benthamite Utilitarianism and Comtean Positivism, their culture, their programs).[1] It is not necessary to review these things here, particularly since Shaw at the point of *An Unsocial Socialist* was only beginning to become a Fabian. He was, however, immediately delighted with the sensibility and class composition of the Fabians (not "manual-working pseudo-Marxists"[2]). And he would shortly reject his own belief in the labor theory of value (having just finished reading *Capital* in French), and adopt the Fabian position.[3] Knowing both of Shaw's reactions to class and theory prepares the reader of *An Unsocial Socialist*, at the minimum, for the very different kind of socialist hero figured in this novel. He is "unsocial," an aristocrat uninvolved in worker agitation and moving instead within his own class orbit. Furthermore, the reader is prepared to witness Shaw only weakly adhering to the labor theory of value at this point. Shaw's Fabian interests, however, figure into this novel in other, subtler ways, informing its project, and, this chapter will argue, deeply affecting the product itself.

The coincidence of Shaw's abandoning his novel-writing career with his involvement in Fabianism (in May of 1884, while he was actually at work on *An Unsocial Socialist*) raises the interesting question, might these events be related? Might there be a connection between the politics of Fabianism and the kinds of difficulties Shaw got into particularly when he was writing *An Unsocial Socialist*? Could he have turned away from writing novels not only because they weren't selling, but because his particular use of the novel form did not work well with his developing politics, because in affirming the novel he might be questioning the politics? One can only broadly speculate on this, and then a case would have to be made for Shaw's later choice of the drama form being more congenial, which we will not do here. But this chapter can, at least, raise these questions in a general way.

Years later Shaw never defended any of his early, now largely forgotten novels. In an inscription he wrote for a 1946 Dublin edition of *An Unsocial Socialist* Shaw said:

> The title of this novel finished me with the publishers. One of them refused even to read it. . . . And all the time I did not know that I was being ostracized on social and political grounds instead of, as I thought, declined on my literary demerits, which, as is now clear, were never in question. (quoted in Loewenstein, 19–20)

Although Shaw here seems to exonerate *An Unsocial Socialist* on "literary" grounds, he also admits to having believed for a long time that the novel was not accepted for literary reasons. He is, in short, less than convincing about his own estimation of the novel's worth. Continuing to take Shaw's cue, critics have rarely attempted to claim any "literary merit" for the novels and never for *An Unsocial Socialist*.[4] Critics, instead, have mined the novels for "content," useful ore being the themes and characters they provided Shaw with when he turned to drama or their "display of the art of personality" (Dietrich, 53).

This chapter does not offer an argument for *An Unsocial Socialist*'s "literary" merit nor does it mine the novel for useful "ore." What this chapter does propose is a reading of the novel as a text rich in its struggle to remold the novel form in the project of promoting Fabian socialist politics. With Shaw's novel we turn away from novels whose project is to contain a radical politics they find alarming—and captivating. The novels studied in the next two chapters adopt a fundamentally different relationship, an advocacy relationship, to radical politics, a politics, interestingly, which is socialist rather than anarchist. These novels are, however, also troubled by the women at their margins.

Part of *An Unsocial Socialist*'s project is to reshape the conventions of the traditional novel, conventions which are inhospitable to writers with radical political projects. In *An Unsocial Socialist*, the socialist and central character, Sidney Trefusis, appends a "Letter to the Author" which follows the novel proper. In it he disparages fiction, claiming that he has been "misrepresented" because he has been fictionalized, forced by writer and reader to fit a particular "romantic" aesthetic (365–7). In several instances within the novel too, characters satirize novel-reading on the grounds that novels never show real emotions. The "aesthetics" of the late-nineteenth-century novel, Trefusis implies, cannot contain him, since the genre has been shaped by the tastes of a sentimental, limited—and female—readership.

One scene in the novel demystifies the powerful cultural notion that there is something sacrosanct, something ahistorical and apolitical about "the aesthetic." Sir Charles Brandon, aristocrat, and Erskine, "democrat" poet, both neighbors of Sidney, who is the son of a wealthy capitalist, come to Sidney's "estate" to view his art collection. Once a symbol of the aristocratic, pastoral retreat, Sidney's estate is crumbling at his hands (he target-shoots at the romanesque statues). And the collection he's invited them to view is not the family portraits, traditional emblem of the aristocracy, but rather photographs of one of his father's houses, emblem of capitalist accumulation. Charles and Erskine have to be prevailed upon to come in the first place since they don't consider photography "art." Sidney is a clever teacher. He first unsettles them by pointing out the prices he has jotted down underneath the pictures. Sir Charles misreads this as a sign of a tradesman's vulgarity; the album he likens to one "house agents" exhibit. Sidney meanwhile makes sure they bring their aesthetic notions into the open. He asks them if they notice the handsomeness, luxuriousness, and comfortableness of the rooms and grounds they see represented, sometimes himself supplying them with adjectives he knows they would use. But Sidney has more educating to do than merely getting his aristocratic listeners to realize that art, here the "art" of fine living represented in the photographs, costs money. Turning the pages of the album, Sidney then shows them pictures of the present condition of the house. It has been converted into tenements. Photos can give only a "fair idea" of the condition of these, however; "you must imagine the dirt and the odor of the place." Some of these tenements, he goes on quickly to say, are inhabited by former workers in his father's mill, who "had created a considerable part of the vast sums of money for drawing your attention to which you were disgusted with me right now" (288–90). Like contemporary Chinese art museums which juxtapose valuable objects with graphs showing their equivalent in labor, Sidney strips away the beautiful exteriors to reveal their dependency not merely on a money economy, but more specifically on the expropriation of surplus value. Not only, however, is *what* is represented in the photographs thereby deconstructed and situated within a capitalist economy, but the ritualized act of viewing representations is interrogated too, revealed as an act of upper-class voyeurs who conventionally separate the "aesthetic" from politics, economics, and history.

This scene is a kind of "play within the play." Coming near the end of the novel, it provides readers with subtle instructions on how to read this novel. To produce such a reading is the purpose of this essay: to examine how the novel deconstructs traditional, "aesthetically" grounded habits of novel-reading. The episode asks us to consider who has been invited to "view" the "collection," what that reader's expectations are, the process of disorientation the reader is made to experience, and what new political, economic, and historical "truths" the novel is trying to teach through both its subject matter and its rhetorical strategies.

Eric Bentley suggests that *An Unsocial Socialist* is the only work in which Shaw overtly displayed his socialism (104). But socialism is not only represented in the speeches Sidney periodically delivers about the relations between worker and capitalist. Socialist theory produces this text in much more radical ways. The "ponderous economic edifice" is not, as Stanley Weintraub claims, erected on "a foundation of whipped cream,"[5] nor, as Richard Dietrich claims, is romance comically "juxtaposed" with the economics (155); there is no dualism here. The novel exposes economic relations in the most unlikely place: at the level of everyday domestic gender relations, the scene of the Victorian novel. *An Unsocial Socialist* is a novel which powerfully and subtly links capital with patriarchy. It is a novel which suggests that the position of workers, who sell their labor, is linked with that of middle- and upper-class women, who sell themselves in the marriage market. But *An Unsocial Socialist* is radical not only at the level of its focus. In disrupting the habits of comfortable viewing/reading, it deconstructs the very notion of "art" itself, situating it within history.

Macherey cautions, however, that the critical reader needs to be wary of reading the text solely within the parameters of its "project," or, using Jameson's term, its "desire." For the text is not what it was "meant" to be. The "product," or realized text, is not equivalent to its "project." There are "absences," "silences," and inconsistencies which the text does not suture; all texts are thus "broken." Shaw's novel's project might be postulated as the interrogation of the "aesthetic" using the Victorian sentimental novel as exemplum. He attempts to reveal that its key components—the hero, the heroine, the marriage narrative, and the middle- or upper-class setting—are ideologemes, complex units of cultural perception which encode and so uncritically reproduce contemporary social relations of class and gender inequality. Shaw's project itself is to be "unsocial," to deconstruct "society." The product, however, reveals that this project speaks from within an historical moment to which it is "blind"; that, however much it tries to speak the new, it is *also* written from within "ideology." Shaw's choice of the specific novel form of the *Bildungsroman*, in particular, while revealing that his project is to deconstruct the Victorian sentimental novel, inadvertently also undermines his project, entangling him in ideology. For this particular novel form readily invites him to image a male hero who, like Gissing's Mutimer, shares traits of narcissism and paternalism with other *Bildungsroman* heroes. The genre, in other words, invites the socialist hero to be male, non-developing, and egotistical—and so troubled in his relationship to women. This invitation undermines the novel's simultaneous attempt to deconstruct the patriarchy, to suggest the possibility of social change, and to question the ideologeme of the free subject. The novel itself, the product, by making this ideology visible, invites us to theorize some of the historical conditions that could have enabled this "broken" novel.

An Unsocial Socialist's implied reader seems to be female. Sidney, like Shaw in his later book, *The Intelligent Woman's Guide to Socialism and Capitalism*, ostensibly respects women's potentially powerful political role. Sidney suggests to Brandon that women are effective politically because they can influence their husbands and children. And in his "Letter to the Author" Sidney says that "mostly" women read (and write) novels, implying that anyone who writes a novel is probably addressing women. Yet these women readers (and writers) are at present apolitical:

> half-educated . . . rebelliously slavish, superstitious, sentimental, full of the intense egotism fostered by their struggle for personal liberty, and outside their families, with absolutely no social sentiment except love. (366)

Man, he goes on, is "turning with loathing from his egotist's dream of independence to the collective interests of society." Man is

> in full revolt against the acceptance of the infatuation of a pair of lovers as the highest manifestation of the social instinct, and against the restriction of the affections within the narrow circle of blood relationship. (366)

For this attitude, woman calls man a "heartless brute." What better genre than the novel in which to reshape women so they take politics seriously? Shaw's novel, furthermore, is full of apparently women-directed sentimental trappings: the setting in a girls' boarding school (*Jane Eyre*, *Vanity Fair*) and a great house (*Mansfield Park*, *Daniel Deronda*); characters who are upper class; and a plot promising to show young girls at the boarding school, especially Agatha, falling in love and getting married.

Shaw's project, in short, as in *The Intelligent Woman's Guide*, is to change his female reader's desires, and to make her like the new "brute" of a male. Just as Sidney invites his friends to view an estate he has ruined and an art object which subtly makes them "faint," so Shaw invites his female reader to explore familiar terrain he has despoiled so he can expose its social and economic roots. He won't make his readers ill (he must keep them looking), just uncomfortable. To achieve this, everything in the novel is a little off center, every episode, every "photograph," is framed either by a price tag or, more importantly, by usually concealed relations of power and exploitation.

First there is the boarding school, early place of socialization for the female—and an early prison. This boarding school is not a place of learning or, more appropriately for Shaw's implied sentimental reader, "romance." This is a world where girls are punished for breaking trivial rules: for behaving in an "unlady-like" way, such as sliding down banisters. The punishment is modern, not corporeal as in *Jane Eyre* or *Vanity Fair*, but psychological. The girls are to be governed by "moral force," "conscience," a governance coerced through the act of writing, "confessing" one's sins in a book, the "Recording Angel." This setting, like the others, has its rebel: Agatha Wylie. Unlike Jane Eyre and Becky Sharpe, however, who try to rebel physically, Agatha, living with modern methods of punishment, rebels verbally: she plays with language, telling "lies" in the book which cleverly assail her superiors. Agatha, too, is highly skilled in repartee, a repartee that dominates the opening chapters. On being reprimanded for her improper writing, Agatha deconstructs the power relations for the reader. She says that this modern form of "governance," this book, is only for confessing one's own faults, *not* for criticizing one's superiors. "Moral Force" is but another, subtler way of enforcing power relations. One implication here is that the ideologeme of the "angel in the house," which presumably the "Recording Angel" alludes to, ensures female compliance, repressing women's free writing—this some thirty years before Virginia Woolf on the angel. Shaw's tone throughout these scenes is, however, light, no Woolfian talk of "killing the Angel" here, no despair. The externals are "comfortable." But deep within, power seems to stunt Agatha. She has nowhere to go and nothing to do but try to maintain her own integrity and help her friends resist. Though she has the "instinct of an anarchist" (67), she has a tiny arena; she will not, in fact, be heard from much longer in the novel. Her strand is taken up by a male. When she appears later, she will be much subdued. Agatha is a "young new woman" who never blossoms, unlike her spiritual twin, Diana Warwick of George Meredith's *Diana of the Crossways*.

Such are the power relations within Alton College that stunt women, curtailing their external and internal movement, reducing the best of them to rebellious verbiage that must exhaust itself. But not only are the internal power relations of the school exposed to the reader. Shaw also locates Alton within the economic, class-ridden, patriarchal world. Shortly after the reader is introduced to Alton, an anomaly is inserted into the plot: Sidney Trefusis, son of a wealthy capitalist and husband of Agatha's friend, Henrietta. Sidney, in violation of the sentimental novel, has left Henrietta because her feminine charms distracted him from his political work. (The reader only glimpses Henrietta's world briefly; it is another prison for the female, a world where the eccentric and overdramatized characters barely conceal the stifling patriarchal relations of Henrietta's family, who would rather not have her back home now that she's married and who cannot tolerate the social affront of Sidney's abandonment.) Sidney, who coincidentally shows up in the neighborhood of Alton, has decided to masquerade as the "common man," "Smilash," to see if he can organize factory workers to join the international. Shaw's bringing Sidney onto the scene at this point fulfills a particular dimension of his project. Shaw needs a character who can do what Sidney later does when he explains the photographs: a character to deconstruct Alton's economic and gender relations and so situate women's education. Agatha cannot do this. As a female she is confined within her own private world, lacking both Sidney's freedom of movement in the public political sphere and his political education and authority to discourse on surplus value (as when he picks up a necklace and defetishizes it for Henrietta).

Sidney eventually reveals his identity (although not his being married) to Agatha, who "takes a liking" to Smilash. But at this point another disruption occurs for the reader, schooled to believe that Agatha should "fall in love" with the man who could rescue her with his money and his larger vision.

> Her imagination was already busy upon a drama, of which she was the heroine and Smilash the hero, though, with the real man before her, she could not indulge herself by attributing to him quite as much gloomy grandeur of character as to a wholly ideal personage. (63)

The reader is warned: romance is only a novelistic fantasy for Agatha. But then the plot teases again: Agatha says she "falls in love" one day after a storm has brought Sidney to the gates demanding refuge for a poor man and his family. The narrator restrains us again: "girls, like men, want to be petted . . . when they are . . . in low spirits" (134). After Smilash says he loves her, Agatha, in a subsequent letter she writes to Henrietta (who by this time knows that Smilash is her Sidney), confesses she does not love him quite as he seems to love her.

Shaw's parody of the sentimental romantic novel intensifies. Henrietta, braving a winter storm, flies to Sidney in a rage. As if to punish him, Henrietta catches cold and dies upon returning. Here Shaw has a wonderful opportunity to allow Sidney to realize he is a cad and grieve openly for the wrong he has done Henrietta; yet Henrietta, whose death symbolizes female martyrdom, is the only one who is punished: she dies. Sidney suffers no remorse and barely grieves over her death. This scene is particularly difficult for Shaw to pull off: for the implied sentimental female reader, desertion is one thing, lack of "heart" over a wife's death quite another. Shaw, wanting Sidney the "brute" to be at least partially "understood," does give him a moment of grief—he has feelings, it turns out, but has to contain them. Quickly, however, Shaw fills the scene with "distractors," pictures which frame and so distance sentimental mourning. Henrietta's father is only concerned with his daughter's death, not, as Sidney thinks, the deaths of his many tenants in his slums; the doctor is concerned with whether Sidney will blame him; the family is incensed at Sidney's choice of a modest tombstone; and, more to the point (thinks the sentimental reader), now the field is clear for Sidney to marry Agatha, whose brain and temperament more nearly match his.

At this point, the reader should know better. The plot indeed does ultimately have Agatha and Sidney marry, but by the time it happens their relationship is so decentered from the plot, their sentiments so unromantic, that the reader barely cares. The second part of the novel is designed to wear out the sentimental reader's expectations, and indeed it does. It tries to demonstrate that the "infatuation of a pair of lovers" is not the "highest manifestation of the social instinct."

While the first part of the novel delivers a series of rapid shocks to Victorian conventions, the second is calm, marked by a shift of time of several years and a shift of scene to another, potentially pastoral great house belonging to one of Agatha's newly married friends, Jane Brandon. Jane has invited Agatha and a third friend, Gertrude, to visit so she can help them find husbands, although Agatha isn't looking. By another Victorian plot coincidence, Jane lives near Sidney, who has by now assumed his rightful place as heir to his father's fortune. At this point in the plot, Sidney has given up his attempt to unionize the workers and has become soured on individual acts of conversion (since he invariably gets the worker into trouble and so has to turn to philanthropy to help him). Sidney's eccentricity has given way to apparent conventionality. Sidney, like Agatha, is not looking for a spouse, but their observance of the social forms of visits and luncheons throws them together. The sentimental reader generates the organizing questions of the section: will Erskine get Gertrude (will the snobbish Gertrude accept a poet?) and will Sidney get Agatha? The complication is introduced in the form of Gertrude's attachment to Sidney and his seeming attentions to her.

But the calm, settled, "conventional" nature of this section is, again, "off." The section is entropic. What should be passion and self-growth is mere petulance, or, worse, mere talk about growth and change. This section is a parody of Jane Austen's novels. The characters meet in an endless series of conversations which either vent their petty annoyances and jealousies (Jane, who hates her husband Charles; Erskine, who is jealous of Sidney and fearful of Gertrude's rejection; and Gertrude, who is jealous of Agatha); or which express their philosophies on correct behavior (Sidney, à la Mr. Knightly, tries to get Gertrude to recognize her faults, or, alternately, to convert Charles and Erskine to socialism, and Agatha, an Anne Elliot with more sting, tries to get Jane to behave more appropriately in public toward Charles). It's not entirely clear that either Sidney or Agatha succeeds (Sidney, in this "Letter," does say that Gertrude has "improved" but the reader never observes this process; the reader never discovers whether Jane improves). As Shaw thus parodies Austen's emphasis on marriage as the potential correction of one's faults, so he parodies Austen's theme that in marriage, love and money can mix; most of the admirable marriages in Austen's novels also solve the economic question. Shaw's women, like Austen's, live in a world where the society pressures them to marry and where most women (excepting Agatha) see marriage as their primary goal in life. The price always appears beneath the photo: there is nothing else Jane, Gertrude, or Agatha can do but marry. But unlike Austen's novels, in Shaw's the economic motive can never be successfully integrated in a marriage. This is necessity out of which virtue is only made in fictions like Austen's (the reader is never given a glimpse into either Gertrude's or Agatha's marriage).

The few reprieves from the talkiness of the second section come in the form of Gertrude's accidental near self-poisoning and Sidney's occasional altercations with the poor who are ever on the perimeters of the great house. The major reprieve from this tedium, however, comes at the end: Agatha, in jest, proposes to Sidney (even a woman's proposal cannot be made forthrightly), and he, charmed with the idea, talks her into it. He then, tongue-in-cheek, promises Gertrude (who feels jilted because she thought his talking to her signalled courtship) that he'll always keep a place in his heart for her and persuades her to marry Erskine for his sake! These are the pairings the reader long ago expected, but Shaw's project, to demonstrate the silliness and social roots in all this attention to matrimony, has pulled the punches from the climax.

After the reader finishes *An Unsocial Socialist*, having become radically disoriented toward the Victorian novel, having been taught to dethrone the hero, the heroine, marriage, and the bourgeois setting, Shaw ensures that we call into question not only what is usually represented in novels, but the act of reading, of viewing the "photograph" itself. Having heard various characters take pot shots at novel-reading as a waste of time, the reader now hears Sidney in the Appendix deliver the final blow, deconstructing the act of reading as the activity of the hopeless, of those who, like the voyeur, can only look at pictures, believing they can do nothing about them. He tells the author:

> allow me to express my regret that you can find no better employment for your talent than the writing of novels. The first literary result of the foundation of our industrial system upon the profits of piracy and slave-trading was Shakspere. . . . But the poetry of despair will not outlive despair itself. Your nineteenth century novelists are only the tail of Shakspere. Don't tie yourself to it: it is fast wriggling into oblivion. (373)

Critics have interpreted this as Shaw, disgusted with his lack of public success, signing off as a novelist. But this interpretation fails to grapple with the obvious fact that Shaw continued to produce "art" using Shakespeare's very genre, the play. Shaw/Sidney's statement is more accurately read as a self-parody, a comment on the position of the contemporary socialist artist—and particularly, as we shall see, of the Fabian socialist, living before the "age of despair" is over—who, like William Morris producing his beautiful tapestries which can then only be purchased by the wealthy, has to do what he does best, even if it is only to talk to a few "silly" women.

Shaw knew he "talked" far too much for the taste of his contemporary readers and perhaps too much for ours. He has Agatha try to anticipate our criticism by saying of novels, "I wish the characters would not talk so much" (316). In such ways, the novel is aware of some of its own abnormalities. But it is not such self-conscious textual abnormalities we need now to probe, but rather those areas of the text to which it is "blind"—those areas which receive little or no attention by the characters—those areas perhaps far too deep, and too sensitive to be spoken. These areas inadvertently expose the *product*, that which the text actually says that it might not have "meant" to say.

The novel clearly has to be the genre for *An Unsocial Socialist*'s material, given Shaw's project of de-sentimentalizing a female reader. But Shaw's use of the traditional novel form also mires him in the ideology of his era. Like all parody, the novel is imprisoned within the very discourse it criticizes. And, like all parody, the novel secretly is attracted to that which it criticizes.

As I have argued, *An Unsocial Socialist* is a text which speaks to readers steeped in other Victorian novels; it is what Bakhtin calls a "dialogical" text. Another way of saying this is that *An Unsocial Socialist*, like Gissing's *Demos*, must be studied intertextually with the *Bildungsroman*, the dominant form of the novel in the nineteenth century. Michelle Massé observes that key elements of the prototype are the pilgrim and the journey, where the pilgrim, either chosen or self-elected, moves through experience not in order to reach a known end (as in the Christian quest) but rather in order to attempt to consolidate the self as it once was in childhood, where the self was "the standard of the world" (182). This novel, thus, is a search for beginnings. The pilgrim may marry or find a career, but this signals limitation rather than liberation, or he may disclaim assimilation altogether by assuming the martyr role. Because the pilgrim interprets each experience in terms of its potential to consolidate the self, the pilgrim is narcissistic.

Whereas *Demos*, disliking Mutimer's ambition, works to constrain the narcissistic hero, *An Unsocial Socialist* playfully parodies him in Sidney. Sidney has no adolescence. He has no nostalgia or desire. He is not at all, in fact, self-reflective. He is absolutely secure. Having no anxiety about the boundaries of self, he need not fortify them. As a kind of "transpersonal" narcissist, he is radically distanced from the typical *Bildungsroman* hero. But the very writing of dialogical discourse entangles Shaw in the discourse of the other. Sidney, while he is decentered by Shaw in the above ways, still occupies the center of this novel *as a character*. It is Sidney's various quests for a political arena and a satisfactory marriage that structure the plot. Shaw is entangled in the ideology of the centered, questing subject and, in this case (since all goes Sidney's way), the ideology of the free subject.

Sidney's character, like Mutimer's, derives from a particular variant of the *Bildungsroman* hero: the self-elected "saviour of the masses," a type popular with political novelists of the era for many of whom socialism and Christianity were closely related. Speaking from within the framework of Christian and ethical socialism, many writers featured heroes who, though isolated and often ridiculed, sought to act as exempla for others. James Adderley's Stephen Remarx, in *Stephen Remarx: The Story of a Venture in Ethics* (1893), provides a typical example of the Christ-like socialist: Stephen, like Marx, argues for an end to social injustice and, like St. Stephen, is stoned for putting his religion into practice. Shaw's Sidney, however, is more like

Margaret Harkness's character George Eastmont (*George Eastmont: Wanderer*, 1905), who is informed by no particular Christian vision yet nonetheless defines his role as "saviour." Sidney is, characteristically, somewhat tongue-in-cheek about his role, although he never gives it up. "Saviour" heroes, among narcissistic heroes, project a more comfortable narcissism—their forerunner, Jesus, legitimates their stature.

If Shaw's dialogue with the *Bildungsroman* narcissist entangles him in an ideology of the autonomous subject, it also entangles him in patriarchal ideology. The hero, the teacher, is male, the student female. The one speaks, the other is silent. The genre has not invited a female "saviour," or a female transpersonal narcissist, although it did in the mid nineteenth century spawn female *Bildungsroman* heroes such as Jane Eyre. Shaw accepts the convention, suggesting that he inadvertently desired to contain women's power, that his socialist politics did not go this far. The patriarchal tutelage model of this text is one of its most uncomfortable dimensions.

The text, however, is more embarrassed by this problem than it is with that of Sidney as a free subject. Two scenes in the novel starkly reveal the repressiveness of the male tutor though they try to hide this using Sidney's eccentricity. Each occurs at what are perhaps the most sensitive points in any text: the beginning and the end, both marked sites of textual desire, the one where desire is first expressed, the other where the text tries to make the situation come out right. In the beginning of the novel, Agatha is the centerpiece of the the plot. She is bright, witty, a fascinating character. But Shaw silences her. As soon as Sidney appears in her life she is silenced. Later on she is wooden, not even recognizably the same character. The character Agatha suggests that Shaw tried another approach, perhaps tried to create a female Sidney, but could not.

Near the end of the novel, Sidney turns to Gertrude, taking her on as his pupil. He will try to show her, a representative of all silly females in the world, that she should respect herself. Shaw's inclusion of this gratuitous episode is extremely revealing. Another play within the play, the scene has, in its seeming endorsement of the tutor–student model, the inadvertent effect of revealing the troublesome dimensions of this male–female relationship. Sidney is partially flirting and a doubt remains as to whether Gertrude ever learns. Gertrude seems to rely on Sidney for her self-worth (even when Sidney tells the reader in the Appendix that Gertrude has become a socialist, we wonder if this is because he is one). In thus implicitly throwing into question the effectiveness of the tutor–student relationship,

Shaw destabilizes his entire educational project for the implied female reader of this novel. It is not accidental that at the end Shaw brings in the "other" woman, Agatha, so she can propose to Sidney and try to right the male–female imbalance the plot has created: Agatha who never becomes a socialist, Agatha who can never be changed by a tutor but only silenced. Yet Agatha's re-entry effects only a partial recuperation of Shaw's desires for anti-patriarchal politics. Agatha has waited too long in the wings of this text, the absent center everywhere pointed to but almost unrepresentable, hidden from our view.

Parody, however, does not entangle Shaw altogether unwillingly in a certain ideological framework. The novel is also that which he *desires* to speak about, however much he opposes such "trivia." In other words, parody is attractive. To determine what is attractive about this parody to Shaw we have to ask Macherey's question: what can't the novel speak that it needs the excuse of parody?

Centrally what this novel cannot speak is that there is nothing for Sidney to do except what he does: try to urge aristocrats to sign letters and to de-sentimentalize women. Although Sidney's wealth depends on tenements, he thinks it fruitless to divest himself. And Sidney's socialism rejects the possibility of the wealthy man either stimulating trade unionism or converting individual workers. Sidney is thus, ironically, confined to being the very voyeur of the tenements he criticizes and to doing limited political work in the drawing room.

Why, then, one might ask, doesn't Shaw write a novel about those who could agitate more effectively? For Shaw, however, it is not only that the capitalist can't work among workers: no one can. Workers, we learn from this novel, are a slavish sort; the best of them imitate the views of their upper-class teachers, the worst are feudal. Sidney is all there is. Sidney, a forerunner of *Major Barbara*'s Undershaft, is the Carlylean hero: only the capitalist, because he has a driving will to conquer, can be the agent of socialist change. There will be no revolution as such. The force of capitalism itself will lead to state socialism. So what is there for a Sidney to do now but wait, and try minimally to urge other members of the upper class, helped along by women, to join him? The discourse of the drawing room, the material of the sentimental novel, is all there is.

Thus far we have examined *An Unsocial Socialist* as a production. Its *project* is to interrogate the "aesthetic" by deconstructing the Victorian sentimental novel, situating its discourse within patriarchal capitalist social relations. Yet the *product*, the completed text, reveals too that which the novel did not wish to say: that the patriarchy, social entropy, and the free, centered subject remain incompletely deconstructed. At this point a Machereyan analysis urges opening the borders of the text to ask the question: what history could have made possible such a text? Or, put in Bakhtin's terms, with what "history" is the text in dialogue?

One of the first things that strikes even the reader unsympathetic to Shaw's socialism (a reader such as Dietrich) is the confidence this novel shows about Marxism, visible for Dietrich in Shaw's ability to reveal capitalist social relations in the untraditional settings of the boarding school or country house. Put another way, Shaw's novel shares the optimism of late-nineteenth-century socialists in the inevitability of socialism. This deterministic view, shared by others such as William Morris, produces literary texts that are not strident or very preachy (the tone of Sidney's short speeches, for example, contrasts markedly with the speeches made in Robert Tressell's *The Ragged Trousered Philanthropists*, written between 1902 and 1911 near the end of this period of optimism). Rather, the texts of the 1880s are, understandably given this optimism, comedic and utopian in form.

However, Shaw's deterministic view, like Morris's, is not absolute; why write novels if some useful "education" for the coming of socialism won't result? Unlike Morris, however, who writes *News from Nowhere* to intensify people's longing for socialism so it will come more quickly, the political purpose of Shaw's tutor–student model isn't at all clear. This ambiguity is what I will argue is *the* secret at the heart of this novel; this is the source of the novel's entropy and its patriarchal overtones.

Let us first, however, explore what the narrative strategies of the novel do imply is important education for the reader. They suggest that the reader needs to know both that labor creates value and, more dominantly, that female socialization cripples women. Shaw's interrupting Sidney's "story" at Alton and Brandon's to allow him to discourse to Henrietta about labor's creating the value of her necklace or to Charles and Erskine about labor's creating his father's wealth reveal that he wants his reader to understand the classic Marxist theory of value: it is *only* labor that creates value. But the more important knowledge the narrative desires the reader to gain concerns women, not labor. Agatha's problems with power and all the women's economic relation to marriage receive more attention.

Juxtaposing these two concerns of the novel in this way, the reader perceives how "broken" a text this is. Shaw is unable to read Marx's labor theory of value in any extended manner, so these scenes concerning labor only dot the narrative on its fringes; when they erupt the reader is surprised. There is no rich relationship expressed between this theory and women's oppression.

What does this brokenness suggest about Shaw's socialism? For one thing, it implies that he even at this time only weakly supported the labor theory of value. Other Fabians had already rejected this concept in favor of a more moderate one that suggested that such things as consumption and rent also created value, although Shaw argued with them for a time. This Fabian modification is what enabled their view that the nonrevolutionary, nonviolent achievement of socialism was possible. Shaw's insufficient ability to write the labor theory of value into the text portends his eventual theoretical abandoning of the concept.

On the other hand, the brokenness of the text suggests that he could not fully figure women's oppression in relation to the economy. Shaw emphasizes women's oppression primarily at the *ideological* level, at the level of the silly notions women are taught, not at the material level. Political economy and ideology, hence, stand as two poles of this text, each groped toward, neither fully elaborated nor concatenated.

An even larger secret is hidden in the brokenness of this narrative, however, one that speaks too of Fabianism and indeed of much of the British socialist movement in this era. It is a secret obsessively repeated in many of the middle-class novels about radical politics. Neither the working class nor women are really knowable: they remain the objects of inquiry, not the speaking subjects; they are not positioned as fully integrated into the radical political movement. However active they are, the groups do not acknowledge them. It is women's and labor's relative invisibility within the movement that generates the patriarchal tutor Sidney; he both acknowledges their invisibility and perpetuates it. The text is clearly anxious about this role of Sidney's. This is one reason that the narrative is protracted and that it gestures toward providing a romantic ending: marriage typically signifying the joining of subject (here the male) with the object (female). That their marriage cannot be represented speaks of Shaw's ideological impasse.

The central issue this novel raises is that it politically has no raison d'être. The education it proposes is limited. Sidney, the wealthy capitalist, cannot teach the workers anything, nor can he really teach women. Agatha is beyond him and Gertrude comes to socialism outside the parameters of the novel. Fabianism, as the most deterministic and elitist of British socialisms, as the one most comfortable about benign evolution given the right leaders, could perhaps not produce other than such a narrative. Perhaps writing *An Unsocial Socialist* taught Shaw that the realist domestic novel could not comfortably accommodate his politics; such writing only invited exposure of its contradictions and blind spots. Perhaps Shaw did not give up writing novels after all merely because he had difficulty publishing them.

5

William Morris's *News From Nowhere*: The Figuration of Desire

Like several turn-of-the-century writers, William Morris answered Edward Bellamy's socialist utopia, *Looking Backward* (1888), with a utopia of his own. *News from Nowhere*, which first appeared in serial form in *The Commonweal*, the Socialist League's paper, in 1890, was certainly an outgrowth of many of Morris's earlier expressed ideas. Yet the enormous popularity of Bellamy's book in his native America as well as abroad (the book sold hundreds of thousands of copies in a few years in America alone, and went on to be published in five other languages by 1891) had to have provoked Morris into writing. Although Morris's novel did not achieve the level of popularity of Bellamy's in his own time, history has reversed this situation. Morris's novel is not only the best known of the socialist utopian novels to come from England during these years, but it is also one of the best-known novels in the utopian tradition. The study of a utopian novel is something of an anomaly in a book such as this, which is primarily concerned with realist fiction; to adequately study socialist utopias at the turn of the century this book would have to consider the utopias of H. G. Wells, as well as the several, now-forgotten anti-socialist utopias Bellamy's book occasioned.[1] Yet I think it important to include here a discussion of Morris not only because of the novel's stature, but also because it allows us to open up the question of the impact genre has on the production of politics. What happens to the articulation of public and private sphere politics within the utopian genre?

If Shaw's *An Unsocial Socialist*'s project is ambiguous, that of Morris's novel is not. Its aim is to cultivate the reader's *desire* for socialism. Although Morris, like Shaw, believed socialism was inevitable, he, unlike

Shaw, also believed its coming could be hastened if people longed for it badly enough not only at the level of intellect, but also at the level of senses and emotions.[2] Literary art, providing the possibility of appealing to all these levels, is thus the appropriate vehicle for realizing Morris's project. For his genre, Morris selected the social variant of the romance mode: the utopian novel. Utopia predicates the fulfillment of desire on a felicitous social organization, not on the private individual finding romantic love or completing a career.

News from Nowhere, by being cast in the utopian mode, promises, thereby, to avoid some of the difficulties created by *An Unsocial Socialist*, which attempts to recast the *Bildungsroman*'s bourgeois free subject as a selfless saviour of the masses, but which ends up as well producing a self-appointed (and ineffectual) patriarchal tutor of the working classes, women, and the reader. In the utopia, by contrast, the hero from the present (bourgeois) order, the figure who witnesses the new society, is, ostensibly, only a student, like the reader, not the locus of attention. And the reader's gaze is, seemingly, directed not toward the personal fortunes of this witness but rather to the panorama of the new world in which the witness has landed. The genre, in short, promises to open up a space beyond bourgeois individualism and even beyond patriarchy not only in what is represented but in how it is represented, in the narrative process the text employs.

To cultivate a desire for the new—communism—Morris's text necessarily begins from within desire as it is now defined, as it is historically constructed. Although utopia is highly *conscious* of the new in that it ostensibly projects that which has not yet come to be, any utopia also has a "political," or "historical," unconscious. Superficially serene, Morris's text is always negotiating between these poles of new and old, future and present. From *News from Nowhere*'s specific staging of this struggle we can begin to theorize some of the historical conditions of its possibility.

Genre, for Macherey, not only reveals the text's "general ideological intention," or project. It also provides a structure for the novelist, a structure which may assist or hamper the novelist as he or she goes to write a particular text. Genre provides such dimensions of the text as its general concern (utopia is concerned with the "good" society); reader expectations about areas to be explored (utopia promises a panoramic tour of social institutions); and a number of controlling character positions, or functions, which may be housed in separate characters or combined. One of these functions in the utopia is the representative from the reader's world who asks appropriate questions; the character Guest assumes this role in *News from Nowhere*. Another is the explorer of the new world who may be a traveler or a visionary. Often representative and explorer are housed in the same character as they are in Morris's novel, since Guest is also the traveler. Then there is the guide, he or she who shows the representative/explorer around the new world. Dick is Guest's principal escort through the world of Nowhere. And there is the explainer: in describing how the new world works, he or she often indirectly voices the explorer's own views. Hammond is the chief explainer in *Nowhere*, although Ellen shares this role with him toward the novel's end. Although these functions may appear in various combinations, some separation between representative/explorer and guide/explainer functions seems necessary to ensure the exposition's authority (i.e. the newness or "otherness" of the utopian world). The more privileged functions of representative/explorer and explainer have usually been housed in male characters, since males have historically generally been thought to have the authority to make such socio-political critiques. The relationship between these two sets of functions is that of student to teacher; knowledge, rather than adventure, conquest, or love, is the aim of the relationship. A third core function in utopia is often housed in a woman character as she becomes a love object for the representative/explorer, symbolizing his desire for the new world. This is Ellen's chief position in the text. To what extent Morris's novel, in inheriting the generic character functions, becomes entangled in their historically patriarchal ideology or manages to transform this ideology remains to be seen.

For Macherey, the stage of *figuration* follows upon the selection of genre, or the stage of *representation*. At the stage of figuration are collected the specific signs in which the project can be read. In this passage from representation to figuration are produced the gaps, the inconsistencies in the product, which make visible the ideological nature of the project. But in Morris's case, where the textual project is consciously radical, the project of proposing new ways of seeing and thinking, it is necessary to proceed somewhat differently with the analysis: to attend in the project to *both* that which is revolutionary and that which works to conserve existing ideology.

The following reading of *News from Nowhere* focuses on its production of "character" and character relationships as the text attempts to construct new communist "selves," or, to use a phrase less steeped in the bourgeois reification of "self," new "subject positions" for individuals living in a communist society. Morris, in "The Hopes of Civilization" (1885), said about such people, "another people will be dwelling here in England, who, although they may be of our blood and bear our name, will wonder how we lived in the nineteenth century" (162). What the following reading argues is that *Nowhere* both constructs new subject positions and produces old (ideological) ones.

The closing scene of the novel provides a metaphor for this way of reading Morris's text as approach and retreat. Guest, the traveler from our world, is just about to enter a church where a feast is about to begin. All his new friends are already assembled. Guest says,

> I stood on the threshold with the expectant smile on my face of a man who is going to take part in a festivity which he is really prepared to enjoy . . . they were smiling, but their beautiful faces were each turned towards the neighbours on either side, who were talking to them, and they did not seem to see me. . . . A pang shot through me, as of some disaster long expected and suddenly realised. . . . I felt lonely and sick at heart past the power of words to describe. I hung about a minute longer, and then turned and went out of the porch again and through the lime-avenue into the road, while the blackbirds sang their strongest from the bushes about me in the hot June evening. (399–400)

Just as Guest is about to pass over the threshold, past the limits of the ideology which has shaped his way of seeing into an entirely new perspective on himself and others, he is isolated, cut off, thrown back into his own history. The utopian possibility arises, then subsides. Such is the recurring rhythm of this novel.

One dimension of *Nowhere*'s project is its extraordinarily challenging task of figuring "another people," people who exist in an entirely different relation to themselves and others. Morris centers his construction of the new people around their relation to work.

One of the most glaring absences in *Nowhere* is that there is little of the mapping of either the nature or genesis of any technical or political "institutions" (factories, voting assemblies, and the like) that is characteristic of the utopian genre.[3] Some of these institutions exist somewhere out on the margins of Nowhere's world. Hammond, for example, tells Guest about "units of management" or "communes" in which members of that unit vote upon issues of interest to all; a simple majority decides. But no one, including the author-producer, is particularly much concerned about how they operate. These institutions apparently function smoothly and unobtrusively and have seemingly little impact on the characters. *Nowhere*, instead, foregrounds the mention (and not always the representation) of the new people as they make seemingly "free" decisions about not being "self-centered" (239).[4] They decide, for example, when to "work" ("work" is the same as "leisure" here) and what work to do. No one makes them do anything nor, Hammond makes a point of saying, are there codes of public opinion to pressure anyone (270). When the text speaks of work (as it does often since work, the making of beautiful objects and strong bodies, is central to this utopia), it is always in terms of "if a man has a *liking* for pot-making" (227; emphasis added). Guest first encounters an example of this new attitude toward work when the boatman who has been rowing him gives up his position to a friend who has been "on the look-out for a stroke of work" (191); again, work is always entirely voluntary. Strategically the text is adept at creating examples of "felt" freedom through work to which the nineteenth-century reader might respond. Morris's examples are all drawn from the world of crafts, from a largely bygone world of hand agriculture (haying), or from a world of pleasant physical activity (such as sculling). Most of Morris's middle-class readers would already have an unalienated relationship to such work (they would pursue crafts or sculling only in their leisure time without external constraints). In this way Morris hopes to play on what the reader already experiences as pleasurable work and then argue for all work's being potentially like this.

Morris's communist "subject," a subject who experiences little or no conflict between what is socially necessary and individual desire, is clearly not the "subject" of bourgeois ideology. He or she is not promoted as the individualist self with an autonomous subjectivity. The narrative, furthermore, does not tell any one character's story nor represent any single center of consciousness. There is no tunneling into an individual character. Nor is Morris's new subject its opposite: the inchoate, fragmented self created by late capitalist consumer society, theorized by post-structuralism, and represented in postmodernist art.

News from Nowhere, in short, sets out to produce an almost unimaginable "human." Morris's choice of the utopian form and his particular adaptation of making his vision a dream help defer the reader's incredulity, since the dream-utopia legitimates vague characters. Furthermore, the narrative is structured around Guest's ambling through Nowhere and so "characters" are seen only fleetingly as the narrator passes them. There are in fact few characters even named in the text, among these Dick, his wife Clara, Hammond, and Ellen, all more fully represented thang Boffin, Bob, and Anna. But Dick and Clara have no discernible "traits," only a personal history of marital troubles. Even the two more prominent "characters," Hammond and Ellen, are not highly individuated.

As the text attempts to figure its desire for "new" humans, as it attempts to protect such humans from the reader's incredulity through genre and narrative form, *Nowhere*, at the same time, constructs traditional humans. The figures emerge partly as projections of authorial desire, as mirrors of William Morris. The high ambition of the project cannot be sustained.

Many readers have observed that the characters wear fourteenth-century dress and shun mass-produced factory goods in favor of handcrafts, all well-documented tastes of Morris. More subtly though, the characters mirror the narrator's desire for one kind of new human. The narrator repetitively uses the same adjectives to describe the characters and he notices the same things about them. For example, they are "kind and happy looking" (193) or "kindly in expression" (200); they are "shapely and well-knit of body" (193) or have "beautiful arms, which she had bared for her work, firm and well-knit from shoulder to wrist" (198); they are "thoroughly healthy looking and strong" (193); "gaily dressed, especially the women" (203); "pretty" (204, 205). Most often, the adjective "pretty" and the descriptions particularly of the body refer to women; the narrator is often arrested by their beauty, a point which we will shortly probe further. Such descriptions of these "new" humans, although designed partly to deflate the bourgeois notion of "character," at the same time foreground the perspective, the desires, of the witness figure: a male witness figure.

Hammond is one of the two more visible "characters" Guest meets on his journey. He is the rare character in Nowhere who both sees the whole panorama of Nowhere and who also knows history. As the explainer figure of utopia, as the sage, he generically has not only visibility but authority, for his job is to teach both Guest and reader about the whole of the new order and to tell him/us how they got there. Here the generic expectations tend to work against Morris's project. Morris's project in Hammond is to rewrite the subject position of the learned patriarchal authority, the great man, in communism. As was also true in the case of his figuration of "another people," however, Hammond is not entirely a new model. He is not altogether a figuration of a new kind of non-authoritative sage. He too is also a mirror of Guest himself and a projection of authorial desire.

In order to teach its contemporary reader how to imagine an altered status of the learned man, *Nowhere* minimizes Hammond's status in his own world. The other characters clearly respect Hammond's knowledge of the past, but they do not in any way look up to him. They see him as someone to turn to when curious strangers come by.

Nowhere enables this different position of the intellectual by changing the *status* of learning and particularly the learning of history. The people of Nowhere are not interested in history and so are not apt to revere Hammond. The behavior of the characters reveals this and Ellen, later in the novel, makes this public attitude (which troubles her) explicit.

> "But I think sometimes people are too careless of the history of the past—too apt to leave it in the hands of old learned men like Hammond. Who knows? Happy as we are, times may alter; we may be bitten with some impulse toward change, and many things may seem too wonderful for us to resist, too exciting not to catch at, if we do not know that they are but phases of what has been before; and withal ruinous, deceitful, and sordid." (383)

The society is in fact curiously "anti-intellectual." When one of Nowhere's inhabitants questions Guest about the old times, Dick says,

> "Hold hard, Bob; this questioning of guests won't do. Why, much learning is spoiling you.... The fact is, I begin to think that you have so muddled your head with mathematics, and with grubbing into those idiotic old books about political economy... that you scarcely know how to behave. Really, it is about time for you to take to some open-air work, so that you may clear away the cobwebs from your brain." (196–7)

The inhabitants of Nowhere do know ideas, but there are acceptable and unacceptable ways to present them—never should one "go on." The pleasure of the present should not be sacrificed. In fact, Nowhere offers a negative example of a character who does "go on." Ellen's grandfather (sometimes called her father in the narrative), dubbed a "grumbler" by the others, serves also to focus Nowhere's position on learned men. Unlike Hammond, he has not learned his appropriate place in Nowhere: to offer knowledge only when it is solicited. Instead, the grumbler has taken to complaining about the altered status of his knowledge. He bemoans the passing of the old times in which "splendid works of imagination and intellect were produced" (336). He is criticized by Ellen, who says,

> "Books, books! always books, grandfather! When will you understand that after all it is the world we live in which interests us; the world of which we are a part, and which we can never love too much? Look!" she said, throwing open the casement wider and showing us the white light sparkling between the black shadows of the moonlit garden, through which ran a little shiver of the summer

> night-wind, "look! these are our books in these days—and these," she said, stepping lightly up to the two lovers and laying a hand on each of their shoulders. (336–7)

Not only does book knowledge, and particularly the knowledge of history, have little status in Nowhere. Teachers do not have any structural authority in Nowhere either. When children learn, they do not learn through a hierarchical tutor–student relationship. "Most children, [says Dick] seeing books lying about, manage to read by the time they are four years old" (209). Children learn languages merely by hearing their elders. When Guest, in this conversation, asks about how children learn history, Dick tells him that they learn it if they want but few in fact care much about it (210). When Dick then describes Hammond as living "a good deal" in the museum where he was custodian of the books, of which "he looks upon himself as part" (232), the reader is not prepared to receive Hammond with any awe.

Not only does the structure of Nowhere's world work to minimize Hammond's authority. The structure of Nowhere's narrative, too, minimizes Hammond's role. He is not Guest's constant companion in the journey through utopia. Rather, Hammond is isolated from the others and he is with Guest only during a stage of Guest's journey, and a transitional stage at that. Within *Nowhere*'s panoramic or spiral organization typical of utopia, the associatively organized glimpses the reader is afforded into clothing, homes, markets, and the like as Guest takes his tour, there also emerges a developmental, linear structure centering on the narrator's process of absorbing the new world. In the first part, Guest literally (and metaphorically) crosses the river into the earthly Eden of Nowhere (Suvin, 191). At this stage he sees inadequately as he attempts to take in the sights of the new world: he meets and sees a number of people, begins to ask a few questions, and tries to conceal his own identity. When he is sufficiently awakened, realizing this is not his own dream, he is taken to Hammond for the second stage. Hammond, the narrative structure makes clear, is a kind of way station. He is not, himself, the fullest expression of the utopia as he sits in his chair and speaks of the past. Guest refers to him as a "blanket . . . against the cold of this very new world, where I was . . . stripped bare of every habitual thought and way of acting" (286–7). After Guest (and the reader) have become "protected," have had their intellectual desires satisfied, as indeed they must if Nowhere is to achieve a level of plausibility, it is time for Guest to penetrate more deeply the world of Nowhere. He moves on, in the third and final movement, back to the utopian landscape in which he can more deeply experience sensual and aesthetic fulfillment. There is, in other words, none of the affective atmosphere of Nowhere around Hammond. The section seems designed to arrest, even bore the reader, even as it satisfies the intellect. Hammond's section is dominated by a closed rhetorical structure of question and answer, where Hammond makes rather long, sometimes overbearing speeches, whereas the flanking sections display the narrator learning by "open-air" experiences—precisely the mode of education the novel explicitly endorses.

Yet, *Nowhere* is troubled by the attitude the inhabitants have adopted both toward learning and toward authority. This is partly revealed in the recurrence of the issue, as is visible in the discussion above. By bringing it up obsessively through different characters, the text seems to long to settle the problem but cannot. Ellen's words on history, although Guest seems not to hear her words (instead noticing her "beauty and kindness"), are echoed within the text by Guest's questions to Hammond. Furthermore, her words echo a statement Morris makes in his essay, "The Socicty of the Future," an echo which tends to enhance her authority as a spokesperson.

> But perhaps you may think that Society being thus happy and at peace, its very success would lead it to corruption once more? Yes, that might be if men were not watchful and valiant; but we have begun by saying that they would be free, and free men are bound to be responsible, and that means that they shall be watchful and valiant. (202–3)

The issue that Guest/the implied author is wrestling with has to do with the stability of Nowhere. On the surface, Nowhere's inhabitants seem totally secure, as if they fear no destabilizing force that a knowledge of history would help them confront. Nowhere here corresponds to Marx's vision of a communist society in which our history would be viewed as an interesting but irrelevant "pre-history." But at a deeper level, the issue worries the outsider who cannot imagine a stable world outside of "pre-history" and so cannot imagine a world in which a knowledge of the evolution of history wouldn't be critical.

Nowhere, more subtly, is also anxious about the absence of authority in the utopian world. This is visible in the way the text works to reclaim individual authority, particularly Guest's authority. *Nowhere* foregrounds this figure. Guest's progress in immersing himself in the new world is the centerpiece of the novel's three-part structure. What Suvin says of Bellamy's *Looking Backward* could also be said of Morris's novel: "The construction of a social system for the reader is also the reconstruction of the hero" (194).

The fuller characterization of Guest also privileges him. He is the only character to whose struggles the reader is privy. The inadequate characterization of the background characters, who mirror Morris's proclivities, serves to highlight Guest, the one who gazes. Even Hammond is not portrayed as a character totally independent of Guest. When Guest first sees him he says,

> I was now looking at him harder than good manners allowed of, perhaps; for in truth his face, dried-apple-like it was, seemed strangely familiar to me; as if I had seen it before—in a looking-glass it might be. . . . (234)

Furthermore, Dick, the second explainer in the text, is a kinsman of Hammond. Finally, Morris attributes to Ellen, in the passage quoted above on history, his own words. The implication is clear: every character of some authority in Nowhere seems partly to mirror the implied author.

It is true that the text attempts to undermine its attention to the narrator Guest by casting him as somewhat inept. He is awkward with others. He presents himself as an ineffectual old man. The frame of the novel, especially, displays this inept side of the narrator. In the frame the reader learns that the narrator has returned from a meeting where six views of socialism have been advanced. He remembers what he should have said on the way home, then has a dream to compensate, the dream form further suggesting his weak discursive abilities. Furthermore, in the frame he is clearly awkward about using his own first person for his narrator. Hence he meanders through "our friend," a man "our friend" talks about who has the experience at the socialist meeting, and then finally reaches the "I" (181-3).

From another perspective, however, all of this can be read as a clever rhetorical device, or, if nothing so intentional as this, then a symptom of a kind of self-absorption. In any case, even as *Nowhere* draws the reader's gaze outward toward a new society where there are no authorities, it also draws it back to the witness, the witness who is still entangled in bourgeois concepts of self-development and interested in maintaining at least narrative, if not social or political, authority.

The desire *Nowhere* figures is also connected with gender issues. On the one hand, the implied author sincerely desires an end to the oppression of women—in work, in divorce settlements, in childbearing and rearing. This is apparent from aspects of the structure of the utopia. On the other, the narrator, his persona, unintentionally establishes woman as the object of his own unreconstructed desire, his gaze, his tutelage, not as a subject in her own right. Radical as *Nowhere* is in many dimensions of its vision, it produces a view of woman as much a projection of bourgeois male fantasy as in any of the other texts explored so far.

A good portion of the discourse of *Nowhere* is centered around the altered status of women, revealing Morris's preoccupation with gender inequity. *Nowhere* is eager to assert, along with Engels, that the oppression of women ends with the abolition of private property. Housework and mothering in Nowhere are accorded totally equal status with other labor. Divorce laws, hurtful to both men and women, have been abolished. Women have been freed from restrictive clothing. Even sexually Morris hints at a revolution: it is Clara who had an "affair" while married to Dick, one which causes pain but brings no shame on her. Finally, *Nowhere* in its narrative structure seeks to establish the equal status of women by allowing one of the authorities, the last of Guest's teachers, to be a woman, Ellen.

The narrator/implied author, for all this, is unregenerate. Morris's text says more than his implied author does: the oppression of women does not simply, mechanically end when private property is abolished, as Hammond believes. *News from Nowhere* is, partly, a "respectable" male's fantasy of communism breeding more attractive women for men.

Guest continues to objectify women, seeing them not in terms of an old standard of beauty, but now a new one more to his "tastes": a woman who is healthy, kind, and tanned. As he walks through Nowhere, Guest is nearly obsessed with the "prettiness" of the women. Here is one of his descriptions of "one of the girls" (nameless, although her male companion here, Dick, is not):

> her skin was as smooth as ivory, her cheeks full and round, her lips as red as the roses she had brought in; her beautiful arms, which she had bared for her work, firm and well-knit from shoulder to wrist. (198)

Only for a moment does the reader get a glimpse of *her* response to Guest's suggestively intimate stare: "she blushed a little under my gaze." Instead, the narrator's desire is what is repeatedly foregrounded. "Almost everybody was gaily dressed, but especially the women, who were so well-looking, or even so handsome, that I could scarcely refrain my tongue from calling my companion's attention to the fact" (203). Or, "Are these the regular country people? What very pretty girls there are amongst them" (204). When Guest first meets Ellen, he even uses a simile which objectifies her: the book.

> I for my part could not help staring at her, and thinking that if she were a book, the pictures in it were most lovely. The colour mantled in her delicate sunburnt cheeks, her grey eyes, light amidst the tan of her face, kindly looked on us all as she spoke. (337)

During their second meeting, Guest realizes she is different from other women ("the most unfamiliar to me, the most unlike what I could have thought of" [371]). But it is only another "register" of charm and interest, not a new way of relating to women. He, after all, says, "I kept wondering what she would say or do next to surprise and please me" (371). Later he can't even pay attention to what she says, for her "strange and almost wild beauty had put it [her question] out of my head" (338). When Ellen offers her thoughts on history (quoted above), Guest replies only, "her beauty and kindness and eagerness combined forced me to think as she did" (384). Guest's amorousness, by our standards, is very controlled in the text. He is always indirect, genteel, and brief in his adoration of the female body. And yet, as these examples reveal, his concerns are obsessive and his language highly suggestive.

Nowhere's production of woman does little to counteract Guest's pervasive gaze. Ellen, grandchild of a "grumbler," is the only one of Nowhere's women to speak out on a matter of importance—and then Guest doesn't hear her. No one else apparently pays much attention to her views either. Clara, the other woman character in the novel, is much more deferential than Ellen. She usually asks questions of the men, and she accepts men's attention to women's physical beauty.

These "excesses"—Guest's obsessive gaze and the presence of unacknowledged or submissive women—frame, or "backlight," Guest and the producer of the narrative, the implied author, revealing their patriarchal ideology. Two scenes from *Nowhere*, in particular, however, even more powerfully backlight this ideology because they are concentrated in one area of the text rather than being diffused throughout: part of Guest's dialogue with Hammond and the closing scene of the novel.

The first disruptive scene occurs during Hammond's dialogue with Guest on "the woman question." The reader witnesses two male characters (and mirrors of each other) "settle" this question by elucidating the conditions which have "ended" inequity between the sexes. *Nowhere* structures this scene as two men saying "all there is to say" (and sometimes laughing "heartily") about women, when there are clearly women who should be able to speak for themselves. By using men, *Nowhere* visibly reproduces the more subtle objectification of Guest's gaze. Hammond, haughty in his view of the "woman question" ("I believe I really do understand 'the Emancipation of Women Movement' of the nineteenth century. I doubt if any other man now alive does"), tells Guest about how they have solved this problem. Although the division of labor along any class lines has been totally eliminated, it has not been for women. The exclusion of women is anomalous, disruptive, and profoundly disturbing. Nowhere goes to even further extremes in postulating woman as other: personal/sexual relations between the sexes are the *only* area of human life unreconstituted by communism.[5]

The setting and Hammond's ideas combine to make their display almost offensive to the contemporary reader. Hammond says, "of course you will see that all this [the woman question] is a dead controversy now . . . . The women do what they can do best, and what they like best, and the men are neither jealous of it or injured by it." As is not true of other labor in this novel, what women like best appears second in the list. What they "can" do best is keep house and raise children. When Guest mentions that he sees women waiting on men and ventures to suggest this is a "little like reaction" (meaning reactionary), Hammond proceeds to rely on an old Norwegian folk tale called "How the Man Minded the House" to argue that men are unfit for any sort of housekeeping. Hammond's recounting of the folk tale, prompting them to have a good laugh over their own ineptitude for housework, seems particularly gratuitous and intensifies a kind of men's club atmosphere about the whole scene. Hammond keeps "chuckling" throughout the conversation until Guest begins to question him on nineteenth-century ideas held by "superior" women (again in quotation marks) concerning the emancipation of intelligent women from begetting children. Hammond then "grew quite serious again." He becomes angry at these women, calling this a "strange piece of baseless folly" and then "warmly" delivers the following:

> "So that, you see, the ordinarily healthy woman (and almost all our women are both healthy and at least comely), respected as a child-bearer and rearer of children, desired as a woman, loved as a companion, unanxious for the future of her children, has far more instinct for maternity than the poor drudge and mother of drudges of past days could ever have had; or than her sister of the upper classes, brought up in affected ignorance of natural facts, reared in an atmosphere of mingled prudery and prurience." (all quotations above, 240–3)

Later the sexism more latent in this scene erupts briefly but powerfully as Hammond makes an offhand remark to Guest: "We live amidst beauty without any fear of becoming effeminate" (254).

The consequences of unreconstructed male desire for women, on the part of Hammond, Guest, and the implied author alike (as producer of the structure of narration), are dire. *Nowhere*'s unconscious erupts in its plot. The final scene of the novel reveals the price of such desire.

The third phase of Guest's journey into Nowhere follows his visit with Hammond. Symbolically he sheds his nineteenth-century clothes, ready now to enter fully the new world. *Nowhere* figures Guest's readiness by increasingly focusing his earlier attention to many "pretty" women now on one: Ellen. In the last scene of the novel that takes place in the landscape of Nowhere, Guest and Ellen row down the Thames, a journey which sharply contrasts with Guest's bewildered boat journey at the novel's beginning. The more Guest's desire for Ellen is awakened, however, the more he senses he is about to leave until finally he is abruptly gone, as if banished from the Eden he has finally begun to set foot in. The question is, what is the "sin" he has committed that has banished him?

Ostensibly, of course, the novel must end somewhere. The witness must return to our fallen world. His "sin" is merely being of another time. But the plot ending precisely where it does raises the possibility that Guest's "sin" is connected with some failure in his relationship to Ellen.

The scene opens with Guest blundering and revealing to her his prior knowledge of the Thames. Unlike his other interlocutors before, however, Ellen readily assumes the student role: "you can tell me all I want to know about it." Yet, though curious, she is not passive. She maintains her sense of her own knowledge: "Yet you must understand that the part I do know, I know as thoroughly as you do" (373). When Guest confesses only to her his real identity, she admits to an ulterior motive in wanting to row with him: "I have followed you up from Runnymede in order that I might ask you many questions" (376). Ellen continues to be forthright in her questions and reactions, concerned about public matters (she wants to know history not for herself but in case others need to know it in time to come).

For a moment Guest seems to react to her being "well-knit both in body *and mind*" (378, emphasis added). But then a peculiar thing begins to happen when she claims to know what he is about to say. Perhaps Guest is terrified at the prospect of a new kind of woman—one who is an equal? One with whom he could have a partnership? For Ellen as a separate consciousness at this point begins to fade for him. It is as if the beautiful woman part of her and especially the thought of possessing this beauty begin to take over in Guest's mind; earlier he has referred to this as a day like that of the "Lotus Eaters" (371) and compared himself to Odysseus

(370). His desire, not for union with her as a separate subject, but more for possession of her as his mirror, begins to intensify. As she finishes her long passage on the importance of history and her own desire for children, she says, "What do you think?" (383). He answers, not hearing any of the content of her words, "Of one thing I was sure, that her beauty and kindness and eagerness combined, forced me to think as she did, when she was not earnestly laying herself open to receive my thoughts" (384). The sexual metaphor is all but explicit. Woman is either the Leda to his swan, or the bewitcher, whose beauty makes him do whatever she wants. In either case, Ellen has ceased to have her own "subjectivity" for Guest, imprisoned as he is in his narcissistic desire for possessing or being possessed.

The next chapter, entitled "The Journey's End," opens with Guest's admission of his "gathering fear of where it [his new-born excitement about Ellen] would land me" (384). He has a premonition that something is awry, that his relationship to her is somehow going to expel him from utopia. Ellen proposes he stay with them and says, "I begin to suspect you of wanting to nurse a sham sorrow" (387), and likens him to ridiculous characters in old novels—suggesting to the reader that his expulsion isn't necessary but might be the result of his own attitudes, particularly his clinging to outworn ways of thinking. He begins to expect the landscape to change at any minute. As he sees Ellen "echoing his thoughts" (391), his heartsickness over the waste of his own world grows. Finally, as he is about to enter the church where they have come to feast, he realizes he has not made it over the threshold.

Guest's expulsion from Eden seems, then, to be connected with his heartsickness, not only over the sorrow for his own world but also, as latently written into the last scene in the world of Nowhere, over his desire for Ellen. His *desire* makes him heartsick, *Nowhere*'s unconscious suggests, because it can't be fulfilled. It is an inappropriate desire, a desire from the old patriarchal world. It is the narcissistic desire of a man to deny woman's own subject-ness. The less he sees her as a subject, the more he sees her as *his* receptacle, *his* mirror, or *his* bewitcher, the harder it is for him to stay in utopia.

Nowhere's unconscious reveals that the consequences of such unreconstructed desire are dire indeed. It is, however, a lesson Guest never learns. At the end he can only generalize his problem to say that "all along" he was conscious "that I was really seeing all that new life from the outside, still wrapped up in the prejudices, the anxieties, the distrust of this time of doubt and struggle" (400)—a very different sentiment from the one he earlier expressed when he said that Nowhere "stripped" him "bare of every habitual thought" (286–7). The only hint that he may have somewhere learned the lesson about his patriarchal male desire is his reading of Ellen's look:

> "Go back again, now you have seen us, and your outward eyes have learned that in spite of all the infallible maxims of your day there is yet a time of rest in store for the world, when *mastery has changed into fellowship*—but not before. Go back again, then, and while you live you will see all round you people engaged *in making others live lives which are not their own*, while they themselves care nothing for their own real lives—men who hate life though they fear death." (401, emphasis added)

Ellen could well be speaking here of his inappropriate relation to her. We cannot know. *Nowhere* has all but contained her real thoughts.

News from Nowhere attempts to stimulate a desire for communism by figuring its new kinds of subject positions, characters in a new relationship to work, to authority, and to each other across gender lines. The text's desire, as well as its difficulty in figuring this desire, provokes speculation on the history which could have enabled such a text. Particularly of interest here is that history connected with the socialist and feminist movements as it might be revealed only in literary discourse.

Centrally apparent is the extent of the separation of these movements. Not only does Hammond's story of "how the change came" not figure the women's movement, but his comfortableness in speaking against "intellectual" women and in speaking for all women reveals the immensity of the separation. This suggests partly the relative invisibility of the women's movement (in 1888 the movement existed though it was not as publicly visible as it was to become during the suffrage campaign of the early 1900s). But Hammond's ideas and his way of stating them also suggest the extent to which socialists at this point had not considered "the woman question" in any but the most perfunctory of ways. Like Shaw's novel, *News from Nowhere* shows no embarrassment in adopting the position of educating "ignorant" women, in Morris's case women readers, about the economy, relying on the assumption that economic liberation would automatically bring about the emancipation of women.

But perhaps there is more to this production of woman than a simple lack of consideration, than ignorance about the public and private work women would have to do. Perhaps Shaw and Morris somewhere sensed these potential changes in women's relationship to men, relations involving frankness and intellectual equality, desired such relationships, yet feared them all the same.[6] So they invoke new kinds of women and new kinds of relationships, yet also try to contain them. Both Agatha and Ellen, as we have seen, hover on the margins of their respective texts, both potentially strong, independent-minded women. It is only by an act of some force that their texts silence them, whether by removing them as Shaw does or submitting them to the narrator's objectifying, diminishing gaze as Morris does. These novels, and especially Morris's, are not only about a longing for communism, but are also about a longing for the relationships between men and women not to undergo too much change. The political unconscious of especially Morris's text, however, reveals that this cannot be. *News from Nowhere* radically suggests that longing for traditional relations between men and women and the longing for living in communism are incompatible. The text has Guest leave utopia rather than learn to change his views; this is how powerful a hold the idea of maintaining traditional gender relations had even on socialists.

Shaw's and Morris's texts' production of woman is, in this respect, different from James's, Conrad's, and Gissing's. The latter writers attempt to invoke the nineteenth-century ideologeme of an ideal domestic and cultured woman in the private sphere as a metonym for the traditional order they wish partly to preserve. Shaw and Morris, on the other hand, do not so much invoke the old ideologeme in toto, as draw woman into a new order—but under male guidance. This way they hope to advance a more "progressive" view of woman's place, yet contain their fear of the loss of those features of domestic femininity that the male finds comforting, namely housewifeliness, commitment to marriage, lack of sexuality, kindliness, and a good mind to make a woman interesting though not argumentative. The tutelage model used by both Shaw and Morris, where the radical male tries to teach the female, serves as a bridge between the radical and conservative dimensions of these projects. Woman needs to be talked to about politics, but she'd best not talk back. The products, however, reveal this "bridge" for what it is: an unregenerate expression of patriarchal attitudes that has dire consequences for both the woman and the man. He may, after all, even be expelled from utopia just for this.

6

Margaret Harkness: Representing Politics in the Slums

Up until this point, we have encountered really only two political novels, James's *The Princess Casamassima* and Gissing's *Demos*, which have focused at all on London's East End slums, site of terrible poverty and seething frustrations at the turn of the century. Neither James nor Gissing, however, is interested in detailing the conditions of slum life, so much as in exploring its effects either on a sensitive, exceptional individual (Hyacinth) or on a typical ignorant one (Mutimer). The slums, for James and Gissing, are an "environment." Although Conrad's setting in *The Secret Agent* is probably the East End, there is little that seems particular and more that seems archetypal about his setting. In this chapter we turn to a socialist novelist, Margaret Harkness, whose aim is to represent these slums, in all their typicality and immediacy, to primarily a middle-class reader. Both her sustained naturalistic focus and her gender promise a different literary production of the moment's public and private politics than we have yet seen.

In the late 1880s and 1890s a number of writers explored London's East End, the late-nineteenth-century metonym for social inequality as Manchester had been in mid century. The East End became the uncharted physical frontier for many motivated by variously philanthropic and revolutionary aims: university graduates, missionaries, statisticians, political organizers, and a number of independent-minded upper- and middle-class women; so acknowledged was this migration that it is even produced in literature (as it is in James's *The Princess*, in the figure of Lady Aurora). Among these émigrées were Beatrice Webb, Eleanor Marx, and the novelist Margaret Elise Harkness. A second cousin of Webb and a friend of Eleanor Marx and other socialists such as Olive Schreiner, Harkness is now the all but forgotten member of this group.[1] Harkness's name, however, has a certain notoriety. Readers of Engels's correspondence may remember her as the recipient of one of his canonical letters on literary realism; Engels criticizes her first novel, *A City Girl*, as "not realistic enough" because it portrays the East End working class as "a passive mass" (April 1888). And she achieved some popularity in her own time. Werner Urlaub claims her novels were more widely distributed than the earlier novels of Gissing or the majority of the social novels of the 1890s. *A City Girl, Out of Work,* and *Captain Lobe* appeared in several editions and *A City Girl* was translated into German, where it was popular among organized workers (243–4). For many years, however, all of Harkness's seven novels and six nonfiction works have remained out of print until Garland Press recently reissued *A City Girl*.

This chapter explores Harkness's social fiction, five novels written between 1887 and 1905, all of which produce an image of contemporary public and private politics among the under- and unemployed. These are not "successful" novels on the whole; that is, these are novels which do not fully confront or attempt to answer the problems they pose. The particular rift in her novels between their competing, half-formed projects and the products themselves suggests the radical inhospitality of the historical moment to fiction such as hers: fiction about the working class, about socialist politics, and about women who are a far cry from middle-class women readers, desperate women who, if they have a "home" at all, find no refuge in it from the harshness of the streets. Harkness, in trying to tell new kinds of stories about new kinds of characters, walks on new and treacherous ground.

Typically the readings in this book have explored the novels' projects and products, then theorized some features of the historical moment which could have enabled them. Here the order is reversed because of the seemingly transparent, even journalistic style of Harkness's fiction. Provisionally constructing a partial "history" in this case will encourage us to read "beneath" the novels' surfaces, without at the same time offering a mimetic measuring stick.

Although by the mid 1890s the British urban working class had become an acceptable subject in novels written by and for the middle class, it was still a tentative one. The working-class fiction of this era, best known of which are the stories of Arthur Morrison, Walter Besant, Rudyard

Kipling, and Somerset Maugham, is slim. Rejecting the triple decker, this fiction usually appears in the short story format, as if such representations could not be long sustained. But too, this fiction is not particularly rich or complex. While it is easy to attribute this to some individual lack of "genius" or "skill," a more promising explanation is that the social conditions, material and ideological, which support any writer were uncongenial. As we have earlier noted, public outcry in the late 1880s and early 1890s over Zola's sexual frankness and his focus on a potentially revolutionary working class powerfully controlled British fictional portraits of this class. Also, the era's literary debates, such as that between James and Wells, worked to repress the production of didactic, self-proclaimed referential, "incomplete" novels about the terrible social conditions of the inarticulate.

Harkness's historical moment was also, however, a treacherous one for a woman writer, as we will see further evidenced in the following chapters. Narrow conventions about an appropriate female voice hemmed her in. Ruth First points out that while many publishers in this era were receptive to books written by women, they still expected them to support traditional values (117).[2] As late as 1931 Virginia Woolf was to rail against the conventions which inhibited women writers, conventions such as those which urged women to flatter men and to avoid representing the body and women's passion; even Woolf, one of the rare ones who began to escape, comments: "If I were to overcome the conventions I should need the courage of a hero, and I am not a hero."[3] Consider, then, the position of the female writer who wants not only to write about untraditional, independent, even outcast women, but who also wants to write about the slums and socialist politics. The fact that Margaret Harkness wrote at all is astonishing.

The facts about Harkness's life (1854–1923) have been, until recently, as buried as her work.[4] They bear mentioning here because they too help point the reader to some of the tensions in her fiction. Harkness published her first novel, *A City Girl*, with the infamous Vizetelly in 1887. This was not, however, her first writing project. Harkness was born into a sheltered religious household which was upper class by rank although financially strapped. Needing to find an occupation, she broke with her family's wishes (and so with her family) in her late twenties and tried to support herself through the financially risky and unconventional career of freelance writing. She wrote a number of journalistic pieces, including "Women as Civil Servants" and, presumably out of financial desperation, two short volumes for the By Paths of Bible Knowledge series. Much more in line with her work in the late 1880s and 1890s, in 1882 she wrote a short article, "Railway Labour," about deplorable working conditions. She also wrote some books and novels, now lost, for which she could not find a publisher.

By the early 1880s, Harkness, then friends with Schreiner, Eleanor Marx, Annie Besant, and Engels, started exploring the East End. In a pamphlet entitled *Imperial Credit* (1899), she explains her motives for going there: "after that saddest event of my life [her father's death] I determined to do something to lessen the miseries of those who to-day have neither land nor money" (1). Yet the precise nature of Harkness's activities in the slums during the first few years is unknown. She apparently did not work for the Salvation Army, although her fiction shows sympathy with their social programs. Whatever it was, her work took her to the very worst districts. Harkness was one of the people to open Eleanor Marx's eyes to the horrors of East End life (Kapp, 261). Some of Harkness's political activities between 1887 and 1891 are known, however. She was a member of Engels's crowd (Kapp, 457), after earlier belonging for a short time to a rival faction, the Social Democratic Federation (Urlaub, 243); Harkness, however, refused to enter Engels's house if Edward Aveling were present, objecting to Aveling's treatment of Eleanor Marx. Harkness became involved in Keir Hardie's, the Scottish miners' leader's, election campaign in 1887–88, and in 1889 helped mediate in the London Dock Strike.

Probably it was the need to make some money that partially urged Harkness to continue writing novels during this period. Olive Schreiner, in a letter to Havelock Ellis, says: "Maggie has no money and she came thinking I would support her" (22 March 1887). Whatever compelled her, shortly after the visit to Schreiner, Harkness began writing novels under the pseudonym John Law that she would use to the end of her life. Though still a highly conventional practice for women writers at this time, we can read in this gesture Harkness's belief that the public narrator of her novels would have more authority as a male.[5]

After the last of the novels based on her East End experiences, her semi-autobiographical *George Eastmont: Wanderer* (1905), Harkness's political interests changed. Already in *Imperial Credit* (1899) she says she is saying "good-bye to the Labour Movement," that her "little bit of work is done," and that she has "other work to do." She gives as reason for this change her having been "got at, abused, and misunderstood by the people who call themselves socialists" because "birth, sex, and temperament have prevented me from coming forward openly among those who are fighting in the labor ranks" (1). Even much earlier, however, Harkness expressed anger at the socialists' divisiveness and their failure to help the poor in any real way. In subsequent writings based on her residence in India and Ceylon between 1906 and World War I, her earlier concern with the working class and socialism and her latent feminism seem to drop away.[6] This suggests that Harkness's radicalism of the 1880s and 1890s was a relatively ephemeral and certainly conflictual thing. The novels bear this out.

It is difficult to read Harkness's novels not because they demand much literarily of the reader, but precisely because they seem so transparent. Her novels, strangely touching, haunting portraits of the lives of the poor and those exiles from the West End who have befriended them, seem to be open windows onto the East End. Indeed, she subtitles both *A City Girl* and *A Manchester Shirtmaker* "A Realistic Story." This means that critically her novels readily invite the sort of vulgar mimetic, "realist" criticism of Engels, a criticism which measures the accuracy of fictional characters and situations in relationship to a model of history. Only by resisting this impulse toward measurement and instead probing textual inconsistencies can we see her novels as attempts to "package" the slums for the middle class, to at once appear to open up the slums to the viewer, yet simultaneously to objectify them, containing what is frightful in them.

Harkness's work has been described alternately as a "curious hotch-potch of literary influences and revolutionary ideas" (Keating, 242) and a not realistic enough portrait of the working class (Engels). In a Machereyan reading, the "curious hotch-potch" and sometimes less than authoritative representation can be interpreted instead as textual traces of the novels' competing desires, or projects. On the one hand, Harkness's novels desire to represent and applaud the underrepresented, a working class surrounded and sometimes moved by radical and proto-feminist ideas. On the other hand, intimidated by the middle-class textual reader they have constructed, her novels desire to contain this representation, to secure within the reader what is fundamentally a conservative, patronizing, paternalistic perspective on both the working class and women's independence. As have many socially marginal writers—women, minorities, political figures—Harkness used her texts to try to repress what she had let out in writing them. Both assessments of Harkness's politics are, paradoxically, right: Keating sees in her novels an "enthusiasm at the awakening class consciousness of the East End workers" (242) and an attempt to "correct the blindness of late-Victorian novelists to the urban workers' revolutionary potential" (245). Conversely, Engels sees reactionary politics in Harkness. The novels' vacillation can be read as a production of late-nineteenth-century political tensions. While middle-class leftists welcomed a roused working class and independent women, they also feared this energy and desired to manage it. The foray into the East End, Harkness's novels suggest, was not a disinterested undertaking.

One of the projects in all of Harkness's novels is to tell the story of the working class, to represent the inadequately or unfairly represented. Harkness conceives of her reader as blinded from knowledge of the working class, including working-class women and their champions, by a number of stereotypes which she sets out to dismantle; as she puts it, she wants to create "intelligent observers" by "rousing" her audience out of their "everyday existence" (1888, 39). As this implies, Harkness's textual reader, the one to whom Harkness speaks both through her own public narrator and through her choice of textual strategies, is not working but middle class. All this is not merely to edify her readers but to warn them to take corrective action; like other novelists and chroniclers of her era Harkness is impelled by a sense of urgency. As an East End doctor in *Captain Lobe* warns, "if things go on like this we must have a revolution" (190).

The stereotypes Harkness attacks shift in the course of the five novels. The first, *A City Girl* (1887), dismantles the stereotype that East End women are immoral—a daring subject in 1887 although Harkness avoids frank sexual details. The novel concerns a young girl, Nellie, who has steady work as a finisher of trousers for a "sweater," a middleman who farms out unfinished factory-made clothing for finishing at home. Nellie, living with an alcoholic mother and a brutish brother, modestly dreams of being a "lady" (because the novel, after Zola, hints her real father was a gentleman). She falls in love with a West End married gentleman, Arthur Grant, whom she meets while attending a Radical meeting with her fiancé, George. Grant and Nellie have an affair and Nellie becomes pregnant. Harkness carefully breaks this to her reader: Nellie has fitful dreams and one day she even trudges through a snow storm to Grant's West End house just to gaze at him through a window. Stunned at the expression she sees on his face as he looks on his baby, she murmurs, "he never looked at me like that; never" (98) and turns back. Only after Harkness has won over the reader's sympathy to Nellie's loneliness does she finally reveal her pregnancy: the harsh "sweater" calls her immoral. The novel then sets out to show that Nellie has the stamina, with practical help from the Salvation

Army, to try to bring up her baby alone, without telling Grant and ostracized by family, employer, priest, and suitor. Harkness assumes her audience, possibly shocked by such East End stories, might be like Arthur Grant himself: unaware Nellie could both be in love and feel intensely protective toward her child. Grant thinks "hands took babies as a matter of course" (177). Interestingly, Grant is treated not as a villain, but only as ignorant and self-indulgent—a contrast to typical contemporary feminist attacks on male sexuality.[7] Nellie is clearly as much to "blame" in Harkness's story as is Grant. Near the novel's end when Grant runs into Nellie carrying their dead baby and discovers it is his, he also discovers his ignorance of Nellie's feelings, has some remorse, and even wants to make amends. He is counseled by the Salvation Army captain to let it go at providing money for the child's burial. George, having been re-educated by the captain about his own sexual double standard, asks Nellie to marry him and they go off to take a joint job in the country.

In the next novel Harkness sensitively handles the issue of the under- and unemployed. *Out of Work* (1888) shows a country carpenter, newly moved to London, who is forced to become a "casual," or temporary dock worker, the lowliest of the unskilled occupations. Jos Coney's unsuccessful attempts to find steady work among thousands of unemployed structure the novel; in this way the plot seeks to undermine the stereotype of the unemployed voiced by Jos's petty-bourgeois fiancée's mother: that "idle habits" are responsible (36). Eventually his fiancée, Polly, breaks off with him and Jos returns to the country where he dies of starvation.

Harkness's third novel, *Captain Lobe* (1889; later edition entitled *In Darkest London*), shifts its focus from inadequately or unfairly represented East End protagonists onto the Salvation Army, stereotyped in its own time most forcefully by Shaw in *Major Barbara* (1905). As Salvation Army workers tour the slums, the reader is offered both a sympathetic glimpse of the Army's practical work and a wider panorama of deteriorating social conditions than the other novels provide—a panorama which surpasses Gissing's *Nether World* (1889) in the stark detail with which it represents East End life. We see women committing suicide because they have too many children, people scavenging shoes for fuel, factory daughters keeping their families alive. The novel particularly shows the strength of women Salvation Army workers, "slum saviours," who enter districts where "respectable" church people and even the police won't go. Even H. Rider Haggard's sympathetic portrayal of the Army some years later (*Regeneration*, 1910) does not recognize the heroism of these women workers as Harkness's novel does.

With *A Manchester Shirtmaker* (1890) Harkness turns briefly from the London East End to the Manchester slums, though there is little to distinguish this industrial city from London. Harkness shows a recently widowed impoverished seamstress, Mary Dillon, forced to sell her sewing machine to feed her baby. Desperately wanting her baby to be "happy" but recognizing it is starving, she finally overdoses it with opium she has stolen. In this novel Harkness confronts the stereotype that mothers who murder children are depraved by depicting such actions as the result of poverty. Incarcerated in a psychiatric hospital, Mary Dillon is so distraught by her own act that she kills herself.

In the last of her social novels, *George Eastmont: Wanderer* (1905), Harkness explores a different kind of stereotype, one also of interest to Shaw and Gissing: the aristocrat turned man of the people, an eccentric. Harkness, unlike Shaw, treats the convert seriously, applauding his commitment. The dedication page proclaims this novel to be an account of Harkness's own experiences in the dock strike. It may be more: it may be an account, using a male persona, of her own difficult entry into working-class culture and politics and a cover for her own desires to be a saviour of the masses. Eastmont, who has given up his upper-class family and his military commission to work among the poor as a socialist, un-happily marries a working-class woman and then finds he cannot whole-heartedly support the dock strike because of its violence. He helps resolve the strike by asking the intercession of Cardinal Loraine, a thin veil for Cardinal Manning to whom this novel is dedicated and with whom Harkness was associated in her own attempts to resolve the strike. Isolated, Eastmont wanders to Australia to join a settlement farm. Upon receipt of his grandfather's fortune, he returns to England at the novel's close with the idea of starting an Owenite farming community on his lands, where he hopes he can both learn about workers and help train them in communal living so that they will be ready when socialism comes. This idea of preparing the workers' domestic lives had some currency in this time (see the discussion of *Margaret Dunmore or, A Socialist Home* in the next chapter).

The authority for Harkness's project of dismantling middle-class stereotypes about the working class and its champions depends upon her being able to convince her reader that her portraits are "true." One strategy she uses is to deny she is writing fiction at all. Hence novel-reading is satirized. *Out of Work* shows the Elwins' servant, Mary Anne, avidly reading romances involving the aristocracy, blind to the failing romance involving ordinary people, Jos and Polly, going on right under her eyes. Another device Harkness uses to de-fictionalize her novels is to imply she is representing "people," not characters. Thus, she chides novelists who will appropriate for their romances the "character" of the "labor mistress," whom she has introduced to the public in *Captain Lobe* as a "person."

> The strong-minded proletarian spinster will come before us half a year hence in a variety of garments. She will be put in the novelists' character-box, and be made to dance with their other puppets. Before she becomes common property, readers are invited to look at her once again. (117)

Harkness also tries to create the illusion that the topography of her novels is "real." Hence she peppers her fiction with historical markers without translating them for the ignorant reader, places like the People's Palace, a particular doss house (or common lodging house), a workhouse, workmen's clubs, as well as specific historical events—the Trafalgar Square riots, Bloody Sunday, the dock strike.

Finally and more subtly, to consolidate her authority Harkness imitates the discourse of social scientists and journalists. Her novels, in their attempt to be panoramic of the East End, are influenced by the new social science of Charles Booth, who sought to make the slums visible to the middle class through detailed reporting of quantitative statistics. Yet Harkness, unlike Booth and more like his mid-century predecessor, Henry Mayhew (*London Labour and the London Poor*), does not want thereby to forgo telling the individual "story." So she frequently interrupts, often even burying, her central story line to allow a marginal character the spotlight. Because of her overall attempt to provide scope, however, the descriptive texture of her novels is thin—much as one might find in a newspaper sketch. Unlike a novel like George Moore's *Esther Waters* (1894), which is thick with descriptions of Esther's domestic situations (a thickness which obscures the narrator's ignorance of both her and the slums from which she comes), Harkness's terrains are stark, hearthless. So the reader quickly glimpses a workhouse, where Jos in his cell tries to split granite with a hammer; or a garment factory, where two hundred factory girls "rattling the reels of cotton and the scissors" and a half dozen men "armed with large knives" (59) terrorize a "sweater" who is trying to take their work away.

This is not to suggest that Harkness's descriptions are thereby ineffective. The accretion of her spare scenes, augmented by the countless sketches of marginal characters, creates a powerful, tangible vision of the fragmentary, homeless, though not always bleak lives of East End in-habitants. The following is an example of one such scene, a glimpse into a common lodging house taken from *Out of Work*. I will quote this passage at some length both to provide an example of Harkness at her best stylistically and to reveal a typical thematic note, that the poor, in spite of their roughness, help each other.

> Men and women stood there cooking their supper; emptying into tins and saucepans bits of meat, bones, scraps of bread and cold potatoes they had begged, stolen, or picked up during the day. Hungry children held plates ready for the savoury messes, and received blows and kicks from their parents when they came too near the fire, or interfered with the cooking arrangements.
>
> Crouching on the floor, gnawing a bone, was a man closely resembling the 'ungry man, who about a month before had disturbed the panegyric of the godly nation in the Wesleyan chapel, who had wanted to see the corn and wine of which Mr. Meek spoke so figuratively. His face was soddened by drink. He had swollen features, palsied hands, and trembling feet. He had probably begun life in this Christian country as a homeless boy in the streets; and would most likely close his days in the casual ward of some workhouse. Then "Rattle his bones over the stones,/He's only a pauper, whom nobody owns!"
>
> The lodgers threw him scraps, and laughed to see him tearing his food to pieces, devouring it like a dog, on the ground. Near him, resting her head against the wall, sat a young woman. She had a baby on her knees, a little thing, almost naked. Its chiselled limbs shone in the firelight. The mother's eyes were shut, and her heavy tears fell on it; so she did not see a shrivelled hag, with ragged clothes, and grey matted hair, watching her. Once the hag drew near to touch the baby's rounded knee with a claw-like finger. She drew back again, muttering. A minute later she joined the old man on the floor; and the lodgers made coarse jokes, while the two quarrelled together for crusts and potatoes.
>
> Jos stood by the fire for a few minutes. Then he went to the door, and sat down there on a bench by a table. He buried his face on his arms, and tried to forget his surroundings. Presently he heard a voice ask, "Aren't you 'ungry?"
>
> He looked up, and saw a girl offering him a basin with a pewter spoon in it. He shook his head.
>
> The girl looked disappointed. "Eat it," she said.
>
> She was scarcely more than a child, a little thing with large dark eyes, and black hair falling about her face.
>
> "Ulloa, Squirrel!" cried the deputy, who was passing by, "the police is a-coming."
>
> The girl took no notice. She put the basin down before Jos.
>
> "You'll never want for a meal if you're friends with the Squirrel," remarked the deputy. "I'd rather trust 'er than any one I know to steal me a dinner."
>
> He left the house, and the girl seated herself opposite the young carpenter, leaning her elbows on the table, resting her chin on her hands.
>
> "Eat it," she repeated, fixing her great dark eyes on his face. "I'd breakfast."

In spite of the narrator's occasionally irritating satiric overvoice ("the panegyric of the godly nation," "this Christian country"), Harkness's lean, short sentences convey the desperation in this gathering. Too, she vividly, without objectifying her characters, represents dialect, several years in advance of the writers of the Cockney School. Finally, she here handles the generosity of the poor without intrusion or sentimentality, so allowing them dignity.

Part of the "truth" about the working class that Harkness desires to show is the currency of both socialist and feminist ideas and their generally salutary influence. Socialists, middle class or poor, unpredictably pass in and out of all her novels, making short speeches which advocate a major redistribution of the wealth. The reader may stumble across a socialist in a doctor's office, on a bridge, in a Salvation Army captain's lodgings, as well as in the more expected space of the political demonstration. In this way, Harkness tries to naturalize the discussion of socialism, to show it is an integral part of daily slum life. Harkness's public narrator, however, never herself risks advancing socialist ideas (for fear perhaps of offending her implied middle-class reader), confining herself instead, as above, to sneering occasionally at laissez-faire political theory and religious hypocrisy.

Though all the novels mention socialism, Harkness's concern with it seems to intensify. *A City Girl*, *Out of Work,* and *A Manchester Shirtmaker* all represent, in passing, socialists and radicals. Yet such characters in these novels have little political effect on the lives of the central characters. Jos hears several speeches by socialists and even is arrested in the Bloody Sunday demonstration, yet does not become more class conscious. In *A Manchester Shirtmaker* Mary learns little from witnessing the factory girls' revolt. Sometimes the early novels even subtly criticize political characters. At the end of *A Manchester Shirtmaker*, a socialist doctor in Mary's sanitarium makes dour predictions about the future at the very moment Mary kills herself. It is even a Radical, one unconscious of East End women's feelings, who fathers Nellie's child.

With the later novels, *Captain Lobe* and *George Eastmont*, however, the narratives isolate the ineptitude of existing political groups as the reason for socialism's failure to take hold and they explore more openly other paths to socialism. *Captain Lobe*'s focus on the Salvation Army is not accidental. Rather, this novel favorably explores the Army's practical ability to deal with the social problem—as the fractured political groups cannot. Yet the novel ridicules traditional religion for ignoring the image of Jesus as a poor homeless carpenter, an image everywhere to be found in the East End. The Salvation Army, only in its capacity as slum worker—not as "salvationist," is the best alternative. A mysterious unnamed lady, a character who has much authority as a seeming persona of the narrator, voices the novel's ideology of the necessity for Christian socialism, for working in this world to bring about equality and to feed the poor; if people were true Christians in this way, she suggests, they would then necessarily be true socialists.[8]

Harkness did not sustain the idealism she displays in *Captain Lobe*, however, with its suggestion that improving practical religion is critical for the evolution of socialism. Agnosticism dominates the last of these social novels, written sixteen years later. Eastmont, once religious, has turned to politics. While he too reveres Jesus the socialist and seeks counsel from Cardinal Loraine, he does not brood on the possibilities of religion in the present crisis. What *George Eastmont* does offer is the more radical, though ambiguous, injunction to "be a socialist." True socialism, Eastmont believes, will not, however, evolve through existing political groups. Though Harkness's earlier novels suggest that these groups are inept and fractured, *Eastmont* dramatizes this more fully. The socialists with whom Eastmont is affiliated early in the novel turn out to support a violence he detests. And they seem to have little hold on the people. During one political demonstration, the people suddenly turn to cheer the army when it comes to disperse them. Furthermore, the labor movement some of them join after the dock strike, he argues, is politically limited since it helps only a few workers enter a labor aristocracy, leaving other, unskilled workers behind. Eastmont also takes issue with some Fabians, arguing that their notions of evolution are too gradual. Eastmont charts, instead, a different path to socialism, one that combines paternalism (he fashions himself a "saviour of the masses" [15]) with a strategy of collectivizing the land rather than factories.

Harkness's novels, however, not only thus attempt to argue the "truth" of their particular (and changing) perspective on religion and socialist politics; they also seek to show the sometimes sordid truth of contemporary relations between the sexes and to "naturalize" at least a mild form of feminism. *A City Girl* and *A Manchester Shirtmaker* both feature the difficulties single mothers face raising children and both criticize particular social institutions, here hospitals and male-dominated courts, for their insensitivity to motherhood. When Nellie enters the hospital with her dying baby, she cries out for a nurse who is a mother to help her; not only are there none, but she is ignored. Mary pleads with the court to understand why she killed her child: "if you were women you'd know what it is to see your child hungry" (159). All of the novels subtly criticize women who seek to live through their husbands and who are unsympathetic to either poverty or politics. *Out of Work* punishes Polly for not understanding Jos's poverty by marrying her off to an "upright" Methodist. Eastmont's working-class wife, in the only represented marriage in the five novels, ironically has no understanding of what Eastmont is doing, dazzled as she is by his being a gentleman; she is killed off—though the narrator shows a flash of sympathy for her empty, boring life which led to her opium addiction. More politically conscious than the other characters, Eastmont refers to this as "the woman question," a question which he will study because "their ignorance is fatal to the labour movement" (219); the novel shows, though, that his "their" is a hasty generalization based on his own marital experience. The other woman in the novel, Miss Cameron, is not ignorant but politically astute. And Harkness's novels gesture toward praising the strong, individual woman, whether she be poor and struggling, a slum saviour, an upper-class political woman, or a socialist "labor mistress" bent on educating herself. The labor mistress, Jane Hardy, is one of the most interesting of these. The narrator describes her as a "pioneer of their sex in questions connected with female labour—eager to work on equal terms with men, defiant of all special legislation for women, sometimes caricatures of the screaming sisterhood, but often setting these people an example" (1891, 278); Harkness clearly is unsympathetic to militant feminism, but nevertheless supports female strength, hard work, and independence. Finally, Harkness occasionally represents a female subculture: Nellie develops a relationship with the Salvation Army worker who takes her and her baby into her home. Ruth in *Captain Lobe*, owner of the coconut chip factory at which Jane Hardy works, is guided by Jane, as are all the factory girls whose homes she regularly visits not as some stern overseer but as moral guide and friend. Miss Cameron in *George Eastmont* tries to help Eastmont's wife.

Harkness's novels reveal these various radical projects—their incursions into working-class life to show a new "truth" and their uncensorious, even sometimes welcoming representation of socialist and proto-feminist politics. Yet the products work to undermine these projects. The novels' progressivism does not entirely hold, constrained by the conservative middle-class textual reader they pervasively address. The forceful presence of this reader bespeaks not only Harkness's own relationship to her class as well as her possible need to sell her novels, but also the gender constraints she experienced. Some rare writers can perhaps escape some of the blinders of class and gender; Harkness did not escape what was expected of the middle-class woman writer at this time, namely that she accede to the patriarchy's condescending attitude toward women as well as toward the working class.

One influence of this textual reader can be seen in Harkness's sensationalizing the story of the working class. Melodramatic plots engage the middle-class reader's sympathy and interest for a working-class subject, while yet keeping this subject at a distance. This means Harkness treads a thin line; she needs to balance the idea that the lives of the poor are filled with intriguing "events" (they are not dull and "mean") with her project of writing nonfiction, hence plausible and "ordinary" stories. Hence in *A City Girl* Arthur Grant first discovers he has fathered Nellie's baby when he runs into her as she is fleeing the hospital carrying their dead child. Yet Grant works in the hospital. In *Out of Work*, the young waif "Squirrel" we saw in the above passage, who comes to love Jos, drowns herself when she discovers he has left London to return to the country. At this very moment Jos, walking in the country, picks up a dead squirrel and, remembering its namesake, buries it. In spite of this highly sentimental moment, Harkness has convinced us that Squirrel, lonely and desperate, lives only for Jos and that Jos, however oblivious he seems, has some feeling for her. Just after Mary in *A Manchester Shirtmaker* kills her baby, a five-pound note arrives from her husband's middle-class family which ignored him when he married her, a foundling. Though Harkness taunts the reader with the conventional "outs" of melodrama—the wealthier inlaws, the foundling, even a mysterious loafer who occasionally watches Mary from afar, they come to naught. The money is only enough to buy her husband a tombstone and bury her child. *Captain Lobe* has fewer coincidences or sensational events than these novels. But it too addresses a more popular audience. Thinly under the surface of the panoramic plot organized by a character's walks, runs a conventional marriage plot: Lobe loves Ruth, the young factory owner who wants to give it up to become a slum saviour for the Salvation Army. The foreman of Ruth's factory, however, Mr. Pember, poses a small obstacle. Described by Ruth as a "serpent," he wants to marry her to keep his position when she comes of age. Lobe and Ruth, however, finally marry without much difficulty. George Eastmont's ill-chosen working-class wife conveniently dies of an opium overdose early in the novel and the plot then tempts the reader to ask whether he will receive his fortune.

However, the novel does not feature these potentially climactic moments; they, again, are there only to lure the popular reader. For Harkness, melodrama is only a strategy; it is not a sign of any larger providence at work (as it is for Dickens, for example).

Harkness's characterization is, similarly, influenced by her conventional textual reader. Her protagonists are never ugly, coarse, or upsetting. Though Jos becomes drunk and his appearance slovenly the longer he is out of work, he maintains his manners. Captain Lobe is not an unpleasant evangelist, but is deferential, kind, and sweet. Eastmont is never haughty. Interestingly, Harkness's characters are not permanent members of the unemployed (some of whom the narrator refers to as "scum"), nor are they foreigners or Jews, but only those recently fallen into poverty. In this way Harkness makes it difficult for a conservative reader to blame the victim. Too, though the violence of the slums may be reported, her central characters are never violent as are Stephen Crane's (*Maggie of the Streets*), Rudyard Kipling's ("Record of Badalia Herodsfoot"), or Arthur Morrison's ("Lizerunt").

Harkness also feels that the implied reader requires conventional heroines. Her female protagonists are pretty, sweet, passive things. So, for example, the narrator says of Nellie: "About her face and neck were the blue shadows which usually accompany auburn tresses. These blue shadows were wonderfully pretty to look at" (15). Mary Dillon is madonna-like: "fair hair lay smoothly on her forehead. Not a trace of colour was in her cheeks, her lips, also, were colourless. Heavy, waxlike lids half covered her eyes, which were grey, and fringed with black lashes" (4). Squirrel too is angelic, ministering to Jos's every need. Lobe, whom the narrator describes as a "saint" (28), says of Ruth:

> her clear white forehead looked like an ivory tablet, upon which Time had written no false word, no evil thought, nothing but love and truthfulness. Her grey eyes were fearless and honest. Her voice was soft and sweet, an excellent thing in women! And her golden hair seemed to set her face in a halo of holiness. (28)

Harkness's public narrator often aligns herself with this conservative textual reader. The narrator is sometimes remote and even condescending toward her characters. Harkness's need to objectify her characters leads her to *type* them: the dock worker, the East End mother, the labor mistress. Though her novels try to dismantle conventional stereotypes of the working class, they perpetuate others. While Engels, who celebrated the type as the cornerstone of realist fiction, may have influenced Harkness here, her use of the type also signals her need to distance, even diminish a character. For example, Harkness's typically intrusive narrator describes Jos's brains: they are "of the same calibre as the brains of other young carpenters who had not the intellectual capacity of an educated man" (114). Or, she describes the labor mistress as a quaint specimen of a "socialist" who knows a string of words without their definitions, who "lives far away from the British Museum Reading Room, where she might graze among a herd of likeminded ladies" (117). Typification here is a form of condescension: the narrator cannot see complexity in these characters. They are at this moment pitiful objects for her.

Finally, the conservative reader whom Harkness chooses not only encourages melodramatic plotting, "respectable" characters, and condescending narrative intrusions. This reader also works to repress the radical elements of the texts, allowing them little expression. For one thing, political activity cannot be represented or shown to have anything but a minimal effect on the central characters. *Eastmont* shows a mindless crowd. *Out of Work* shows Jos unaffectedly passing through the Trafalgar Square riots. Similarly, neither the protagonists nor the narrator even reflect on the political speeches the characters hear in all the novels.

Importantly, Harkness's controlling textual reader affects the texts' production of a vision of socialism. The transition to socialism is a comfortable, paternalistic one: a few wise men will bring it about. Both *Captain Lobe* and *George Eastmont* say leadership of the ignorant "masses" is necessary. For example, in *Captain Lobe* the narrator says: "He could not see that the people take pleasure in their filthy existence, he could not understand the satisfaction they get by fuddling their brains in public-houses and by coarse love-making" (211) and "they feel as masses, not as individuals. . . . They have no confidence in themselves, any power of forming their own opinions" (213). Or, in reference to working-class attempts at self-education, the narrator says: "A self-educating woman is very pathetic, much more pathetic than a self-educating man. . . . The East End is full of people who seek to educate themselves with the help of secularist and socialist lectures" (110). But in *George Eastmont* disgust for the masses and disappointment in their stupidity is even more pronounced. While sometimes this disgust is political, often it is aesthetic. Like the scornful reaction of Gissing's narrator of *Demos* to Richard Mutimer's pitiful attempts to educate himself and become well-mannered, *George Eastmont* opens with scenes of Eastmont's disgust at his working-class wife's personal habits: her table manners, her clothes. When the workers lift him high on their shoulders after a demonstration, he feels they now are "scum" (39).

It is not accidental that Eastmont is the arch-socialist hero of all these novels. As a male and an aristocrat he is completely nonthreatening to a middle-class reader. Eastmont need not struggle or engage in any mass activity; his position comfortably enables him to make his own contribution to socialism—which will be a long time in coming and whose agents the novel never specifies. The message to the middle class is that it need do nothing to advance socialism. The novel ends just when the difficulties could begin: just as he sets up his scheme.

Another powerful repression stimulated by the complicity between narrator and textual reader is that of radical and independent women. So, for example, Harkness's more potentially striking women—the mysterious socialist lady and the socialist labor mistress in *Captain Lobe*, and Miss Cameron, the unmarried Fabian in love with Eastmont—are fleeting characters, never allowed center stage. Then too, they are shown as lonely, colorless, even a bit silly. Such women might alienate the middle-class reader used to young, pretty, apolitical Victorian heroines. Even the mildly rebellious working-class heroines end up conventionally. Nellie, having tried to bring up her illegitimate baby, loses her child and gets married. Mary, after killing her baby (a possible mark of unconscious anger), similarly comes to a respectable end: she kills herself.

The projects of Margaret Harkness's novels might be characterized as radical in their attempt to open up the slums to her middle-class reader, slums seething with political disruption and in which traditional gender roles are in disarray. Yet the products nevertheless partly work to contain these potentially disruptive projects when they occasionally have recourse to traditional plotting and conventional characterization, particularly of women, i.e., when they invoke the familiar ideologemes of paternalism and domesticity. The novels generate both sympathy and pity, respect and condescension, toward the poor. They both naturalize and distance radical politics. They both represent and marginalize "new women." They stage, in short, some of the understandable difficulties of a middle-class turn-of-the-century woman writer who journeys into the "other" world of the slums.

7

The "Outsiders": Women and Socialism

Many of the novels engaged with the socialist and anarchist movements, as we have seen, rely upon the paternalistic trope of the male saviour hero, here transformed into a "saviour of the masses." His ally is the dependent domesticated woman, who is often his student. These paired images have emerged as key ideologemes of turn-of-the-century fiction about radical politics, useful for their ability to promise stability whether the novels criticize or celebrate radical change in the public political sphere. However, in the margins of all these novels, in their products, hover traces of the disruptive late-century figure of the new woman. This new woman challenges earlier Victorian representations of a domestic femininity acquiescing to paternalism. Traces of the new woman have appeared in James's Princess's political ambitions and sexual attitudes; in Shaw's Agatha's rebelliousness toward authority and imperviousness to romanticism; in Gissing's Adela's desires for education and her attraction to other women; in Conrad's Winnie's primary emotional affiliation to her brother, not her husband, and her murderous anger at that husband; in Morris's Ellen's intellectual capabilities and qualities of forthrightness and comradeliness; and in several of Harkness's less developed women characters. In fact, it appears as if the use of the paternalist, usually saviour, figure (whether handled with admiration or contempt, whether produced by radicals or conservatives) emerges partly as a strategy for containing the threat posed by this new woman. For her aim is to negotiate her financial and emotional independence from the male and, as she increasingly organizes with other women in the later years of the century, to develop a militant women's political movement designed to dismantle the patriarchy.

The next two chapters turn to a number of novels, mostly written by women, which do throw a particular kind of new-woman character more into the foreground of their texts: a new woman who has political or proto-political interests, as well as the more typical new-woman interests in challenging acceptable female social behavior.[1] These novels, not surprisingly then, less frequently feature the male saviour figure. This chapter explores a group of little-known, long out of print, novels written by women which feature a woman or women characters who, even if tentatively, long for a fundamental, large-scale change not only in the organization of society but in domestic arrangements as well; their forum is socialist politics. The next chapter focuses on women who are represented in connection with the women's suffrage movement. There is a discernible difference between the tenor of these two groups of novels.

The characters in the first group of novels are not represented as being part of a political movement in which they can effectively act to fulfill some of these longings. They are in the position, rather, of mostly observing the men in their lives act within the socialist movement, sometimes ostensibly though ineffectively on their behalf. The women characters of these novels are, hence, vaguely drawn and their plots assume peculiar, evasive shapes as they seek compensatory satisfactions for their inability to take action.

What the novels studied in this chapter broadly suggest is the power the socialist movement of the 1880s and 1890s exerted on women's imaginations, yet its simultaneous inability to empower women, to affect their self-representation profoundly. On the one hand, socialism encouraged women to begin to interrogate more openly the ideologeme of the domesticated, protected female by arguing that *all* social arrangements, including domestic ones, are historical. Books such as Engels's *The Origin of the Family, Private Property and the State* and August Bebel's *Women and Socialism*, both appearing at this time, specifically encouraged women to view marriage and the family as historically situated, and hence as alterable features of a wider social and economic landscape. Yet, by privileging the industrial sphere of labor as the site of revolutionary activity, and not the home, developing socialist theory designated class and not gender as the important locus of attention. Women's oppression in the family, as Rowbotham analyzes the early socialist perspective, was only a *symbol*, an indication of the state of society; it was not designated as a site within which she herself could effectively act to change history. Revolution would involve women only insofar as they were members of the working class. The social relations of production, not the relations of reproduction, were what counted. Since early socialist theory did not specify women in domestic settings as agents of change, it robbed many women of a sense of their value and agency. The women characters in these domestically set novels, not surprisingly, remain by and large passive in their relationship to socialist men.[2]

Studying these novels which figure women in relationship to socialism generates a different perspective on the novels concerning the women's suffrage movement that we will study in the following chapter, a movement in which women began to see themselves as agents in changing all aspects of their lives, private as well as public. Although from a contemporary perspective these suffrage novels are inadequate in their representation of women, they appear far more radical when compared with these, what might be called precursor novels.

The novels studied in this chapter take their place within the genre of new-woman fiction that emerged in the 1880s and 1890s. Although a number of these new-woman stories have now been forgotten, several well-known novels written during this time prominently feature such women, novels such as Thomas Hardy's *Jude the Obscure*, George Meredith's *Diana of the Crossways* and George Gissing's *The Odd Women*. But none of these better-known novels foreground women associated with a militant, radical political movement, one which provides at least a potential arena in which not only women's practical lives, but also and more subtly the very nature as well as the object of women's desire could be remolded. The best-known novels feature, instead, new women whose new arena is that of a new domestic arrangement or a career. But, however much the better-known novels foreground such new women, Sue Bridehead, Diana Warwick, and Rhoda Nunn are all contained, even punished, in the plots. These novels take back what they give. Gissing offers the widest social canvas of working women, yet even his braver novel is highly problematic. Although *The Odd Women* is sympathetic to the condition of "odd" (i.e. unmarried) women and the aims of new women, and although it surpasses Hardy and Meredith in representing communities of women making a living by themselves, the novel characterizes this women's world as painful, narrow, undesirable. Gissing severely restricts the *sphere* of women's action—and the *scope* of women's desire. The "odd," unmarried, passive Madden sisters nearly starve. Mary Barfoot, the other new woman along with Rhoda Nunn at the center of the novel, "new" in that she actively tries to make an independent economic place for women, desires nothing more than promoting the material welfare of other genteel women of the middle class who have no financial resources. The narrator in fact applauds her because of her "quiet work [that] was probably more effectual than the public career of women who propagandize for female emancipation" (54), yet he demonstrates neither the social "effectualness" of such work nor any salutary effects on Mary herself. More significantly, Gissing cannot devise a narrative around her. Rhoda Nunn, the other new woman at the novel's center, receives much more of the narrator's attention, including half of the story line. But Rhoda's "story," like that of the only "normal" woman, Monica, who shares the story line with Rhoda, is centered on her failed relationship with a man. *The Odd Women* thus suggests that "oddity" and "newness" are functions of non-existent or frustrated heterosexual love. While Monica's story involves choosing to escape a stifling male protectiveness (and so becoming "odd"), Rhoda's story is structured around the plot of the ordeal. Gissing subjects Rhoda to a test of her own suppressed desires for masculine love in Everard Barfoot. Her claim to being a legitimate new woman, in Gissing's construction of her, depends upon her ability to renounce enormous desires, which she does (though even this strength he undermines by having Everard marry someone else). Gissing can conceive of no other kind of narrative in which to situate Rhoda. Although Gissing does not offer any hope for male–female relationships, there is something almost sadistic in the spectacle he produces of Rhoda's emotional trial. *The Odd Women* is devised to stimulate the reader's pleasure in Rhoda's proud suffering. His new woman is large, interesting, but it is the painful suppression of her desire for the male that the reader is asked to take pleasure in. As in H. G. Wells's *Ann Veronica*, discussed in the next chapter, the new woman is fascinating for some males not because she is genuinely autonomous, not because she takes pleasure in work, in friends, in her community, but because she still essentially needs a man. Her attempt at autonomy makes her a potentially more interesting "catch" for the male. Everard doesn't get her, but she is still available for the narrator's pleasure. As Deirdre David points out, Gissing's narrator describes Rhoda in terms of her powerful, though repressed, feminine sexuality.[3]

Alongside these better-known new-woman novels by male authors, however, is a group of novels written by women that explore the relationship between middle-class women and socialist politics; although middle-class political women appear briefly in several of Harkness's novels, she does not focus on them, nor explore the relationship between women's political work and their domestic arrangements. The few novels explored here (which surely comprise only a sample of a yet to be discovered group[4]) do, it is true, end traditionally by telescoping in on the individual male–female relationship. But what is significant about them is that they weave their domestic plots as firmly as they do with public politics and that any distancing from or denunciation of socialism they may ultimately develop has none of the powerful sardonic edge of the conservative male writers such as Gissing and Conrad. The relationship the novels produce between women and socialism is a generally tolerant and central, if ambivalent, one. On the one hand, as in the other novels studied in this book, turn-of-the-century socialism emerges as an almost exclusively male club. These novels highlight women's "outsider" status (as Woolf was to characterize women's position some years later in *Three Guineas*). Part of women's "outsider" status is created by the male socialists' failure to expect women to be as active as they themselves are and by their own residual paternalist attitudes. But another part of the women's "outsider" status derives from needs and desires that socialist politics as presently articulated do not address. These novels, for example, feature women who either cannot or will not cross class lines to work or live among the poor, so giving up the cultured life, luxuries, and a settled home (the male socialist in this literature often renounces his class comforts). Here are women who still need some features of both conventional morality and traditional domestic arrangements, as well as interpersonal relationships that the male zealot claims not to need. Socialist practice does not seem, in this respect, to offer women any help in navigating these waters. Yet, on the other hand, these novels suggest that the old domestic arrangements are intolerable, that some radical change in the sphere of women's lives is necessary. For this reason the novels make socialism and socialists the centerpiece, however flawed, of plot, of characterization, of theme.

The novels' power is adversely affected by this deep ambivalence toward socialism. Like Margaret Harkness's narrators, the female narrators of these novels usually identify with their female characters' reservations where socialism is concerned. This identification produces often scanty, inadequate characterization, plot evasions and abrupt shifts, and stylistic "thinness"—all perhaps to avoid stepping into what could be the potentially refreshing yet potentially threatening waters of radical politics.

Because of the understandable timidity of these writers, these novels are generally not as rich, not as powerful as those of the male writers who feel "at home" confronting public politics. Such an explanation for the novels' thinness sets aside the issue of "artistic skill," although it is important not to rest an explanation for a novel's "weakness" on this alone; the narrators' evasions may derive as much, if not solely, from their relationship to their material as from some aesthetic weakness. Socialism in the 1880s and 1890s seemed to offer a "way out" for women, particularly the promise of equality in employment outside the home. But at the same time socialism failed to offer women a way to actively transform the private sphere. It is not surprising that these novels hang back, even at moments backsliding into celebrating the traditional place where women had any power at all: the home.

Although these precursor novels are uneven, they provide a counterbalance to those of Morris, James, Conrad, Shaw, and Gissing which all position the female as the other. We can use the strategies employed throughout this book of looking for signs of the novels' failed projects in order to begin to recover some of the potential wealth repressed in these now forgotten novels. We can tentatively begin to theorize from these texts some of the contours of women's relationship to socialism in this historical "moment" of the 1880s and 1890s. Although all the novels in this book in various ways produce the gap between women's concerns and radical politics, these novels do so most acutely and so signal more loudly the beginnings of the political break between feminism and socialism that begins with the development of an independent women's suffrage movement around 1900 and which erupts more visibly during the second-wave feminist movement of the 1960s and 1970s.

The precursor novels studied here are Constance Howell's *A More Excellent Way*, Olive Birrell's *Love in a Mist*, and Gertrude Dix's *The Image Breakers*. Howell, who supported campaigns against sweated work,[5] published her novel in 1888. Of the three novels, *A More Excellent Way* finds the least in socialist practice to recommend it to women, given that women love domestic comfort; are undereducated and so do not understand it (making them prey to domineering political men); and live in a society which punishes outspoken women. The main plot revolves around a gentleman socialist, another saviour figure, whose political ardor the narrator occasionally warms to while simultaneously she removes him from the security of a middle-class home and marriage, which also attracts her. Caught in an either/or logic of socialism or comfort, the novel finds viable neither the ascetic, renunciant gentleman socialist nor the quiet, undereducated middle-class lady imprisoned at the hearth. This is a novel which even at the level of its project, its manifest desire, is deeply confused. To not be confined, Howell would have to both criticize prevailing socialist aims and practices and upset prevailing notions of femininity, neither of which she is able or willing to do. It is her timidity that weakens this novel.

The novel begins, however, with a very different plot, a plot in which is visible all the latent potential of this novel. Agatha, living in a middle-class English home in India, has decided to try to revive her boring marriage. Educating herself, she begins seriously reading some of her husband's books on Freethinking which he rarely reads, so that she can converse better with him. Reading, however, opens her eyes, gives her a different focus for her desire than mere domestic bliss. She begins advocating atheism as the only way for the masses to revolt against the tyranny of the upper classes. Though the narrator tells us she was ignorant of the women's rights movement and of radical politics, Agatha also shows a natural sympathy for oppressed women. She desires to spread her views among people. To her husband's horror, she begins to act on her new views by refusing to attend church or educate their son, Otho, in Christianity, both of which he feels it is her job as a woman to do. If all of society were as atheistic as she is, he argues, the revolution he fears will occur. He threatens to take the boy from her if she infects him. She never tells Otho about her views until he reaches twenty-one, not only because of her husband's power while he is alive, but because the state, as well, could take her son from her because she thinks as she does.

Such is the extraordinarily promising donnée with its budding political female hero, but Howell's plot is no *Awakening* with a political focus. The reader is never made privy to the process of Agatha's "conversion" so it is not powerful; the plot does not have husband and wife battle it out, so developing Agatha and forcing a probable separation or divorce; nor does the plot allow Agatha to do the political work she wants. Rather, Howell has Agatha fall ill, and with a suspect rapidity moves mother and son to England, kills the husband off, makes Agatha wealthy, and walls her up in a snug house. Agatha is left sending checks to the Freethinking cause. Her isolation overdetermined, Agatha never has to confront her husband on the one hand, or society on the other. In this way Howell avoids divorce, the renunciation of wealth, and a radical political female character. Agatha disappears from the reader's view but not before she in one brief scene has converted her son to Freethinking, now for her a social and not a theological program. The plot now has a new protagonist: Otho. The plot thereby offers an oedipal fantasy (on the mother's side) as a "solution" to Agatha/the narrator's conflicting desires for radicalism and conventionality: the adoring son believes in her views and will act them out; he will be a better champion for her than her husband was. Agatha is Howell's recommendation to the restless middle-class woman: be freethinking, but restrained in your actions. Let a man act out your politics. Agatha has to be abandoned because she could become potentially too freethinking, too powerful a mother hero who teaches her son radical ideas, for the middle-class reader Howell addresses. The novel therefore abruptly truncates Agatha's story and shifts to the son. Radical socialism in a man is more socially acceptable for Howell and her implied reader.

The second, main plot, however, subtly reveals what it does not wish to reveal: that Agatha's turning over her political work to her son is not a good idea. Not only is the son ineffective, but he can't understand the situation of women. Otho converts to socialism by joining the Social Democratic Federation, historically the most anti-feminist of the socialist groups. Just as the author will not or cannot represent his mother's conversion, so she avoids his. The rest of the plot develops two lines that finally intersect: on the one hand, Otho, now a rich gentleman, courts a pretty, empty-headed, middle-class girl whose aunt is pressuring marriage so her own daughter can marry a lord without competition. On the other hand, Otho becomes increasingly committed to being a socialist in practice, which means for him giving up most of his money to the poor and lecturing to his family and the public with speeches that often draw at least the narrator's approval. The plot offers a twist on the typical renunciation-of-wealth theme carried to extremes in James Adderley's *Stephen Remarx*, where Stephen gives up all of his wealth to found a socialist commune. Otho decides to give up only some of his money so he won't have to work and so compete with other workers. The two plot lines clash. His fiancée consistently refuses to understand his interest in socialism. When Otho tells her he (by his own decision) has given up most of his money and therefore she will be deprived, she refuses to marry him and he goes his own lonely way, off to the country where even his old landlady won't take him in any more because of his radical views.

What is curious about this second half of the novel is that Howell gives Otho such an empty-headed fiancée after he's had such an independent mother. Somewhere he needs a middle-class home, a traditional wife, a passive female he can try to convert: he is like his father after all, as well as a true representative of the SDF's gender politics. The paternalism in current socialist discourse revealed in Gissing and Shaw is repeated in Otho's part of the novel. Howell does not make Evangeline as smart as Shaw's Agatha, however, so presenting an opportunity for Otho to declaim frequently on socialism. Evangeline's utter inability to understand his ideas, however, foregrounds even more starkly than Shaw's novel the futility of the male–female tutelage model, as well as the ineptness of the SDF's political strategies.

Another way of interpreting Evangeline's presence in the plot, however, is that she is a decoy figure for the implied author, a gentle caricature of her own conventionality that she wishes at once to deny yet protect. Agatha is her more ostensible hero so Evangeline must be chastened, yet Agatha also has frightened Howell. The narrator says of Evangeline, "she was gentle, caring, loving, but she was selfish" (195). In the narrator's description we can detect not only her approval of certain Victorian "feminine" traits, but also her understanding that it is women's restricted education which prevents their larger sympathy. In fact, in many places the narrator reveals a special understanding of women's inferior social position.

Because Howell's novel wrenches apart the socialist from a home and love, because Otho is left alone, the saviour outcast, at the end Howell is not fully recommending the existing socialist path where men lead the way. Yet, similarly, Evangeline's life, the life of the middle-class woman, is at a dead end. While she might not be better off with Otho, since it would be a paternalistic relationship and the beginning of the novel has alerted us to the problems in such a marriage, the middle-class orbit where women desperately compete for husbands is certainly stifling her. Agatha's potentially more radical socialist way, a way sensitive to the needs of women, the way the novel cannot talk about, seems to be all that is left.

Olive Birrell's novel, *Love in a Mist* (1900), similarly worries about socialism from the perspective of the middle-class woman. Again the socialist is male: the female protagonist's (Sybilla's) father, Lincoln. The plot is structured around the daughter of the socialist, so offering us another example of socialist politics looked at from a woman's point of view. In this novel the question that propels the plot is whether Sybilla will leave her home and renounce her father's politics to marry Keith, an old family friend who has no sympathy for such politics. The novel explores not the issue of any broader reapportionment of social wealth, but rather the issue of "love." Does human love mean renouncing one's wealth and eliminating class lines—a "levelling" socialism, as Sybilla's father Lincoln attempts? Or does love mean extending human sympathy and treasuring family, all the while keeping individual wealth and acknowledging class distinctions, a sort of Christian sympathy? The novel's project is to solidify the latter viewpoint. The daughter's decision to marry Keith, and give up her father's levelling views but not her father's sympathy for the poor, signifies the novel's desire and is the sign of its project.

Sybilla's widowed father, Lincoln, has given up all of his wealth and settled himself and his two children in a boarding house he owns. Here he attempts to break the circle of his nuclear family by involving all the residents in household tasks. Lincoln spends most of his time preaching socialism. Sybilla's suitor, Keith, an old family friend recently returned from India who believes in class distinctions, enters and courts Sybilla. Sybilla, who has been raised not to care for finer, "frivolous" things, immediately feels her poverty and begins, tentatively, to desire such things. She almost marries Keith but this would mean leaving her younger, misguided brother behind so she declines the offer. As is true of so many of these plots, by novel's end Birrell invokes a deus ex machina to move her plot forward in ways she otherwise could not. Brother and father both die, the father at the end renouncing his socialism in favor of Christian love. All obstacles are thus removed for Sybilla. She and Keith are then, not surprisingly, reunited without Keith's having changed and with Sybilla, disappointingly, now ready to accept him as her father and protector. The only thread remaining from the earlier part of the novel is that Sybilla will not live as luxuriously as she could and she won't mock poverty. Now she will help to bring the poor up rather than trying to go down to meet them as her father did.

The "happy" ending reveals that the project of this novel is more solidified than was true in Howell's case, Howell's being a potentially more radical novel (which is why it finds more in current socialist practice to criticize). The project of Birrell's novel is to work away from a more radical socialism and from untraditional familial and gender relations toward a different ideology, one of Christian sympathy rooted in traditional domestic patterns. The wife here will supply Keith's deficiencies. The novel's product, however, that which it does not quite know how to say, or is unable to say, reveals much ambivalence toward the desirability and possibility of Sybilla's vision and their forthcoming marriage.

For one thing, what is produced before the mechanistic plot takes over and she is to be married is a female character who has some freedom and independence in her father's house. Her father is not interested in protecting Sybilla, so she virtually has the run of the house and of her brother. Sybilla's character is the most lively in this early portion of the novel.

Further, in the first half of the novel the narrator is clearly uncomfortable with the suitor Keith. In fact, the novel, even when it lionizes him, can never represent him. He is cold, unfeeling, snobbish and provokes the reader's anxiety. Rather than representing him, the narrator represents the humbler passionate people clustered around Sybilla's household: the socialist bookbinder, the religious Hudson enamored of Sybilla, an aging woman so jealous of Sybilla she attempts to prevent her relationship with Keith.

Most seriously, though, *Love in a Mist* is confused about whether Sybilla's decision to reject levelling socialism (signaled by her leaving the communal house and marrying Keith) will in fact allow her to connect with the poor. The novel strongly suggests, rather, that class separation, as well as the nuclear family, *prevents* widespread human sympathy. Keith, for example, never understands a character like Hudson. Only Sybilla, living as she has, really acknowledges him. Her father, Lincoln, it is true, has not promoted social or domestic harmony with his political views, but at least his way of living promoted more interclass connection and sympathy. Furthermore, the novel does not present the only character who preaches love alone (and not egalitarianism), the religious Hudson, as a model. It is not surprising that the narrative postpones Sybilla's marriage in a futile attempt to work out the possibility of interclass love while maintaining existing class lines. The novel's deferral of Sybilla and Keith's marriage tells us that Birrell is not sanguine about what it will accomplish.

Birrell, in *Love in a Mist*, tries to work out the contradiction between her desire for social stability and the maintenance of gentility, on the one hand, and her desire to extend human sympathy on the other. Sybilla (the Sybil?) is clearly at the center of this novel's search, making this novel closer to a woman-centered plot than is *A More Excellent Way*, which silences Agatha early on. Neither her father nor her fiancé nor Hudson who loves her has the answer. Birrell is unable to invent a *new* story, to see a clear path, for this genteel, "proto" political woman, this disappointing, shadowy, finally weak character. Birrell seems not to be able to risk having her stand up for herself for long and so tucks her back into the conventional mold. Sybilla has, however, come a long way from Otho's empty-headed fiancée who is only interested in luxuries, and unlike Otho's mother Agatha, Sybilla does not rely on a male (the son Otho) to play out her vision. Her vision is yet waiting to be both articulated and acted upon.

Gertrude Dix's *The Image Breakers* (1900) similarly focuses on middle-class women who become involved with socialism. Dix was apparently herself involved in the socialist movement in Bristol,[6] and she wrote at least one other novel, *The Girl From the Farm* (1895). The most complex of these three precursor novels, *The Image Breakers* focuses on two women friends, Rosalind Dangerfield and Leslie Ardent, each of whom not only becomes involved with socialist men but also is a socialist herself, at least at certain points in the novel. Unlike the other two novels, then, Dix's women characters are much more visibly intelligent and political. Furthermore, her narrator appears to know much more about the varieties of socialist practice and is willing to figure the women as involved in such practice, as well as more openly criticize the socialist movement for its failure vis-à-vis women. *The Image Breakers* thus reaches far beyond the other two novels. Although a deeply flawed novel, intermittently sentimentalist, relying on improbable character changes and rapid shifts of place, and often uncertain about its own desire, about its project, the intensity of the novel's restlessness reveals tensions severely muffled in the other novels. The novel has a "modern" quality to it, deriving partly from its characterization of women. *The Image Breakers* acknowledges women's sensuality, their passion for women as well as men (stopping short of overtly representing lesbian or free-love heterosexual relationships).[7] Furthermore, Dix's novel explores the tension within women between their sensuality, which makes them vulnerable to men and men's desires to contain them in marriage, and their own desire for integrity, a space for concentration, in short for a meaningful place in the world outside of marriage. Both female characters struggle for most of the novel, before acceding to marriage, to develop careers. *The Image Breakers* rivals Gissing's *The Odd Women* in terms of the forcefulness of its representation of the difficulty women are having at the turn of the century in making a meaningful and financially independent life outside of marriage. And in its not choosing "spinster"-like single women for its central characters, *The Image Breakers* has more to recommend it in terms of its representation than does *The Odd Women*. In its acceptance of female sensuality and its interrogation of communal living (for a portion of the novel), Dix's novel seems to be speaking to the late-century cultural movement connected with the Fellowship of the New Life. This progressive circle, influenced by Edward Carpenter (*Love's Coming of Age* (1896)) and involving such well-known figures as Havelock Ellis, Olive Schreiner, and Rebecca West, was dedicated to ideas such as communal living, the expression of sexuality, and the development of the new woman; furthermore, this circle did much to try to connect socialism with the liberation of women.[8] Since Carpenter had an important influence particularly on the Bristol socialists of whom Dix was one (Bristol also being one of the most significant of the socialist groups in the late 1880s),[9] it is not unreasonable to suppose that she is at least somewhat in dialogue with Carpenter's ideas in this novel.

Marriage, *The Image Breakers* teaches the reader early on, severely constricts women. The novel reveals this through a double plot, each centered on the two women friends. As the novel opens, Rosalind is married to Herbert Dangerfield, a one-time socialist turned capitalist. The note is sounded: merely holding socialist ideas is not enough (this note will later be amplified in the other male characters.) Rosalind tries to do political work while married but her husband's social position constrains her; the people in the movement won't trust her. Rosalind leaves her husband to enter a platonic union with a political friend (at least for most of the novel's duration—the novel is silent about the ultimate fate of their relation; all the reader knows is that their celibacy causes a strain between them). Her partner, Justin Ferrar, is a "utopian" socialist, one who wants first to set up a model community, which fails, and who later turns to writing books. Rosalind becomes disenchanted with both the narrowness of his vision, feeling that it doesn't speak to the lives of ordinary working women, and with his motherly and sexual demands on her. Disavowing his financial support upon recognizing that he liked her only to serve his own ideal, she tries to burn his book and goes to work in a stained glass factory, the effect of which on women Dix graphically depicts. Rosalind does not stay at the factory long though; Dix cannot finally envisage such an end for her middle-class woman. In a dramatic, conventional, and disappointing twist, she has Rosalind returning to her husband, ostensibly to protect him from anarchists who plot against him, saying that although she had broken her vows, "the Higher Power kept her still in bondage to what cannot be loosed or broken" (390).

The second, contrapuntal plot strand, that concerning Rosalind's friend Leslie, is the more interesting one and is given more attention in the novel. Leslie, early in the novel a socialist, decides to leave the protection of her aunt's home and seek employment in London, not as a governess but in her field, graphic drawing. Her journey is difficult and, interestingly, her socialist politics are no longer mentioned; again, contemporary socialism does not seem to speak to the needs of women, for work again in this case. Not long after she arrives she meets Redgold, who introduces her to someone who can give her some work. Although he is in some ways the image of a "modern" man, a man an independent woman would be attracted to, his whole relation to women still speaks of control. The rest of Leslie's story concerns her struggle to manage at once her strong attraction to Redgold and her desire to have a career. For Redgold wants to marry her and cart her off to the country. Redgold too is a socialist but, like his counterpart Ferrar, his socialism is stained, here not by utopianism but by opportunism, for he is trying to get elected to parliament and so makes some shady connections that come to deeply trouble Leslie. Leslie promises to marry him and "tries out" her role as his admirer. The novel even daringly implies a sexual relationship. But Leslie finds she can't work, she can't concentrate. She is afraid of marriage, understanding the consequences of financial dependency. She begins to feel that Redgold is content with little things, whereas for her the inner life is the real life.

Leslie then breaks off her engagement and Redgold is pursued by another woman. As part of Dix's rather complex portrait of him, he is not a cad or a simpleton. Though attracted by the other woman's homage, he comes to realize that he wants neither her slavery nor his own political slavery. He resolves to seek the more independent Leslie. He finds her, melodramatically, at a socialist meeting (which breaks up in an uproar). They agree to marry after he returns in six months, a separation she says will be good for her, for it will allow her to grow stronger. This plot of the novel ends here, with the promise of their marriage. Again, as in Birrell's novel, the deferral of marriage, yet its promise, is necessary.

Although the project of this plot strand, as does the other, reaffirms conventional ideology (engagements should not be broken, or, more largely, marriage is a woman's end), both of the men in this novel clearly need the female. Redgold, in particular, needs the "new woman" rather than the slavish devotion of a conventional woman. Dix cannot plot what their new relationship will look like—she doesn't even go so far as to promise Leslie a career—but she does project that a "new" kind of relationship is necessary between man and woman.

Along the way toward reaffirming conventional legal and socially acceptable heterosexual relations, *The Image Breakers* (as does *Demos*) hovers on the edge of exploring, even applauding, female homosocial if not fully lesbian relationships; unlike *Demos*, however, these women are not punished for their affection. Rosalind and Leslie's relationship is never allowed much room in which to flourish and Redgold, to be expected, comes between them, both Rosalind and he vying for Leslie's attention. But they counsel each other at critical moments. Rosalind even says to Leslie at one point: "Dear sister woman, you know that it is only by our making a stand—we women together and the men who see with us—that the world-sickness is to be cured" (274). Their bonding is touched with a sexual energy in one brief scene of parting: Leslie hugs Rosalind and "felt herself enfolded in a quick and passionate embrace, that made her heart beat violently with a strange confusion and fear" (172).

The female bonding hinted at in this novel, a bonding that, as Rosalind says, needs to have a political dimension other than that of the men's kind of socialism, does not flourish in this novel. Dix cannot represent it although this novel subtly and consistently desires such a community of women as the other two do not. It remains for the women's suffrage movement to provide such a larger public political community for women. As we shall see, however, the novelists who work within the historical context of the women's suffrage movement are surprisingly still deeply uneasy about the implications of this political community for women's private lives, for love and marriage.

Before turning to these novels whose discourse is concerned with the women's suffrage movement, however, there is at least one other pre-suffrage novel I have located, written by a woman, which portrays women's relationship to socialism in a radically different way from the preceding novels: Jane Clapperton's *Margaret Dunmore or, A Socialist Home* (1888). The novel features a wealthy unmarried woman, Margaret Dunmore, who has failed to find romance and instead has found a female friend—"I knew no one of the opposite sex whose presence thrilled me as Miss Jose's did, or with whom I would have cared to live" (159) (another discreet allusion, if not to female homosexuality, then at least to strong female homosocial bonds). Margaret decides to give over two-thirds of her money to start a "socialist home," a commune where a number of lost middle-class people will live and where many of them will work. All pool two-thirds of whatever they have. The commune is self-consciously modeled on many of the American models, such as the Shaker community. While marriage vows are sacrosanct, the rearing and education of children is collective, as are all household tasks. This means class and gender prerogatives are destroyed. The novel focuses on both explaining how the commune is run (through devices such as having visitors come by) and on dramatizing the various difficulties the characters successfully surmount (e.g., jealousy, men who can't give up their patronizing ways, children who aren't sufficiently responsible). The plot ends as the commune is given money to expand both its buildings and its work in its nearby city, Liverpool, where it hopes to build a "People's Palace" to teach the poor how to love life and each other and so prepare for socialism.

This novel is anomalous in a number of ways in relation to the other novels studied in this chapter. First, the socialist movement it alludes to is not the more familiar one of groups such as the Social Democratic Federation or the Fabian Society. These latter groups focused on organizing the unemployed and workers, using lectures, demonstrations, and strikes, and on changing the composition of parliament. In this way they hoped to hasten the socialist revolution. All such public agitation is not even alluded to in this novel. Rather, the socialism this novel defines is primarily *domestic* in character. The novel argues that people need to be prepared at the level of their interpersonal relations for the great change into a socialist society that the novel is sure will come (a new society that their personal transformations will, furthermore, help stabilize). Therefore the novel shows how to be a good socialist among one's family and friends—at "home." The novel does this by featuring a successful experiment in a socialist home, a commune where unrelated family members live and work. The novel deprecates all acts of violence, public and private, and only goes so far (insofar as it speaks of wider socialism at all) as advocating public lectures for the poor which will show them not how to unite, but how to have the "right conduct" in their homes. The novel sympathetically alludes to the People's Palace venture in London, to the theory of scientific meliorism, and to the philosophy of "altruistic humanism." *Margaret Dunmore* is an answer to Gissing's argument in *Demos*. It features loving interpersonal relations and asserts that these by themselves will transform the structure of society (which Gissing doesn't believe).

Second, this novel is anomalous because it has a collective protagonist, the members of a socialist commune, and because it is quasi-utopian in structure. That is, it is set two years in the future (1890) and it thus takes as its narrative project outlining for the reader how such a socialist home could be run, a home it paints in all the rosy hues characteristic of the utopian genre.

Margaret Dunmore in many ways hearkens back to the Owenite socialist feminism of the 1840s. This utopian socialism argued that altered domestic, communitarian relationships would eliminate all social oppression (in contrast to the feminist socialism at the turn of the century which argued the liberation of women in terms of structural changes in the industrial economy). Why Clapperton chooses this outworn vision now is an interesting question.[10]

One thing her choice does is free her from all anxiety about women's relationship to this sort of socialism. Running domestic establishments, educating the young, stressing the arts, is, after all, at this time seen as women's province. The socialism of this novel threatens nothing in this province and in fact provides poorer women with the means of having such a province in the first place. Clapperton's narrator throughout approves of tough-minded, hard-working women, women who do not necessarily need men but who will love them well if they are open, loving, and nondomineering. But her narrator always stops short of condoning militancy, as is shown when she comments on the public agitation for women's rights. Her characters throughout retain all their gentility.

Furthermore, Clapperton's choice of an outdated Owenite socialism prevents any anxiety about a socialism predicated on women's renouncing their current source of happiness (their homes, their own work) to follow a male socialist around (as in Howell, Birrell, and Dix). The women in this commune, in fact, rarely have to renounce any luxuries since there is plenty of money for them not to worry and since most of them were anyway of that class figured in *The Odd Women*, the genteel poor.

The novel, however, has latent tensions which reveal that it is a nostalgic text, that it is writing out a dead vision of socialism. One tension the novel glosses over is the philanthropic angle. Though Margaret is the founder, she is not revered as a saviour figure nor does she have such aims. The novel tries to be thoroughly anti-class, and specifically anti-paternalist. At one point, one of the male characters wants to introduce Margaret to a man he has met who has "systematized a reform—I mean, a theory and practice immediately applicable! Our hiatus, Margaret, is filled by his—scientific meliorism." (197) He eventually joins the group. But the other members will not let him alone be the spokesperson of their ways. One woman takes him on:

> "it was like the conceit of his sex, to think society built up by the working-men: I say it is built by the mothers; and I would keep the men out of our hall until all the women have been there, and know how we feel with them, and think for them, and what we would have them do." (203)

She succeeds. Yet in spite of this affirmation of its collective spirit, the novel's silence about any monetary tensions, any anxiety to curry Margaret's favor for example, is odd. Margaret's gift of money to keep the home going is the single unacknowledged problem in the novel. Such experiments depend on the rich philanthropist—the rich who are few and far between.

Second, *Margaret Dunmore*, in many ways more powerful than Morris's *News from Nowhere* in delineating how things could work on a daily basis, is a novel that knows that its scheme will not work on an extended basis. We learn near the novel's end that more and more people have to be turned away—the addition of one wing cannot stem the tide. The novel ends here, at the point where the commune might become too big.

Finally, *Margaret Dunmore* is unconscious of the inadequacy of its public strategies. The temperament and the visions of the poor who join the commune are changed not merely by hearing new ideas, but by being able to live without monetary anxiety and with a supportive, non-nuclear community. At the point that the commune plans to stop living for itself alone (necessary, the members claim, to get started) and go public, preach to the poor on how to live (yet without giving them monetary support or a nurturing wider community), these contradictions would surface. The novel, not surprisingly, ends here after the disquieting comments of an additional male philanthropist who has joined them: he has gone to America to see all their experiments, but says their life "scarce seemed to touch the broad question of national poverty" (189).

Margaret Dunmore does provide a new, if socially small, arena for women's as well as men's newly formed desires. The old ones, for a mate, are gratified but both the women and men find larger horizons than merely pleasing each other. Just as historically, however, such communes have been rare and often short-lived, so there are few novels which see this as the solution to the social question in general and a way for women to grow in particular. The turn in the twentieth-century novel was more generally toward representing women still living within the old domestic situation but now struggling within a larger arena of their own politics, a politics which came to be centered around the struggle for the vote.

* * *

If all of these novels, in their heterodoxy, do offer a composite portrait of women's relationship to socialism in the 1880s and 1890s, this portrait seems to be of a far different hue from ones offered in contemporary historiography, such as Sheila Rowbotham's *Women, Resistance and Revolution* or Olive Banks's *Becoming a Feminist*, both of which discuss women's relationship to socialism. Very different as these two histories are in their methodology (Banks's is an induction from the biographies of the most well-known feminists of the era), their narratives are similar in depicting new women energetically making their way with relative coherence as a group despite their plurality of concerns. Each history, however, focuses on different sites of activity. Rowbotham stresses that women in the 1880s made the "woman question" a vital one on the left by pushing for education, legal changes, and birth control. Furthermore, women, through their involvement in the New Life cultural circle initiated important discussions on the relationship between public and private life. Rowbotham points out that these radical programs and ideas upset many socialist men at the time, underscoring the inadequacy of socialist theory in confronting reproductive issues. Yet her argument is that women, nevertheless, put gender relations on the historical agenda of socialism, even if the agenda was not to be acted on for another eighty years. Banks's argument is less broad, though she seems less sanguine about the long-term effect of turn-of-the-century feminism on socialism and is negative about socialism's effect on feminism. She sees the decline of this first wave of feminism as in fact related to its alliance with a socialism that focused on class rather than gender. Banks sketches the various strains of feminism (most feminists, she claims, were socialist) and the position of the various socialist groups on the "woman question." For example, the Fabians and the Socialist League were not anti-feminist as was the SDF. The other socialist group, the Independent Labour Party, even used women as speakers and organizers.

These novels, by contrast, do not offer up women who are so radical or so purposeful. The "history" the novels imply is more confused, more blurred—and certainly nonlinear. This could be partly because the contemporary historiography focuses on feminist consciousness, whereas the political positions of these novelists and most certainly of their implied readers were far less radical, as the texts reveal. Although, as Rowbotham argues, feminism did stimulate a new consciousness of men's and women's relationships, not all women authors or readers could comfortably adopt feminist or feminist/socialist perspectives. This discrepancy between the perspective of the contemporary histories and that of the novels could also, however, be connected to their different genres, as well as their different moment of historical production. Novels tend to focus on the individual and on his or her fractures, not on broadly mapping the past to make it a precursor to our own sense of what the present is. Furthermore, productions made within a particular moment need to repress certain frightening dimensions (such as how willing women were to openly express a desire for change) that later, retrospective productions can comfortably talk out. Novels work to control not only what is anxious in the public sphere, but what is anxious in the private sphere as well. Although the novel connected with the women's suffrage movement produced a somewhat different image of a woman, a woman more open in expressing her desires for a radical change and who acts more decisively in bringing these changes about, even these novels do not offer the same spectacle of energetic, directed women seen in contemporary historical accounts or even in other, nonliterary documents produced within the era.

8

The Novel and Women's Suffrage

This chapter will focus on a sample of novels which begin to offer at least glimpses of another way for women than that offered in the fiction of the 1880s and 1890s studied in the last chapter: a larger world, other objects of desire. This palpable change in fiction was enabled by the historical possibility of women's involvement in that public political arena created by the campaign for women's suffrage, a movement whose history is already well documented.[1] The chapter will focus on interpreting three novels relatively well known in the period: Elizabeth Robins's *The Convert* (1907), H. G. Wells's *Ann Veronica* (1909), and Virginia Woolf's *Night and Day* (1919). This is not the only fiction of the period which discoursed with the topic of women's suffrage. But these novels, in their diverse handling of the topic, reveal some of the crises of representation provoked by an even "newer" kind of woman: a now politically militant woman.

Each of the projects of these novels, not surprisingly given the newness of the public political arena for women, is concerned with integrating the public with the private arena. As do the pro-socialist novels, these novels too seek to normalize, to situate what is radical in their vision. And, as before, the domestic is the favored arena for promoting the reassurance that all these proposed changes are not really that threatening. To fulfill this project of integrating the public and private new woman, as well as of packaging her in a less threatening way for the reader, each of these new-woman novels, not surprisingly, situates political women within a romance plot, much as the saviour-of-the-masses novels do. The centrality given this romance plot, however, is what needs to be explored. Is this romance plot the ground, the escape, or only the vehicle of a metaphor for a specifically female desire for a new political order? Furthermore, in what terms is the character of the political new woman represented in this plot? Is she given any male saviour, paternalistic traits? Or is she at root the familiar woman of domestic ideology, passive, still enslaved by a longing to be protected by a man in marriage? In other words, is the domestic arena, along with the old ideologemes which define and support it, radically redefined in these novels? As throughout this book, studying the conjunction of the project and product in each novel enables us to construct features of the "history" which could have produced it.

Elizabeth Robins's *The Convert* (1907) crosses over the threshold at which the earlier writers stopped: that of making a woman acting independently in a political arena the center of the drama. Here there is no abrupt truncating of the plot of the rebellious woman as in Howell, no embryonic political woman buried in home and marriage as in Birrell, and no, underrepresentation or suggestion of the ineffectiveness of the political activity of women as in Dix. Rather, *The Convert* enacts a central fear at the heart of Edwardian middle- and upper-class culture: that women will reject marriage and a patriarchal domesticity, with its ideology of male protection/female submission, and will choose ("convert" to) political activism in their own interests, namely suffragism. This novel undoubtedly was able to cross this threshold because feminism, considered avant-garde in the 1880s and 1890s, was by the early twentieth century a more established part of political life. And, as Elaine Showalter observes, writers could no longer ignore the issues, given the new militancy between 1905 and 1914 (1977, 218). More and more middle-class women were beginning to think and sometimes "do" such things. This novel, however, addresses those women readers who are still sitting on the fence, as well as those sympathetic males who might help the cause of women's suffrage in parliament; the novel's project, that is, is to "convert" its readers.

The Convert employs an exemplary convert, Vida Levering, as the vehicle through which to convince its reader of the power and necessity for women of the movement for women's suffrage. The novel seeks to show that the movement is compelling for women and necessary for eliminating their private pain, pain deriving from their lives with men. Part of Vida's story is her developing political desires, part her waning romantic desires, presented as a threat to women engaged in politics. Unlike Gissing's *Demos*, however, the trial of the woman's desire for the man does not structure the plot; this novel, rather, explores new dimensions of the female psyche which Robins felt the suffrage movement needed if it were to be successful. Women had to be made aware of the potentialities of their consciousness. The novel thus attempts to open a space for women's other desires and other joys to structure the action—the joy of escaping the confines of upper-class life, the joy of gaining self-confidence by speaking in public, the joy of experiencing a community of women.[2] As in Virginia Woolf's *Night and Day*, suffragists are represented as single women, women who have left behind the personal goals of husbands and children. Historically it does not yet seem possible for a woman to integrate the two spheres of domesticity and political action.[3]

The central plot concerns Vida's becoming political as she is increasingly drawn into the women's suffrage movement. The plot is cyclical: the novel opens with the protagonist Vida and her sister stealing away from their upper-class home to gaze at a women's suffrage open-air meeting; the novel ends with a younger woman similarly drawn to attend a meeting at which Vida herself has now become the speaker. The novel's plot thereby implies that the movement is mushrooming. All these women discover, as they listen to speeches, that the suffragists are not the ogres their men and the media have cast them to be. The speech, as has often been true in many of these novels, is the primary channel through which Robins makes her case for the worthiness of the cause. In fact, these particular speeches make extremely sophisticated arguments: likening suffragism to the Chartist movement, observing that women are already working outside of the home in larger numbers (as was historically true by the 1890s), and arguing women's political contribution to the Liberal Party, which has reneged on its promise of political support. Punctuating the speeches that structure this more static, montage-like plot are the jeers of an extremely hostile crowd. The jeers help Robins accomplish several things: (1) they reveal the terrible hostility feminism has engendered; (2) the jeers are so personally insulting that they discourage the reader's identification with those who make the jeers and so tend to weaken any pull the objections might otherwise have; and (3) they allow the objections to be raised and then dealt with.

As Vida starts to attend more and more of these meetings, the reader learns more about the movement. Not only are the arguments sophisticated. Poor women are involved, women whose clothing and manners don't trouble the narrator or Vida. Vida even works on opening a shelter for homeless women. Many women learn to speak in public for the first time. The reader comes to understand what the other novels don't show us as fully: the movement is not just for the vote, but for a radical change of the economic and social lives of women. We learn too that neither the Salvation Army nor the other socialists much approve of the suffragists.

In so many ways, then, this novel tells the story the other novels at times wanted to tell. It shows that women can be in political plots versus marriage plots; Vida is not seeking marriage but the larger arena of public life. Interestingly, Vida does not seek to run the movement. Though she has grand dreams for what the *movement* may accomplish, she is not a "female saviour" figure, akin to Harkness's George Eastmont or Shaw's Sidney Trefusis, nor does *The Convert* represent any other such women characters. Historically the women's movement was dominated by several strong personalities (particularly the Pankhursts). Yet, surprisingly, fictionally the ideologeme of the protective saviour, the paternalist, does not seem to be invoked when that leader is a woman. Nor is his more likely female counterpart invoked: the mother.

The Convert, however, founders. It is unable to create a thoroughly new narrative out of these promising materials and so to represent as convincingly as one would like a new arena for women and a different structure of female desire. The product backlights the project, revealing the limiting conditions of history, revealing the ways in which the project is ideological, a utopian wish, a way of seeing that yet has something of the imaginary about it as all projects do. The material of the novel asks for a different narrative focus than it gets. Either Vida should be figured as a kind of Lukácsian epic hero, a large individual character whose conflicts are at the same time representative. Or the novel should center around a group protagonist. *The Convert* seems to "know," in the way that texts have of displaying their unease, that such is the figuration the project calls for, but the product, the actual figuration, waffles. *The Convert* seems unable to decide which route to follow; it is timid both in its representation of a strong Vida and in its representation of her colleagues. What ends up propelling the plot is neither the reader's awe at Vida's accomplishments (and so her being a true exemplum, as Lukács's epic hero is), nor the reader's awe at the collective power of women. Rather, the reader is *curious* about an opaque Vida; though the novel does not quite position the reader as a voyeur (since there is not even a hint at salacious material here), it comes as close as it can in that it urges us to probe Vida's personal life in order to discover why she has become involved politically, as if this were the only story to tell about suffragism. Why, we ask, is she interested in suffragism, for example, and the lot of poor women?

The narrator throws us crumbs along the way: for example, we learn that Vida herself was homeless for a while. The largest "secret" about Vida, however, the one Robins usually uses to move her plot forward, is that Vida has had an abortion. All this is ostensibly presented to account for Vida's interest in the lot of unprotected women but the reader, schooled in romantic narratives and not schooled otherwise by Robins, tends to shift focus to a familiar and politically unfortunate question: is the father Geoffrey Stonor? Uncovering the "name of the father" unwittingly becomes one of the primary "engines" of the novel. The reader then becomes concerned with the issue, will Vida and Stonor reunite? The product has, unwittingly, reduced Vida to the status of an abandoned, if not notorious, woman and so, at least on one level, invokes our pity rather than our awe at her accomplishments. The political unconscious of Robins's novel undermines what it consciously offers.[4]

The novel attempts to stay on track, to avoid becoming derailed by this fascination with the romantic which contradicts its overt politics. It refuses to look much at Vida's emotions. It offers a surfeit of speeches, as if to dull our curiosity about Stonor and command our interest in the movement. And it has Stonor become engaged to a young woman, Jean, who herself seems to be a young Vida, since she is the one who goes to a women's suffrage meeting near the novel's end to hear Vida speak.

But nowhere is the novel's attempt to rescue itself from the romantic plot more bizarre, more unfortunate, than at the end. As the scene opens, Vida has told Jean about her past sexual relations with Stonor, relations that produced a child. Jean asks Stonor for the truth, which he gives her, though he thinks her an "ignorant child" (280) because Jean has it in her mind that Stonor must repay his debt to Vida even if it means that Jean will lose him. What Stonor doesn't know as he goes into the room to talk openly with Vida about his debt is that Vida aborted the child—he thinks it died. Vida's aim in telling Stonor about the abortion is not to get Stonor to marry her (the narrator convinces us she really no longer loves him; after ten years she has "other things to think about" (287)), but rather to try to blackmail him in repayment for her suffering. He is about to stand for parliament and she wants his support for women's suffrage. In exchange, she will not "take Jean" from him for the cause. Stonor, however, chafes under her attempted blackmail. He makes an argument that seems to have the narrator's approval:

> "You don't understand men. They can be led; they can't be driven. Ten minutes before you came into the room I was ready to say I would throw in my political lot with this Reform."
>
> "And now?"
>
> "Now you block my way by an attempt at coercion. By forcing my hand you give my adherence an air of bargain-driving for a personal end. Exactly the mistake of the ignorant agitators in Trafalgar Square. You have a great deal to learn. This movement will go forward, not because of the agitation outside, but in spite of it." (301)

Vida then backs off and Stonor gives way.

For this brief scene Robins has painted Vida as having human feelings yet as keeping her sense that her own life is not her concern now. Robins has also shown a new frankness in relations between men and women (e.g. Stonor and Jean's frank conversation about his past with other women) and changes in the patterns between women (e.g., Jean's adherence to the principle that Stonor owes Vida a debt first). At the same time, Stonor has an authoritative presence here. He has his way; he delivers a pointed and serious criticism of the movement, and particularly of agitation, that sticks because he is, at the same time, supportive of the movement. The outsider man seems to be more reasonable than the women. Finally, and more seriously, the novel has achieved its ending in the place most novels do: with the putative hero and heroine working out a truce designed by the man. The novel cannot utterly disentangle itself from romantic ideology.

Robins, finally, is very distant from her almost puppet-like characters. While, as in many of the novels so far studied, one might argue this results from her lack of skill as a writer, I think one could also continue to make the argument that the material itself was too frightening for the novelist to handle, too frightening both for the writer and for her sense of her reader. Showalter comments on the threat the movement posed to women writers:

> women writers found themselves confronted through the suffrage movement by a number of challenges and threats: by the spectre of violence, by the ruthlessness of female authoritarianism, by the elimination of class boundaries, by a politics of action rather than influence, by collectivism, and by the loss of the secure privacy in which they had been cultivating their "special moral qualities." The shift was too abrupt to be liberating. . . . (238–9)

The Convert theoretically opens a place for a woman to take a different path from the romantic one and it does sustain this plot throughout most of the novel. The suffrage movement exists there as a beacon, an anchor, for the protagonist. What the novel does not do is imagine as fully as we as late-twentieth-century readers think it could the possibilities of female desire for a life beyond man, because such an imagination invoked terror as well as joy. Such an imagination of these other desires was not to begin to be produced in fiction until Virginia Woolf some ten years later—Woolf, the only major female novelist even close to the turn of the century. But before turning to explore Woolf's *Night and Day,* which also features a suffragist, we need to consider the kind of response suffragism provoked from the patriarchy, the kind of enclosure the patriarchy typically attempted as a result both of the movement and of the changing representation of women in novels such as *The Convert*. The central example of this in the period is H.G. Wells's *Ann Veronica*. Wells takes Gissing a step further in the attempt to contain the threats posed by new, now militant women.

H. G. Wells's most infamous novel, *Ann Veronica* (1909), has been read in its own time and in ours as a feminist text. Odette Keun, once a close friend of Wells, praises *Ann Veronica* in her memoir as a "deliverance" for women.

> Into this foul and insupportable nightmare leapt [Wells] . . . to thrust and cut and hack . . . at the tentacles, the octopus, the whole evil, stupid, brutal frame in which we were imprisoned. . . . We were being delivered. (quoted in Costa, 91)

More recently John Batchelor has described *Ann Veronica* as "an entirely serious feminist novel" (84), in its championing of sexual liberalism and its critique of sexual possessiveness. And indeed both the novel's plot and its public reception seem to suggest its progressiveness. Macmillan, Wells's usual publisher, wouldn't touch this novel which features a young intelligent woman disobeying her father to run off to London to secure an education and woo the (married) man she loves. Denounced from the pulpit, banned from the libraries, the occasion for the establishment of "Watch Committees" to censor "poisonous literature" (yet read all the more because of this opposition), *Ann Veronica* seemingly provoked his readers' fears of socialism and feminism alike.[5]

Yet *Ann Veronica*'s progressivism is shallow. The novel champions not women's liberation, but sexual emancipation. The novel works not to open up feminism, but to contain it.[6] Its project is, rather, to display to a male reader the fascinations this new woman holds for him. The novel constructs a spectacle of a new woman which it yet works to contain within traditional patriarchal boundaries. Unlike her docile sister, the mid-nineteenth-century woman at the hearth, young Ann Veronica has no father protecting her (she has thrown him over); she is, in short, available. She is an intelligent, quick-witted companion, feisty enough to be undemanding (she is not wooed by wealth or the promise of protection), and, best of all, she can love passionately, even to the point of openly declaring this passion to an already married man and then agreeing to run off with him. *Ann Veronica* is a tamer version of Grant Allen's *The Woman Who Did* (1895), where the woman opts for free love, in the end rejecting marriage as Ann Veronica does not when circumstances allow it. But Wells's novel is produced from the same voyeuristic vantage point as is Allen's: that of the male spectator surveying the delights the "liberated" woman has to offer him. As a correspondent of Wells, Richard Gregory, tellingly puts it to Wells: "The worst of reading a book like this . . . is the desire to experience a woman like V" (quoted in MacKenzie, 251). The novel, as Norman and Jeanne Mackenzie see it, "is the escapist's dream fulfilled. The married man runs away with the beautiful and intelligent girl to live happily ever after" (249). I would add to this characterization, the married man could assuage his guilt by calling Ann the seducer and yet he can have her in his thrall all the same. Wells's novel enacts another desire at the heart of Edwardian culture: the male desire for quasi-liberated women. Secondarily, however, the novel also enacts another fear, that which some of its women readers might have about new women like Ann Veronica stealing their husbands.

The indicators that this novel's project is to present the advantages the new woman has to offer men are found in its woefully inadequate characterization of Ann as a complex character, as one who genuinely has a consciousness of self (as does Woolf's Katharine or even, though less well-developed, Robins's Vida). In addition, the insistence of the novel's plotting on Ann's relationships with men, an insistence that sometimes necessitates abrupt turns in the plot, reveals the novel's obsessive need to contain the female within the male. In this novel marriage is not a "rescue attempt," not a solution to a situation the writer cannot think to close any other way; rather, marriage is the very project of *Ann Veronica*, not so much because it is legal and respectable, but because it is woman's place. Whereas Gissing contains the threat of the new woman by making Rhoda a nun, Wells contains the threat by marrying her off.

Briefly, the plot displays young, rebellious Ann Veronica (her personality is much like Shaw's Agatha) chafing under her father's strictness about what parties she should go to (her most serious problem) and under social pressures to marry a wealthy but boring man. She wants to continue her schooling, though the reader rarely sees her seriousness about her studies—in contrast with even the glimpses Woolf gives us of Katharine studying mathematics in *Night and Day*. So Ann Veronica, on her own, flees to London to find work. Unlike Leslie in *The Image Breakers* or numerous women in Gissing's *The Odd Women*, however, Ann Veronica has no "luck" finding work. In fact, on her first walk about London she is followed by a man, warning Ann Veronica and reader alike about the impossibility of a woman going out on the streets alone. Instead she is quickly "saved" from penury both by surreptitious gifts of money from her aunt and a "loan" from an older male friend, Rammage; her monetary dependency on family and a man is thereby speedily reinstated. With this money, having substituted one father for another, Ann Veronica resumes her studies in biology.

Rammage (his very name is telling of his style), however, has another form of repayment in mind from her father's (who wants her to be a dutiful daughter by marrying well). In a scene which dramatizes the gender politics of the entire novel and which serves as a decoy for Wells's narrator, Rammage tries to rape Ann Veronica. She escapes, but is haunted by her monetary debt until she can repay him at the novel's end. Meanwhile, she has casually been attending both Fabian socialist and suffragist meetings (little of either their politics or her aversion to their "vulgarity" sticks with her past the chapter). Following Rammage's attack, though, she quickly turns to suffragism. Such is the narrator's accounting for women's politics: it is capricious, precipitated by men such as Rammage. Men, you have only yourselves to blame, suggests Wells, if you insist on forcing yourselves on women. Ann is thrown in prison for participating in a riot, an experience so horrible for her that she "decides" she must have been very bad (her political acumen is pathetic) and decides to "repent" by returning to her father and engaging herself to her old suitor, a man whose narcissism and patriarchal attitudes the narrator mocks.

Wells, however, must have Ann Veronica's sexual passion dominate. So, she falls in love with her biology professor, Capes, a man married to a woman from whom he has long been separated. He reciprocates, following one day in the lab when she makes an outburst advocating women's suffrage; her independence prompts him to see her as a person. Ann decides she cannot tolerate her fiancé after all and decides to flee to Switzerland to live with Capes. The novel ends as they are back in London after four years, now legally married, Capes a promising and wealthy playwright, Ann Veronica waiting in their well-furnished flat for the birth of their first child and reconciled to her family.

The experience of the women's suffrage movement, according to the project of this novel, has helped Ann Veronica make a better choice of husband, her own choice from her heart (and her passion) of whom she should marry and live with in a conventional domestic arrangement. Also, her fleeting experience with the suffragists has helped her be more attractive to the "right" man, the new sensitive man; Capes now sees Ann Veronica as a human with whom he can talk about his failings. The suffragist "experience" was merely an objective correlative for her own rage at her dependency on Rammage, a galvanizer for her own will, a "phase" as Ann Veronica tells Capes. The message to male readers is: let them go, let them dabble in these politics. It only makes women more interesting mates, for the "real women" will still be driven ultimately by their passion to do anything for men they care for, a passion such radical dabbling helps ignite. Dix and Robins, as so many of the contemporary feminists of the time, were, it seems, not outrageous after all: woman's passion may be something to contain at least at the present time—it can make her fall for a male and so possibly into the old relations of dependency.

That a novel like *Ann Veronica* should appear on the heels of a novel like *The Convert* is understandable. This is Wells's attempt to manage the crisis the women's suffrage movement focused, an attempt to manage the new woman, to find in the situation something desirable for the patriarchy. As such, the novel is a containment strategy. But again, as with all the novels studied in this book, what is most interesting about it is what it fails to contain, what it avoids saying, in other words, the way it frames its attempt to appropriate the new feminism for the patriarchy. Although Wells's novel does not open any positive space for women, although he neither constructs a new political arena in which they can act nor frames new desires for women, the novel's impossibility of containing its material reveals that it somehow "knows," in its political unconscious, that its project is futile, even retrograde. The negative space *Ann Veronica* opens up, in other words, reveals that historically a positive space is being created for women.

Two of the more uneven, disruptive moments in the text occur when Ann is in prison and at the end when she is in her new home. Ostensibly Ann Veronica goes to the women's suffrage headquarters so that she can "do" something (241) to help her and all women be free from certain customs, particularly the custom of a woman's not telling a man (Capes) that she loves him. "If one was free . . . one could go to him. . . . I will not have this slavery . . . will not be slave to the thought of any man, slave to the customs of any time" (236). The narrator has at this point worked himself into a position where he has to narrate something about Ann Veronica's subsequent participation in a riot and then her stay in prison. So the narrator is drawn to describe the magistrate who speaks to the women as "you silly wimmin . . . you silly creatures! Ugh!" (252). Then Wells's narrator, however briefly, describes the prison experience. He details the "turbid water that had already been used" (254) in which a fellow prisoner bathes Ann Veronica. Then she is dressed in a "dirty dress of coarse serge," a dress "unwashed from its former wearer." To Ann Veronica, "horrible memories of things seen beneath the microscope of the baser forms of life crawled across her mind and set her shuddering." These representations are, of course, grossly inadequate when compared with other accounts of police brutality and prison conditions.[7] And too, they focus on the aesthetic and hygienic, the personal, rather than the larger political dimensions of which Wells's narrator has no inkling. Nevertheless, the appearance even of these few details, however briefly, reminds a sympathetic reader of the seriousness and violence of these events. They stay in the reader's mind long after the narrator tries to pass by them onto Ann Veronica's pitifully self-abasing "recognition" scene. Wells ultimately uses this experience to make Ann Veronica repent, to separate herself from the movement as she identifies herself as a woman out of place among the suffragists because she is a woman who "likes men" (263), a true woman who "wants a proper alliance with a man, a man who is better stuff than herself. She wants that and needs it more than anything else in the world" (263). In spite of this attempt at recuperation, however, the novel has inadvertently let out that which it cannot quite contain: the horrors the suffragists experienced.

At the end of the novel, similarly, Ann Veronica is to be shown as in utopia, as thoroughly content with her husband, house, and baby. Yet the novel ends on a distressing note. Ann Veronica, kneeling into her husband's arms, is speaking to him alone after her family has left.

> "Do you remember the mountains? Do you remember how we loved one another? How intensely we loved one another! Do you remember the light on things and the glory of things? I'm greedy, I'm greedy! I want children like the mountains and life like the sky. Oh! and love—love! We've had so splendid a time, and fought our fight and won. And it's like the petals falling from a flower. Oh, I've loved love, dear! I've loved love and you, and the glory of you; and the great time is over, and I have to go carefully and bear children, and—take care of my hair—and when I am done with that I shall be an old woman. The petals have fallen—the red petals we loved so. We're hedged about with

> discretions—and all this furniture—and successes! We are successful at least! Successful! But the mountains, dear! We won't forget the mountains, dear, ever. That shining slope of snow, and how we talked of death! We might have died! Even when we are old, when we are rich as we may be, we won't forget the time when we cared nothing for anything but the joy of one another, when we risked everything for one another, when all the wrappings and coverings seemed to have fallen from life and left it light and fire. Stark and stark! Do you remember it all? . . . Say you will never forget! That these common things and secondary things sha'n't overwhelm us. These petals! I've been wanting to cry all the evening, cry here on your shoulder, for my petals. Petals! . . . Silly woman! . . . I've never had these crying fits before. . . ."
>
> "Blood of my heart" whispered Capes, holding her close to him. "I know. I understand." (376-7)

What has happened here (in spite of Ann Veronica's allusion to the crying fits as a result of her pregnancy) is that the image Wells produces earlier in the chapter of their Edenic bourgeois home has collapsed. The love, the wildness, is all in the past, in the moment when Ann Veronica and Capes lived outside of society in the mountains. This is hardly a radical stand for it is still a reaffirmation of traditional heterosexual love, a love in which the female is "beneath the male," but the use of the past tense introduces a disturbing note. Perhaps, though, it is not only bourgeois life that has dulled them. Perhaps the relationship is less than satisfactory for Ann Veronica? Certainly she is the only one who talks; he is not passionate now, only consoling.

Indeed, an even larger dimension of this novel than these two scenes, which suggest some instability, some inadequacy at its core to make its case, is the way the novel features only Ann Veronica. Unconvincing as she is, she is the only well-drawn figure. She makes her way by herself, chooses her man, gets her way. No man teaches her, only other women, if at all. Capes is not at all well drawn, nor is their relationship. He is a fantasy for her and reader alike, and then not in any way a passionate one. While the novel thus overtly celebrates in the end a traditionally hierarchical male-female relationship—with a modified (tamed) "new woman" and a "new man"—the novel never figures this relationship or any enthralling power of the woman's desire for the man. The story is Ann Veronica's story, her orbit, from beginning to end.

This, of course, is the heart of the patriarchy's fear of the feminist movement: women will discover they don't really need not only male protection and money, but men at all. Their selves are in some fundamental way their own, not a man's. However much Wells tries to contain this fear by making Ann Veronica do all the conventional things, however frivolous Ann Veronica is at many moments, the point is his novel celebrates her ability to do them entirely on her own. She is her own person. Like earlier texts, such as *Jane Eyre*, which celebrate individual women's journeys by naming their novels after the women (an important indicator of the novel's attention), *Ann Veronica*, by being only about Ann Veronica's journey, subtly undermines the novel's project of containing the new woman.

With Robins and Wells we have seen the emergence of a more sustained narrative focus on the new woman, a character, furthermore, whose enhanced autonomy is figured as a function of her involvement in political activity. Although Wells especially goes to great lengths to contain the effects of this activity, his novel "lets out" far more than it contains. Rebellious women have now become acceptable figures on the fictional horizon. Over the course of the second decade of the twentieth century was to be produced Virginia Woolf's *Night and Day* which represents such new women in very different ways. Their rebelliousness is tempered, their sense of self even more sure and more full. Nevertheless, their newly constructed selves are marred by the same kinds of conflicting desires we have seen throughout, the conflict between the desire for love and the desire for autonomy.

Virginia Woolf's project in her second and last Edwardian novel, *Night and Day*, written during the war and published in 1919, is to explore how a woman can "be," how she can create a social space, a life situation, congenial for the exercise and development of her large imagination. As such, this novel poses the most profound, if most elusive, question of all these novels, as it simultaneously constructs the most complex and largest woman character of all of the novels studied here. Without any consciousness of its unusualness within its time (there is, for example, no sign of any anxiety or defensiveness), the novel makes Katharine Hilbury a protagonist whose vast yet non-specific desires linger in the reader's memory long after the book is put down. *Night and Day* is a richer, deeper probing of the problem hinted at in Dix's Leslie; both feature women whose undefined yearnings far exceed the options open to them. Woolf's narrator, however, probes Katharine's consciousness much more deeply than does Dix's narrator, who tends to stand farther off from Leslie and limits Leslie's desires to romance and work. One of the possibilities that Woolf explores for Katharine is political activism, particularly the campaign for women's suffrage. Woolf, however, represents a suffragist at work in *Night and Day* not only to give Katharine "options"; the representation of the political movement functions as a critical sign of women's separateness and their ability to anchor themselves in the world on their own, outside of marriage. The representation of women's suffrage is not a side show, but, on the contrary, is critical to the novel's ability to represent Katharine as it does.

The novel is structured as a journey—not a "quest," because, like many female protagonists, Katharine does not set out to "make" or "find" her self; she is not a discoverer. Nor is the novel a journey "out," as in Woolf's first novel, *The Voyage Out*, which used the vehicle of a physical journey to a tropical colony (and so offering a female parallel to Conrad's journey novels) as the objective correlative for Rachel's similarly unconscious development. Here Katharine's journey unfolds inwardly, to her heart and mind. There are, however, many contained physical journeys in the novel, which signify the indeterminateness of Katharine's longing. The novel is crisscrossed with Katharine's walks about town, alone, with friends, sometimes to escape her parents' home, with its strict late Victorian social decorum, sometimes to go to the "rooms" of her intellectual, aesthetic, and political friends (echoes of Bloomsbury). Unlike Ann Veronica's dangerous walks, Katharine's are salubrious and expansive. The point for Katharine (and Woolf) in these walks is not "seeing the world," but giving room to one's imagination through physical solitude and freedom from social decorum.

Katharine, however, is not entirely "free," unanchored, as she wanders. Woolf, as designer, encumbers her from the start with the pressure of marriage. Woolf thereby is still implying the centrality, if not the necessity, of marriage for a woman in this social position. The plot never allows any other option to become a possibility. Katharine's family and her friends expect marriage of her, given her position as a young upper-middle-class single woman, with no visible occupation, living under her parents' roof. Yet Katharine is gifted. Though not visibly formally educated, she studies mathematics in secret in her room. And she is working with her mother on a biography of her grandfather. But it is principally with the issue of marriage, not "career," that she must deal in *Night and Day*: shall she marry? And then, whom shall she marry? As the novel opens, Katharine decides to marry a poet, Rodney. By the novel's end, they have mutually agreed to break their engagement, each finding more suitable mates. Katharine finally decides to marry the difficult, more "lower-class" lawyer-would-be-writer, Ralph Dedham, who has throughout the course of the novel developed an almost chivalric obsession with Katharine. The only character left out in the cold at the end is the suffragist, Mary Datchet, friend of all of them, who has deeply loved Ralph and for a time thought he loved her in return. The way in which Woolf handles Mary, Mary's rejection, and Mary and Katharine's relationship is but one of the many indices of this novel's unconventionality.

A surface reading of the plot, as well as of the novel's images and descriptions, however, seems to suggest that the novel is quite conventional. Woolf's "answer" to Katharine's journey seems to be: choose to marry, marry a man who adores you and with whom you experience a certain "spark," if not abrasiveness; choose to live your life in the couple unit, in personal ease and intellectual pursuit. The way of the political activist, the novel's plot read superficially suggests, will not yield a woman a man or marriage. Woolf's narrator's descriptions of Ralph's view of Katharine compared with her rather arid descriptions of Mary's work further support the seemingly conservative project of the novel as they engage the reader's romantic fantasies, on the one hand, and confirm, on the other, the stereotype of an "old maid" for whom singleness is a retreat from passion. In the following passage, for example, the narrator describes one of Ralph's impressions on seeing Katharine:

> When Ralph Denham entered the room and saw Katharine seated with her back to him, he was conscious of a change in the grade of the atmosphere such as a traveller meets with sometimes upon the roads, particularly after sunset, when, without warning, he runs from clammy chill to a hoard of unspent warmth in which the sweetness of hay and beanfield is cherished, as if the sun still shone although the moon is up. (308)

The simile, one of Woolf's favorite devices in her earlier fiction, draws the reader to Ralph and Katharine's romance. The narrator, in contrast, describes Mary's feelings for Ralph quite differently. Early in the novel Mary says after seeing Ralph,

> the mystery of his nature laid more of a spell upon her than she liked. Moreover, she could not prevent herself from doing now what she had often blamed others of her sex for doing—from endowing her friend with a kind of heavenly fire, and passing her life before it for his sanction. Under this process, the committee rather dwindled in importance; the suffrage shrank. (169)

When she enters Mary's mind, the narrator's language becomes pinched, abstract ("moreover," "under this process"). The next chapter of the novel offers the reader a scene in which Mary's memory of her prior meeting with Ralph battles with her attempt to be present at the women's suffrage meeting. The meeting "wins out," to the narrator's dismay. The narrator says:

> And then, without conscious effort, by some trick of the brain, she found herself becoming interested in some scheme for organizing a newspaper campaign. . . . Once more, she knew exactly and indisputably what is right and what is wrong. As if emerging from a mist, the old foes of the public good loomed ahead of her—capitalists, newspaper proprietors, anti-suffragists, and in some ways most pernicious of all, the masses who take no interest one way or another—among whom, for the time being, she certainly discerned the features of Ralph Denham [since Ralph doesn't sympathize]. (173–4)

Mary is subtly caricatured by the narrator ("some scheme," "exactly and indisputably," etc.). Nor do the rest of the characters in the room, mostly elderly women, fare much better in Woolf's portrait. They speak in platitudes: "shouldn't I be proud to give everything I have to the cause" (177). The narrator refers to one of them in phrases such as "the odd little priestess of humanity" (176). Such descriptions of Mary and her work reveal a narrator who at least in this earlier part of the novel finds all this activism rather silly, a compensation for unrequited love. The narrator is as hurried a visitor to the women's suffrage meeting as is Katharine. This narrator is nowhere near as bitter as the narrator of *Mrs. Dalloway* in describing the obsessed Miss Kilman, but there is already an ungenerous, sneering edge in her voice.

The "night" and "day" of the title perhaps refer to the seemingly absolute contrast of these two worlds of suffragism and romance—respectively, death and life. Or the title could imply that Katharine, by choosing to marry, has moved from darkness into light, night into day. But the very tone with which the narrator has gently satirized Mary's clear sense of "right" and "wrong" suggests the title may be ironic; the cliché the novel's title seems to allude to, "as different as night and day," may not be a reliable way, may be a far oversimplified way, to describe any person or situation. Indeed Woolf's "answer" to Katharine's quest is nowhere near as solid as the foregoing reading suggests. I believe part of Woolf in *Night and Day* did want the "happy ending," the safe harbor of romance for a woman and a new type of domesticity (the literary country cottage to which Ralph and Katharine will repair at novel's end). But Woolf is extremely open-ended: if not unsure about what route Katharine should take, then at least unsure about Katharine's ultimate satisfaction with this route. Woolf's project is exploration, her answers unclear. From this vantage point, Mary Datchet's role in the plot is not at all as simple as that of being a sitting duck.

For every moment during which Woolf entices the reader with Ralph's romantic adoration of Katharine and so stimulates the reader's applause at their eventual union, she pushes the reader back, framing this enticement as a fantasy. The novel, in other words, deconstructs the myth of marriage as uniting two selves and giving a woman's life meaning, even as it re-enacts the myth in the reader's desire and so reinscribes it. In *The Voyage Out* Woolf dramatically has her young woman die before her marriage, partially, in Rachel DuPlessis's reading, as an enactment of her desire to escape from being written into a marriage plot. In *Night and Day* Woolf seems more resigned to marriage; her criticism of the limitations of marriage for a woman is less dramatic, her tone detached, remote. It was to take Woolf some ten more years, after composing *To The Lighthouse*, before she could give up writing novels in which the marriage relationship does not figure prominently and before she could represent in fiction what she only implies in both of her first two novels: "there is no arm to cling to, . . . we go alone" (1927, 118).

Typically, it is at the end of romantic novels that the utopian quality of the union of male and female is at least hinted at. But *Night and Day*'s ending is far different. Observe, for example, these moments as the novel moves to a close. I wish to quote from these moments at some length because the characters' and narrator's language here display the range of Woolf's complex feelings about marriage. In one scene in which Katharine is trying to make up her mind whether to marry Ralph, the two of them discuss their "lapses."

> "Anyhow, there's no reason why we shouldn't see each other."
> "Or stay together. It's only marriage that's out of the question," Katharine replied.
> "But if I find myself coming to want you more and more?"
> "If our lapses come more and more often?"
> He sighed impatiently, and said nothing for a moment.
> "But at least," he renewed, "we've established the fact that my lapses are still in some odd way connected with you; yours have nothing to do with me. Katharine," he added, his assumption of reason broken up by his agitation, "I assure you that we are in love—what other people call love. Remember that night. We had no doubts whatever then. We were absolutely happy for half an hour. You had no lapse until the day after; I had no lapse until yesterday morning. We've been happy at intervals all day until I went off my head, and you, quite naturally, were bored."

Following this really rather humorous scene of their too high seriousness, the narrator summarizes:

They were trying to explain, not for the first time, as their weary gestures and frequent interruptions showed, what in their common language they had christened their "lapses"; a constant source of distress to them, in the past few days. . . . What was the cause of these lapses? Either because Katharine looked more beautiful, or more strange, because she wore something different, or said something unexpected, Ralph's sense of her romance welled up and overcame him either into silence or into inarticulate expressions, which Katharine, with unintentional but invariable perversity, interrupted or contradicted with some severity or assertion of prosaic fact. Then the vision disappeared, and Ralph expressed vehemently in his turn the conviction that he only loved her shadow and cared nothing for her reality. If the lapse was on her side it took the form of gradual detachment until she became completely absorbed in her own thoughts, which carried her away with such intensity that she sharply resented any recall to her companion's side. . . . The fact remained that she had no need of him and was very loath to be reminded of him. How then, could they be in love? The fragmentary nature of their relationship was but too apparent. (500–501)

Then Woolf tries to salvage romance from her narrator's disillusionment above. Enter the sprightly, somewhat zany Mrs. Hilbery, who tries to help her daughter overcome her reservations about marriage.

"If I could help you, Katharine, by the memory of what I felt—"

"Yes, tell me what you felt."

Mrs. Hilbery, her eyes growing blank, peered down the enormously long corridor of days at the far end of which the little figures of herself and her husband appeared fantastically attired, clasping hands upon a moonlit beach, with roses swinging in the dusk.

"We were in a little boat going out to a ship at night," she began. "The sun had set and the moon was rising over our heads. There were lovely silver lights upon the waves and three green lights upon the steamer in the middle of the bay. Your father's head looked so grand against the mast. It was life, it was death. The great sea was round us. It was the voyage for ever and ever."

The ancient fairy-tale fell roundly and harmoniously upon Katharine's ears. Yes, there was the enormous space of the sea; there were the three green lights upon the steamer; the cloaked figures climbed up on deck. And so, voyaging over the green and purple waters, past the cliffs and the sandy lagoons and through pools crowded with the masts of ships and the steeples of churches—here they were. The river seemed to have brought them and deposited them here at this precise point. She looked admiringly at her mother, that ancient voyager.

"Who knows," exclaimed Mrs. Hilbery, continuing her reveries, "where we are bound for, or why, or who has sent us, or what we shall find—who knows anything, except that love is our faith—love—" she crooned, and the soft sound beating through the dim words was heard by her daughter as the breaking of waves solemnly in order upon the vast shore that she gazed upon. She would

> have been content for her mother to repeat that word almost indefinitely—a soothing word when uttered by another, a riveting together of the shattered fragments of the world. But Mrs. Hilbery, instead of repeating the word love, said pleadingly:
>
> "And you won't think those ugly thoughts again, will you, Katharine," at which words the ship which Katharine had been considering seemed to put into harbour and have done with its seafaring. . . .
>
> "But then," she [Katharine] said, ignoring the difficult problem of ugliness, "you knew you were in love; but we're different. It seems," she continued, frowning a little as she tried to fix the difficult feeling "as if something came to an end suddenly—gave out—faded—an illusion—as if when we think we're in love we make it up—we imagine what doesn't exist. . . ."
>
> "We have to have faith in our vision," Mrs. Hilbery resumed. . . . "otherwise, as you say—" She cast a lightning glance into the depths of disillusionment which were, perhaps, not altogether unknown to her.
>
> "Believe me, Katharine, it's the same for every one—for me too—for your father," she said earnestly, and sighed. They looked together into the abyss. . . . (511–13)

At this point they resume a trivial conversation.

Mrs. Hilbury's reassurance, though laced again with lovely lulling similes, is similarly undermined by the narrator's language. The similes are sometimes extravagant ("roses swinging in the dust"); they can't but be read against Mr. Ramsey's overblown epic similes which attract much of the narrator's criticism in *To the Lighthouse*. Woolf here has Mrs. Hilbury, as the representative of the Edwardian era, even imitating something of the posture of Matthew Arnold's speaker in "Dover Beach" (without his patronizing stance toward his "love" or his pretentious philosophical explanation). Like Katharine, the reader is taken out to that "sea of faith"; like Katharine, the reader is then beached. The narrator too desires but knows her desires are illusions.

Marriage is the only serious option Woolf sees for Katharine, yet it is not in this novel an absolutely satisfying one. The novel offers us an excess of desire in Katharine, a longing for something nameless, something impersonal. Her love for mathematics seems to hint at the impersonality of her desire. Yet even her "pursuit" of mathematics isn't presented as an option (she is not disciplined in its study, nor does she "do" anything with it).

Mary Datchet is the suffragist who now in the 'teens does not have to be defended or accounted for, as Robins's and Wells's characters a decade earlier must be. Mary occupies the rather unlovely position, in this novel of inaction, of being the character who believes there is necessary, concrete work to do in this world: "there's always work . . . it's the thing that saves one" (415), and communities of women in which to do it, that one's longing needs to be and can be curbed in the air of larger social life. As such, she occupies a peculiar structural position in the novel. Mary at once absorbs any irritation the reader might feel toward Katharine's claustrophobic amorphousness and inactivity *and* she simultaneously attracts the reader to her more prosaic yet active way of life. As with other writers of the period, James in particular, the Marys of the world do not engage the writer's *aesthetic* imagination (or apparently that of suitors), so there is little "story" Woolf can tell about her except her failed romance with Ralph. But the revolutionary Marys of the world nevertheless attract in the abstract. Mary, a sort of parallel to James's Paul Muniment, attracts the reader not only because Katharine structurally needs a foil, but also because the narrator in flashes presents Mary as brave, reassuring, and potentially as complicated, if not as "mysterious," as Katharine. Mary becomes particularly attractive when she poses no further threat to Woolf's project of steering Katharine away from suffragism and into marriage with Ralph. Our last glimpses of Mary are strong, positive ones. In the scene when Ralph tells Mary he loves Katharine, Mary is presented as dignified, even heroic, in overcoming her attachment to him. The narrator's language is not overblown here as it is when she is gently satirical.

> She had suffered and relinquished, she had seen her future turned from one of infinite promise to one of barrenness, and yet, somehow, over what she scarcely knew, and with what results she could hardly foretell, she had conquered. With Ralph's eyes upon her, smiling straight back at him serenely and proudly, she knew, for the first time, that she had conquered. (416)

Mary later convincingly says in a complex scene with Katharine, one in which Mary experiences under the surface both hostile and caring feelings for Katharine, that she discovers she no longer loves Ralph—that "another love burnt in the place of the old one" (474). Mary is partly braving it out of course—once "the pain of her loss shot through her. Nothing would ever make up—not success or happiness, or oblivion" (478). But the narrator follows:

> But this pang was immediately followed by the assurance that now, at any rate, she knew the truth; and Katharine, she thought, stealing a look at her, did not know the truth; yes, Katharine was immensely to be pitied. (478)

And to some extent the narrator's portrait of Katharine's feelings, as we have seen, corroborates this. Katharine is imprisoned both by her own uncertainties and by Ralph's image of her, an image born of his own desire for a mysterious (i.e., unformed) "lady."

As the novel draws to a close, Katharine and Ralph are standing on the street in front of Mary's rooms. Katharine thinks: "Is she alone, working at this time of night? What is she working at? . . . Why should we interrupt her? . . . What have we got to give her? She's happy too . . . She has her work" (535). As Ralph goes in, Katharine continues to look at Mary's light:

> the light was not moved. It signalled to her across the dark street; it was a sign of triumph shining there for ever, not to be extinguished this side of the grave. She brandished her happiness as if in salute; she dipped it as if in reverence. "How they burn!" she thought, and all the darkness of London seemed set with fires, roaring upwards; but her eyes came back to Mary's window and rested there satisfied. (536)

There is nothing even humorously mocking in the narrator's tone here—as there is in her rendering of Mrs. Hilbury's vision of romance. Katharine here is paying homage to Mary, even as Ralph pays homage to Katharine. Mary seems to have become the new woman on the pedestal, the woman Katharine, by the logic of mid-century ideology, should have been in this novel. For all that Woolf does not let her protagonist really enter Mary's world, but must leave her gazing at it from an admiring distance, Woolf delineates the limits of Katharine's world of marriage and passion and she shows a budding comprehension, an opening sympathy for Mary's world and for Mary as a potentially large and complex figure. This is a story Woolf cannot, for whatever reason, tell, perhaps because she does not understand Mary, perhaps because she feels herself something of an "outsider" to political activism. In the long run, Robins, of all these writers, is probably the least afraid of probing political women, but then her purpose is not to probe character but to urge the reader to understand and sympathize with the suffragists' aims. There seems to be no middle ground: Woolf is interested in displaying these characters but is not very knowledgeable about the suffragists. Robins, who has the knowledge, has other aims in mind than the careful display of character—namely converting the reader.

The project of *Night and Day*, affirming conventional romance, like all the other novels we have seen, is vitiated by the novel itself, the product. From a number of vantage points the myth of romantic love is interrogated and destabilized. Woolf doesn't want to throw it out but she well knows its unsatisfactoriness. The narrative about the non-suffragist, the vestige of the romantic heroine, is the only story Woolf can tell, yet it is a painful, unsatisfactory narrative about loneliness and unsatisfied longing. At its margins hovers a different story of a "way out," a story of the independent political new woman, a story waiting to be told.

One of the literary "conditions of possibility" (in Macherey's terms) of all the novels studied in this book, including those more woman-centered novels studied in the last two chapters, is the domestic novel and the romance plot. Women writers historically have especially foregrounded this literary plot, even as women's social lives have. Throughout the readings in this book we have seen, however, that the plots of male writers also evoke the domestic novel as the backbone of their public political stories. But I've variously argued that in these latter novels domestic relations are used as a strategy to *contain* the male hero's other, public political project of attempting to shape a new world. Whether these novels applaud or dread the new order that their heroes call for, these novels employ domestic relations to manage what is frightening about the new politics. The private, domestic sphere is, in other words, projected as the essential, ahistorical, ideological "ground," the ground not to be explored itself.

As we have also seen, however, the novels by men do in their margins, in their products, reveal that domesticity and a certain view of woman is an ideology. Yet their deconstruction is "unintentional." Furthermore, the men's novels rarely show a woman's other self, the self apart from a man. The novels by women, in contrast, more openly deconstruct domestic relationships and begin to feature women's separate selves.

The women's novels studied here do not, in other words, strategically work to contain the public in the private sphere. Rather, these women writers attempt to recreate or at least interpret differently the domestic sphere in the light of their interest in public life. However unsatisfactory women writers find existing public politics, they do not seek stability in the ideologemes of domesticity and paternalism. These writers, and their characters, try to write themselves *out* of domestic spaces and the romance plot, a plot which often threatens to engulf them, to prevent them from becoming independent, separate selves, fully public political creatures in their own right. The novels do not entirely abandon domestic space or the romance story, but rather interrogate and even subvert it. They truncate (Howell), postpone (Birrell, Dix), or deromanticize (Woolf, Robins) the old romance story and in its place foreground other struggles. By destabilizing and decentering the romance plot, they attack the ideology that marriage and domestic life is a woman's natural and central place.

DuPlessis, focusing on plot, has observed that twentieth-century woman writers have tried to "write beyond" this familiar marriage ending. These turn-of-the-century women's novels, however, write not necessarily "beyond" the ending, in the sense of writing beyond the moment of marriage, probably because historically they do not have other endings yet available. But they do write through the plot into the spaces of a woman's life which marriage cannot fill. This is the space of the "private," separate self, a self that the turn-of-the-century political new woman argues can be developed and sustained only through a transformation of the public body politic itself. The representation of this separate female self is vivid at moments in Dix, even stronger in Robins and most powerful in Woolf. Howell's and Birrell's novels do not overtly represent women's private selves but they do, by centering parts of their plots around single women's lives, point to women as potentially separate.

In all of these women's novels it is, of course, the presence of an active historical political movement, centering on making the private female sphere public and so changing it, which enables the novels' disruption of the ideology of the private sphere. This is the larger historical condition of the women's novels' possibility.

What all these political novels by men and women, taken as a whole, begin to show us is the extraordinary extent to which the "air" of turn-of-the-century England was charged with the threat of domestic upheaval. Although other disruptions, particularly those of class and race, figure as, if not more, prominently in the other histories of the period, the middle-class novel foregrounds gender disruptions. That the male writers contextualize their public political plots within a domestic, private sphere, and that women try to write themselves through, not outside, of this sphere, reveals the extent to which the era's political unconscious needed and desired to work out domestic arrangements. The moment demanded a new balancing of male and female energies, of consciousness, of activity and the like. Each writer, whether male or female, is seeking a foothold. Sometimes this takes the form of a conservative desire, a desire for the reassertion of male dominance over potentially interesting new women (James, Gissing, Shaw, Morris, and Wells). Sometimes the foothold is terror and hatred of the very family itself and of women in particular (Conrad). In the women's texts surfaces not a desire to dominate men, nor a hatred of them, but rather a desire for singleness, for separateness, whether it be escaping to one's own home alone, postponing one's marriage, or burying oneself in political work for women. Both male and female texts, in other words, seem to want, in different ways, to manage an intrusive "other." The intensity of this struggle for management suggests how unknown, fearful, and invasive this other has become.

Turn-of-the-century British political fiction shows the reader that the period's political upheavals were not just about an economic and political reorganization simply in the sense of a redistribution of wealth. These upheavals were also, subtly and profoundly, about a redistribution of power between men and women.

Notes

Chapter 1

1. Both Gareth Stedman Jones's *Outcast London* (sadly, out of print) and Nancy Armstrong's *Desire and Domestic Fiction: A Political History of the Novel* map different aspects of the strategies with which the middle class during the nineteenth century managed poverty and the threat of working-class uprisings. Jones explores the effect the "discovery" of the East End in the late nineteenth century had on disrupting the traditional ideology that charity, or a one-on-one corrective, was viable. Armstrong, whose work focuses on the early and mid 1800s, maps the way the middle class maintained cultural hegemony over working-class attempts at "combination" by targeting an individual's inappropriate home life as the source of both poverty and agitation. In a number of discourses, including the middle-class novel—a chief vehicle for maintaining cultural hegemony—domestic problems and sexual scandal are targeted as the cause of worker agitation.

2. See George Woodcock's *Anarchism*, 439–53, for a succinct discussion of anarchism in England at the turn of the century. Although anarchists here were few in number, the English anarchists, he claims, focused more on art and literature than those in other countries. Some anarchist ideas, in fact, drew the interest of a number of writers (although I think Woodcock stretches his points to include as many writers as possible under the anarchist umbrella). He numbers among them Morris, Oscar Wilde, Edward Carpenter, Olivia and Helen Rossetti, and the young Ford Madox Ford (448). Woodcock feels British artists saw in anarchism the protection for the individual's freedom that they felt was necessary for the production of art. The appeal of the movement to both James and Conrad can perhaps be explained, then, in terms of this cultural movement.

All the accounts I have read of anarchism during this period seem to have different information about the actual activities. Woodcock, for example, claims that no terrorist incident was the work of any anarchist (439). Graham Holderness, in his article "Anarchism and Fiction" (in Gustav Klaus, 1987), claims that all terrorist actions committed during this time were the work of Fenian nationalists. Woodcock, furthermore, locates the source of James's Hyacinth Robinson in Johann Most, whereas Holderness, citing W. H. Tilley, finds James's source in a story, widely reported in *The Times*, about the defecting conspirator.

3. The most authoritative and comprehensive account of the Socialist League branch of the early English socialist movement is found in E. P. Thompson's biography, *William Morris: Romantic to Revolutionary*. Other key accounts which analyze the configurations and positions of the various socialist groups during the era are Paul Thompson's *Socialists, Liberals and Labour: The Struggle for London 1885–1914* (London: Routledge & Kegan Paul, 1967) and Stanley Pierson's *Marxism and the Origins of British Socialism: The Struggle for a New Consciousness*. For an economic and social history of the period, most useful are E. J. Hobsbawm's *Industry and Empire* and Gareth Stedman Jones's *Outcast London: A Study in the Relationship between Classes in Victorian Society*. For a literature-centered discussion of social and cultural history, see both of Raymond Williams's books, *The English Novel From Dickens to Lawrence* and *The Country and the City* (London: Oxford University Press, 1973).

Several analyses of the women's suffrage movement in England have contributed significantly to this study, among them Sheila Rowbotham's *Hidden from History: 300 Years of Women's Oppression and the Fight Against It*; Dawn Morgan's *Suffragists and Liberals* (Oxford: Blackwell, 1975); Olive Banks's *Becoming a Feminist: The Social Origins of "First Wave" Feminism*; David Mitchell's *The Fighting Pankhursts: A Study in Tenacity* (New York: Macmillan, 1967); and Patricia W. Romero's biography, *E. Sylvia Pankhurst: Portrait of a Radical* (New Haven, Conn.: Yale University Press, 1987).

4. For a good, detailed discussion of Booth's procedures and his own contradictory impulses, see Albert Freid and Richard M. Elman's "Introduction" to *Charles Booth's London* (New York: Pantheon, 1968); the book excerpts entries from all three editions of Booth's multi-volume study, *Life and Labour of the People in London*.

5. This list of novels is not, of course, exhaustive. Yet my readings of and about other similar novels written in the period have not convinced me that my generalization about deflection is inaccurate. For a discussion of some of these other, now largely forgotten novels, see especially the essays in Klaus's collection referred to above.

The one better-known novel not read in the present book is Robert Tressell's *The Ragged Trousered Philanthropists* (1914), a novel described by Jack Mitchell (*Robert Tressell and The Ragged Trousered Philanthropists*, London: Lawrence & Wishart, 1969) as the great socialist-realist novel of the time. The novel is rich in its depiction of both the social relations in the building trades and the attempts to organize workers not only for trade unionism but for socialism. Tressell's book has not been included here largely because the present study focuses on the attempt of middle-class writers, addressing a middle-class audience, to negotiate a resolution to the social crisis. I am not convinced that this is Tressell's scene of writing. Also, Tressell's novel is local in its coloring; its social landscape is confined, if intensive. It does not, in other words, attempt to portray the wider public landscape as the novels discussed here gesture toward doing.

6. The mimetic approach to reading the political novel is already becoming, if not already is, a dead horse. Yet, as will become apparent in subsequent notes to the individual chapters, mimesis has generated most of the extant criticism of these novels. Mimesis, briefly, premises an unmediated, or largely unmediated, relationship between the literary text and history. The procedure, generally, is to isolate specific textual signifiers, such as, for example, James's characterization of the political club at the "Sun and Moon," and then compare these signifiers with actual accounts of anarchist clubs. Most, although by no means all, mimetic critics have found turn-of-the-century fictional representations of politics generally inadequate. Some, like Engels, blame both the writer and the "times," as Engels does in his often quoted letter to Margaret Harkness on the publication of her novel, *A City Girl*. Engels first faults Harkness's characterization of the working class "as a passive mass, unable to help itself and not even making any attempt at striving to help itself," but then goes on to say that "nowhere in the civilized world are the working people less actively resistant, more passively submitting to fate . . . than in the East End of London" (*Marx and Engels On Literature and Art*, Lee Baxandall and Stefan Morawski, eds., St. Louis, Mo.: Telos Press, 1973).

The premises of this methodology have been radically called into question by both poststructuralism and neo-Marxism. The literary text is now conceived as a highly mediated production, the privileging of certain textual signifiers over others is radically questioned, and concepts such as "history" and the "actual" now appear as highly problematic, since these always are available to us only in textualized form, and hence themselves are interpretable. To practice mimetic criticism, then, is to privilege one set of texts ("historical" texts) over another ("literary" texts), as well as to dichotomize these two sets of texts and, among other operations, to read "history" or "politics" narrowly from particular kinds of literary signifiers.

7. See William C. Frierson, "The English Controversy Over Realism in Fiction 1885–1895," *Publications of the Modern Language Association*, vol. 43, 1928, 533–50, for a careful tracing and analysis of the debate over Zola.

8. See particularly June Purvis's *Hard Lessons: The Lives and Education of Working-Class Women in Nineteenth-Century England* (Minneapolis, Minn.: University of Minnesota Press, 1989) for a discussion of the ways in which all women were positioned within domestic ideology, although the ideology of femininity differed according to class.

9. The most comprehensive discussion on working-class fiction is P. J. Keating's *The Working Classes in Victorian Fiction*.

10. For discussions of the "new-woman" fiction see especially Penny Boumelha's excellent chapter, "Women and the New Fiction 1880–1900" in her *Thomas Hardy and Women: Sexual Ideology and Narrative Form*. See also Gail Cunningham's *The New Woman and the Victorian Novel*, A. R. Cunningham's "The 'New Woman Fiction' of the 1890s," *Victorian Studies*, vol. 17, 1973, 177–86; and Lloyd Fernando's *"New Woman" in the Late Victorian Novel*, University Park, Pa.: Pennsylvania State University, 1977.

11. Boumelha's book on Hardy is similarly an important work in this field, although it is not specifically Machereyan in its approach, contrary to Moi's assertion. Boumelha, in her introduction, cites the usefulness of Althusser's definition of ideology. Her book dicusses turn-of-the-century sexual ideology, particularly the

impact of Darwinism on concepts of "womanliness" and the influence of the "new woman" fiction cited above. Then she analyzes the relationship between her framing of this ideology and Hardy's shifting, troubled production of women. Not only is the present book theoretically different from Boumelha's in that it closely studies the project/product discontinuity within each text, but it also differs in its larger structure. Rather than producing a narrative of ideology and juxtaposing this with close readings, the present book, outside of providing a few reference points, attempts to focus on novelistic discourse and *from that* infer a "history." This is, it seems to me, what the Althusserian/Machereyan method is all about. It also seems to me the only way we can refuse to be seduced by the mimetic approach in a barely concealed disguise: "matching" the text against some constructed narrative of history drawn from non-literary sources.

In addition to Boumelha's book, which does mention Althusser, another recent essay should be mentioned as belonging to this larger field of related criticisms. This is an essay by Johanna M. Smith, "'Too Beautiful Altogether': Patriarchal Ideology in the *Heart of Darkness*," which appears in a recent collection of critical essays on the novel, Ross C. Murfin, ed., *Heart of Darkness: A Case Study in Contemporary Criticism* (New York: St. Martin's Press, 1989), 179–98. Smith, influenced by Belsey and Eagleton (and so indirectly influenced by Macherey, although she does not acknowledge him), analyzes how the women in this novel function both as a site for Marlow's own patriarchal/imperializing tendencies and as a basis from which the text simultaneously destabilizes patriarchy and imperialism.

Chapter 2

1. See Woodcock, 448–52.
2. Marcia Jacobson (*Henry James and the Mass Market*) argues that this marginalization of radical politics was a result of James's desire to write a more popular novel in *The Princess*. Following the lead of other middle-class writers by exploring the working class, James "shied away from the implications of [its] . . . discovery of working class life. . . . To make political activity more than peripheral to the main story . . . would be to recognize the explosive potential of the exploited working class" (46).
3. Claire Rosenfield's archetypal study of Conrad (*Paradise of Snakes*, Chicago: University of Chicago Press, 1967) observes Winnie's links to this archetypal female.
4. Defending James's knowledgeability about anarchism was a significant critical issue in the 1940s and 1950s. In 1940 Lionel Trilling (*The Liberal Imagination*), who was responsible for reviving interest in this then unpopular novel, praises *The Princess* for being a "brilliantly precise representation of social actuality" (79), full of "startlingly prescient" social observations (66). Oscar Cargill ("*The Princess Casamassima*," *Publications of the Modern Language Association*, vol. 71, March, 1956, 97–117) claims that James learned about anarchism through Turgenev and read widely on the subject. Such critics take their cue partially from James himself, who argued the authenticity of his portrait. Writing to Thomas Sergeant Perry, he says, "I have been all the morning at Millbank Prison (horrible place) collecting notes for a fiction scene. You see I am quite the Naturalist" (quoted in Edel, 147–8).

More recent James criticism, departing from this simpler reflectionist model, focuses on observing the novel as James's record of his own often ambiguous and vague perceptions. Hence, for example, Maxwell Geismar (*Henry James and the Jacobites*, New York: Hill & Wang, 1962) says that the novel reflects all of James's prejudices and fears about anarchism. Trilling himself points out that the novel suggests "that it [present society] may meet its end by violence and that this is not wholly unjust . . . " (59). Edel speaks of *The Princess* representing the predicament of nineteenth-century liberals who desired to change the lot of workers but who hated the violence of revolution. John Lucas ("Conservatism and Revolution in the 1880s," in John Lucas, ed., *Literature and Politics in the Nineteenth Century*, London: Methuen, 1971), criticizing Trilling's assertion of realism in the depiction of the anarchist movement, claims that the novel projects a "baffling vagueness" (208). While he, like others, doesn't go so far as to explore closely the ways the novel reveals its ambivalence toward anarchism, Lucas does say that James knows anarchism can't be accounted for through personal motives even though James tries to do this. Taylor Stoehr ("Words and Deeds in *The Princess Casamassima*," *English Literary History*, vol. 37, March, 1970, 95–135) similarly observes that James's attitude toward anarchism is "ambiguous" (113). And Terry Comito ("Introduction," *The Princess Casamassima*, New York: Thos. Y. Crowell Co., 1976) observes that "the misery on which this society is based and the grace and beauty of its accomplishments, the justice of the revolutionary cause and the meanness of its probable motives, the fatuity of the great and their humanity—all these are seen unblinkingly and held in balance with no 'reconcilement of disparities'" (v). Many of these critics observe James's own consciousness of his ambivalence, citing the letter to T. S. Perry quoted at the opening of Chapter 1. Cargill refers to an article by Newton Arvin ("Henry James and the Almighty Dollar," *Hound and Horn*, vol. 7, April–June, 1934, 434–43) in which Arvin cites letters James wrote indicating he even desired the overthrow of British society (102n).

Conrad criticism has taken similar paths. On the one hand are those critics, such as Eloise Knapp Hay (*The Political Novels of Joseph Conrad*, Chicago: University of Chicago, 1963), who go to great lengths to demonstrate that Conrad's novel "shimmeringly reflects the newspaper attitudes as well as the factual hints" (219). Hay, comparing *The Secret Agent* to *The Princess*, in fact argues that James's theory of revolution is much more vague than Conrad's, although James was far more interested in anarchism than was Conrad. And, while Hay acknowledges James's fascination with anarchism, she maintains that Conrad is "securely confident that the ship of state is not and perhaps never can be seriously threatened" (237).

Other Conrad critics, however, suggest that his novel is not a securely authoritative portrait of anarchism—although they do not then probe the ways the text strives to balance itself. Rosenfield observes of *The Secret Agent*'s "enormous sense of control" that "the very necessity for the control apparent in every line implies a deep sense of commitment and involvement. Where no danger lurks for the author, no verbal guard is necessary" (120), a point also made by Elsa Nettels (*James and Conrad*, 149).

Most Conrad critics, in fact, responding to the novel's extreme decentering practices (its ironic tone, its narrative structure), are bent on affirming some stable center to the novel. H. M. Daleski (*Joseph Conrad: The Way of Dispossession*,

London: Faber & Faber, 1977) claims that the novel, in spite of its extreme irony, posits a norm of "integrity" (170). Or, Avrom Fleishman (*Conrad's Politics: Community and Anarchy in the Fiction of Joseph Conrad*, Baltimore, Md.: Johns Hopkins University Press, 1967) argues that while images of secrecy dominate the novel, the novel nevertheless has a center: it "suggests an ideal of social order by its very representation of a world without order" (212). For some of these critics who see the center in the text (rather than in, say, history), Winnie is the novel's pivot. Daleski attempts to demonstrate that she is in fact the center of the narrative, that her story is parallel to Stevie's story, and that the imagery of self-loss unifies them.

Jonathan Arac ("Romanticism, the Self and the City: *The Secret Agent* in Literary History," *Boundary 2*, Fall, 1980, 75–90), while observing Winnie as the philosophical center of the novel, does not attempt to center the novel. Rather, he explores the novel's difficulty in creating a center in the context of its being an urban novel and so revealing the dif-ficulties the city poses for perception and connection.

Graham McMaster ("Some Other Secrets in *The Secret Agent*," *Literature and History*, vol. 12, no. 2, Autumn, 1986, 229–42) interprets the novel's numerous unanswered questions not as signs of the novel's refusal of politics, but rather as indices of the historical moment as the "ultimate horizon" (229) of the novel. He also observes, in consonance with parts of my argument about Winnie, that she "must be disposed of physically and ideologically to satisfy another [ideologeme]" (240); while her killing Verloc is agreeable to the novel's ideologeme of the rightness of killing a foreign aggressor, it is inimicable to the era's conservative sexual politics.

5. Mark Selzer's reading of *The Princess* (*Henry James and the Art of Power*, Ithaca: Cornell University Press, 1984) is an exception in that he interprets its shifting point of view as an indication of discomfort with "spying" on the lower orders.

6. Hay makes this observation of *The Princess*'s effect when compared with that of *The Secret Agent* (238).

7. Hyacinth is also, of course, an alter ego in other, related senses. Stoehr observes that he is both the man of hasty action and the man who makes a vow and so creates his own reality—types James partly envied. Edel observes Hyacinth is also a double in his capacity as orphan, James being recently "orphaned" by the death of his parents (190). Margaret Scanlan ("Terrorism and the Realistic Novel," *Texas Studies in Language and Literature*, vol. 34, no. 3, Fall, 1992, 380–402) argues that Hyacinth, "striving for originality" and for a "search for a tradition," is a double for James, the writer of a still lowly art genre, the novel (391).

8. Conrad praises extremists in a letter to R. B. Cunninghame Graham (*Joseph Conrad's Letters to R. B. Cunninghame Graham*, Cambridge: Cambridge University Press, 1969) dated 7 October 1907: "At the worst he [the Professor] is a megalomaniac of an extreme type. And every extremist is respectable" (170).

9. See Stoehr's article.

10. Peter Stine ("Conrad's Secrets in *The Secret Agent*," *Conradiana*, vol. 13, no. 2, 1981, 123–40) also observes the misogyny in Conrad's handling of Winnie (130). Conrad's misogynistic treatment of Winnie is by no means an atypical response in this period to women who violated the traditional model of domestic virtue. Bram Dijkstra, in his study of icons of feminine evil in the West at the turn of the century (*Idols of Perversity: Fantasies of Feminine Evil in Fin-de-Siècle Culture*, New York:

Oxford University Press, 1986), observes that such images proliferated at this time as women's political resistance to domination escalated. Dijkstra, in fact, says that this cultural campaign, this "war" against women, facilitated the ideology of Nazi Germany (vii).

Marilyn Stall Fontane ("Joseph Conrad's Secret Agents," *Publications of the Arkansas Philological Association*, vol. 13, no. 1, Spring, 1987, 7–13) also makes the point that Winnie acts as a secret agent within the home. And she observes the particular horror of this: "Winnie, then, as well as Adolf . . . is a secret agent, but it is more hor-rifying that Winnie be one than Adolf because the public has grown used to the idea of political secret agents" (12).

Chapter 3

1. See Pierre Coustiallas's "Introduction" to *Demos* (Sussex: Harvester, 1982) for a discussion of the conditions of publication.

2. See Marcia Jacobson (*Henry James and the Mass Market*) for a discussion of James's relationship with Gissing, as well as with other writers who wrote on the working class.

3. See Jameson's *Political Unconscious*, 186, for a discussion of Gissing's use of Dickens.

4. Given the history of Gissing criticism, one must, however, be careful of introducing biographical material.

The biographical readings of *Demos* take the familiar form of, for example, interpreting the narrator's adoration of Adela as an expression of Gissing's desire, following his divorce from his prostitute wife Nell, for a respectable woman (Robert Selig, *George Gissing*, Boston: Twayne, 1983). John Halperin ("How to Read Gissing" in Jean-Pierre Michaux, ed., *George Gissing: Critical Essays*, London: Vision, 1981, 58–71) goes so far as to say that "to read his books without a detailed knowledge of his biography is to read blind-folded" (58).

More often than not, however, a biographical interpretation of a Gissing novel is introduced to explain what is perceived as a *literary* failure. So even a critic such as Raymond Williams, who tries to read the individual life more largely within the communal life, says that in *Demos* we learn of "*Gissing's* prejudices and difficulties" (*Culture and Society*, New York: Harper & Row, 1958, 175; emphasis added). Jacob Korg (*George Gissing: A Critical Biography*, Seattle, Wash.: The University of Washington Press, 1963) makes the most revealing of such statements. In Gissing's novels, he says, there is always a sense of strain between "*legitimate* narrative interests" and "didactic autobiographical motives" (70; emphasis added).

Not all Gissing criticism is, however, biographical. The most substantial interpretation of *Demos* has been produced by John Goode ("Gissing, Morris, and English Socialism," *Victorian Studies*, vol. 12, December, 1968, 201–26; further references will be to this essay unless otherwise noted). Although Goode wrote a full-length book on Gissing in 1978 (*George Gissing: Ideology and Fiction*) he relies on his earlier article for his reading of *Demos*. Goode's essay is written from within the perspective of Lukácsian mimesis. That is, he matches Gissing's representation and criticism of socialism with other representations in the era. While Goode thereby points to Gissing's inaccuracy in representing socialism and his inadequacy in mounting a conservative attack on it, he does not read this as a sign of Gissing's personal failure but rather of the confused consciousness of the moment. In this way, although Goode's interpretation studies only a portion of Gissing's novel (its confused ideology) and while it suffers from the tendency of all mimetic criticism to make the novel coherent and then judge it for its historical accuracy, his is an example of a judicious mimetic criticism. Following the publication of Goode's essay in *Victorian Studies*, *Demos* became the center of a lively controversy. Alan Lelchuk published an essay in the subsequent issue ("'Demos': The Ordeal of the Two Gissings," 357–74) in which he tries to distinguish Gissing the propagandist from Gissing the novelist. Lelchuk argues that Gissing the novelist makes socialism more appealing than his propagandist narrator desires. Although Lelchuk's reading is not convincingly argued, his point highlights the too rigid character of Goode's analysis. What followed was a debate between Goode and Lelchuk ("Gissing's 'Demos': A Controversy," 431–8). While Goode acknowledges that Gissing has several competing desires in *Demos*, he describes this as a tension that is not rewarding but rather full of "confusion and chaos" (431), suggesting his almost new critical penchant for tension-in-coherence (Goode's subtle commitment to this essentially conservative, coherent, organic definition of art is further evidenced in his reading of Gissing's use of melodrama as only a strategy to sell his novels, not as an important structural part of the novel itself.) Lelchuk's counter-response was a most unfortunate attack on Goode for being a Marxist-socialist interested in judgment rather than in "art," an attack that should be read as characteristic of the spirit of the times.

Other writers mention *Demos* in passing. Adrian Poole, for example (*Gissing in Context*, Totowa, N.J.: Rowman & Littlefield, 1975), says that it is one of Gissing's most important novels "by virtue of its ambitious scope as the dramatization of a total cultural and social crisis" (69). Jameson too only mentions *Demos* briefly in his chapter on Gissing in *The Political Unconscious*, yet his suggestive remarks about Gissing's transformations of the Dickensian narrative paradigms of sentimentality and melodrama and Gissing's ambivalent reliance on the nonpolitical philanthropic model to manage social contradiction are important stimuli of the current essay. Jameson does not dismiss biographical criticism but rather uses it to account for bizarre twists in the plot, moments at which more than the events in the novel seem to "determine" the outcome. And while Jameson reads *Demos* within the context of social history as does Goode, he reads it not as documentary but as a record of contradictory middle-class fantasies about the slums, a contradictoriness he welcomes.

5. Goode observes that Gissing's contemporaries were dissatisfied with his portrait of not only Eldon but all the middle-class characters and criticized him for drifting too close to aestheticism (207). Selig says that George Meredith, then a manuscript reader for Chapman and Hall, "sensed a basic falsity in Gissing's attempts to portray the rich in fiction" and advised Gissing to stick with working-class characters (11).

6. Gayatri Chakravorty Spivak, "Finding Feminist Readings: Dante–Yeats," *Social Text*, Fall, 1980, 73–87.

7. In spite of Paul Sporn's ("Gissing's *Demos*") dismissive remarks about Adela and Stella's implied physical relationship, he accurately reads *Demos*'s representation of marriage as a victimization of women. Gissing sensitively perceives,

says Sporn, that if women are led to marry for money both their characters and their erotic experiences will suffer.

Chapter 4

1. Some of the books that I have found useful on Fabianism are: Deborah Epstein Nord's *The Apprenticeship of Beatrice Webb* (Amherst, Mass.: The University of Massachusetts Press, 1985); Stanley Pierson's *Marxism and the Origins of British Socialism: The Struggle for a New Consciousness*, and A. M. McBriar's *Fabian Socialism and English Politics 1884–1918* (Cambridge: Cambridge University Press, 1966).

2. Quoted in Nord, 204.

3. This is Pierson's interpretation of Shaw's position between 1884 and somewhere around 1886–87 (120–1).

4. At least three contemporary writers on the novels have challenged this trend: Robert Hogan, in "The Novels of Bernard Shaw," *English Literature in Transition 1880–1920, VIII*, Tempe, Ariz.: Arizona State University, 1965, 63–114; John von Behren Rodenbeck, "Alliance and Misalliance: A Critical Study of Bernard Shaw's Novels," dissertation (University of Virginia, 1964); and Richard F. Dietrich, *Portrait of the Artist as a Young Superman*. Dietrich, for example, attempts to make some case for the "intrinsic value" of Shaw's novels. Yet he selects the first, *Immaturity*, as the "best." His criteria are traditional: a plot structure, speeches in keeping with a character, and consistency in characterization. The rest of the novels, in Dietrich's evaluation, "succeed less well"—although they are a "respectable" display of "literary art"—because they are trying to do something new (48).

5. Weintraub, speaking of *An Unsocial Socialist* in his "Introduction" to *An Unfinished Novel* (12) (quoted in Dietrich, 153).

Chapter 5

1. See A. L. Morton's *The English Utopia* (London: Lawrence & Wishart, 1969) for a discussion of turn-of-the-century English utopias which either endorse or condemn socialism.

2. In his essay "Communism" (1893), Morris argues that the working class, if "overtaken by a longing for the change" (231), will hasten the change to the new society. They must, he stresses, "consciously" strive for its realization (231), so intellect is clearly involved, but he repeats often in this essay words like "ardent desire" (229) and "longing," suggesting that other faculties than the intellect are involved.

3. See Darko Suvin's *Metamorphoses of Science Fiction*, 182. Suvin finds this absence of institutions so significant that, working from within a tightly constructed definition of utopia, he argues that *Nowhere* is thereby excluded from the utopian genre. Suvin, rather, places *Nowhere* in the genre of the Earthly Paradise.

4. The text does express some anxiety over this issue. Hammond speaks of those who might be hurt if a vote on which work needs to be done doesn't go their way. These dissenters might choose not to work on a public project. Hammond, however, attempts to gloss over this potentially serious social problem by saying that there is no alternative to Nowhere's simple democracy; everyone must be able to vote, even if the outcome is not unanimous. Guest, here, further probes Hammond's anxiety, suggesting another, more radical alternative—that "every man should be quite independent of every other and thus the tyranny of society should

be abolished" (272). This idea both Guest and Hammond may mean ironically since both "burst out laughing," but then Hammond says, "Yes, yes, I quite agree with you—and so we all do" (272). In other words, Guest/Hammond may briefly be looking to the desirability of greater anarchy in the future. Morris in constructing this novel, however, seems to have stretched his imagination as far as he can in terms of envisioning how communal jobs get agreed upon; it may not, though, be the farthest he would like to go, as Guest's remark suggests.

5. Hammond's ideas here are a curious blend of Engels and Darwin: Engels insofar as he argues that the elimination of private property will resolve "the woman question," Darwin insofar as he argues that women and men have different "instincts" so that there is an essential "womanliness" society cannot touch. Many feminists of the time too, accepting Darwin and appalled at revelations about upper-class men's frequent use of prostitutes, similarly argued for the sanctity of "motherhood." See Penny Boumelha's *Thomas Hardy and Women* for an extensive discussion of the impact of the Darwinian paradigm on notions of "man" and "woman." Also see Elaine Showalter's *A Literature of Their Own* for a discussion of maternal ideology and feminism at the turn of the century.

Morris's focus on individuals-in-concert, versus institutions, is consonant with a statement Morris makes in his essay, "The Society of the Future" (1887). This essay was first delivered in the form of a lecture to the Hammersmith Branch of the Socialist League on the eve of Bloody Sunday, the events of which helped Morris later write the chapter "How the Change Came." Morris says that his ideal is "first of all the freedom and cultivation of the individual will . . . the shaking of the slavish dependence, not on other men, but on artificial systems made to save men manly trouble and responsibility" (192). Earlier in the essay he says that "men in general will feel the obligations of society much more . . . that the necessity for co-operation . . . will be more consciously felt" (189).

6. E. P. Thompson (*William Morris*) says of Morris's portrait of Ellen:

> Into his portrait of Ellen . . . are projected all those qualities he desired to find: and in the suggestion of the emergent relationship between Ellen and the narrator there will be found that tenderness, frank intimacy, comradeship and equal intellectual exchange, which he could envisage between the lovers of the future and yet which he knew he could never achieve in his own life. (169–70)

See also Florence S. Boos and William Boos's essay, "News from Nowhere and Victorian Socialist-Feminism" (*Nineteenth-Century Contexts*, vol. 14, no.1, 1990, 3–32) for a discussion of the socialist-feminist debate in the 1880s and of Morris's relationship to it. They argue that while Morris partially agreed with the socialist-feminist position, he was also less than wholehearted because of "considerations of political expediency and personal acquaintance" (4). Although they, as do I (see my article, "The 'Production' of William Morris's *News from Nowhere*," *the minnesota review*, no. 22, Spring, 1984, 84–104), see conventional aspects of women praised in the novel, they argue that these aspects are on the outside and are residual. They argue for Ellen, in particular, as embodying "something of its [the socialist-feminist ideal's] *inner* consciousness, that sense of harmony with nature . . ."(27). I find this argument problematic because it appears very similar to the conventional notion that woman is already free and transcendent in her inner nature, so that improving her position in the public world is unimportant. Rather than denying the power of the conventionalities in this novel, I argue they trouble it so that the novel makes them visible.

Chapter 6

1. Harkness has only very recently been "rediscovered." Werner Urlaub, whose book came out in Germany in 1977 (see Bibliography), includes Harkness as one of a handful of significant socialist novelists to write at the turn of the century in England. John Goode then wrote a seminal article on her in 1982 ("Margaret Harkness and the Socialist Novel," in Klaus, 1987). Both of these readings of Harkness's novels were, however (in contrast to my reading, a version of which appeared in *Turn-of-the-Century Women*, vol. 1, no. 2, Winter, 1984, 12–26), mimetic in approach; that is, they argued the extent of Harkness's realism. Most recently, again in the mimetic tradition of criticism, Harkness figures prominently in Gerd Bjorhovde's *Rebellious Structures: Women Writers and the Crisis of the Novel 1880–1900* (Oslo: Norwegian University Press, 1987) and her novel *George Eastmont: Wanderer* is discussed in Kiernan Ryan's essay, "Citizens of Centuries to Come: The Ruling-Class Rebel in Socialist Fiction" (in Klaus, 1987). On the historical and biographical fronts, Deborah Nord (*The Apprenticeship of Beatrice Webb*) uncovered much information on Harkness. (Also, see note 4 below.)

2. I have not yet been able to locate information on all of Harkness's publishers. One of them, however, the Author's Cooperative which put out cheap editions, also published materials of the Religious Tract Society (Urlaub, 237–40). There is every reason to expect them to prefer that a female novelist uphold traditional values. Vizetelly (who published Zola and was jailed for it) published *A City Girl*. While there is no reason to think he would shirk from any representation, there was still the issue of what the reader would tolerate.

3. "Speech before the London/National Society for Women's Services," January 21, 1931. Reproduced in *The Pargiters* (New York: HarBrace, 1977), xxxix.

4. The most comprehensive information to date on Margaret Harkness's life has been compiled for an entry in *The Dictionary of Labour Biography* Vol. VIII (Joyce M. Bellamy and John Saville, eds., Clifton, N.J.: A. M. Kelley, 1988, 103–13).

5. See Susan Lanser's *The Narrative Act* (Princeton, N.J.: Princeton University Press, 1981) for further discussion of the terms, "public nar-rator," "textual reader," etc.

6. In Harkness's later writings all that is left of her once radical politics is a slim anti-imperialist thread. In 1907 and 1914 Harkness wrote two books about her travels in India, books which celebrate the humanity of parts of India yet untouched by British cultural influences. She also wrote one interesting novel, set in Ceylon, *The Horoscope* (1914), which is about the tensions between Buddhism and an imperialist British Christianity. Harkness's final novel, *A Curate's Promise* (1921), concerns a curate's decision to join the Salvation Army rather than the army as a chaplain.

7. See Elaine Showalter's *A Literature of Their Own* for a discussion of typical attacks made by women writers of this era on male sexuality.

8. Harkness's blend of Christianity and socialism was historically not at all eccentric. Within a number of the religious sects during this period were groups of

"Christian socialists," people who saw in this path a way of both confronting troubling social questions and of reinvigorating the church, whose membership was declining during this period. See Peter d'A. Jones, *The Christian Socialist Revival 1877–1914* (Princeton, N.J.: Princeton University Press, 1968).

Chapter 7

1. A. R. Cunningham, in "The 'New Woman Fiction' of the 1890s," *Victorian Studies*, vol. 17, 1973, 177–86, observes that interest in the woman question in this period was social rather than political and the fiction followed suit. See also Elaine Showalter's *Sexual Anarchy* for an extended discussion of "new" and "odd" women at the *fin de siècle*.

2. See Sheila Rowbotham's *Women, Resistance and Revolution* for an extended discussion of early socialist theory about women's place in history.

3. Deirdre David, "Ideologies of Patriarchy, Feminism, and Fiction in *The Odd Woman*," *Feminist Studies*, vol. 10, no. 1, Spring, 1984, 117–39. David argues that "the novel's subversion of patriarchy is determined by what it seeks to subvert" (119). So, for example, despite the novel's representation of the possibility of a community of women surviving, it also represents Rhoda and Everard in the pattern of a Victorian sexual relationship and it describes Rhoda and Mary at times in terms of conventional "Victorian myths of female sexuality" (119). David argues that Gissing's novel mythically resolves its contradictions (in Mary's work and the serene liberalism of the family Barfoot eventually marries into), a position with which I cannot agree on theoretical grounds. The novel spills out more than it contains. David also feels that Gissing "wavers between what one might call the novel of patriarchal generation and the novel of feminist celibacy" (121)—again, a reading with which I disagree. There is little in feminist celibacy that he shows interest in. He gazes at it, instead, as a voyeur.

4. I have not chosen to discuss here a novel that is often talked about in the context of radical politics in the era: William E. Tirebuck's *Miss Grace of All Souls* (1895). This novel's focus is somewhat different from these novels which explicitly feature women in relation to socialists or the socialist movement. *Miss Grace* is closer to a late-century version of *North and South*, arguing as it does for a kinder capitalism, with Grace as the mediating angel. When the miners strike, Grace, daughter of a vicar in league with the local mine owners, urges a program of equal pay for equal work (including the owner's work)—in other words, that capitalism is wrong. But when the strike is settled, the old rate is restored, with new owners in place who vow to act differently in the future. The possibility of a more radical change is denied in this novel, and the novel figures no agents (socialists) who could effect such a change.

There are at least two other novels which feature women and socialism, although I have not been able to read them: Clementina Black's *An Agitator* (1894) and Emma Brooke's *Transition* (1895).

5. The source of this information is Brunhild de La Motte's "Radicalism—Feminism—Socialism: The Case of the Woman Novelists," in Klaus, 1987.

6. Ibid.

7. It should be noted here that Dix's novel, in its inclusion of female sensuality, contrasts with another strong trend in women's fiction of the period to deny sexuality in favor of motherhood. Frightened by men's spreading syphilis to innocent women, many feminists shunned such sexuality. See Elaine Showalter, *A Literature of Their Own*, for a fuller discussion of this trend.

8. See Rowbotham's *Women, Resistance and Revolution* and Stanley Pierson's *Marxism and the Origins of British Socialism* for discussions on the New Life movement.

9. Pierson, 103.

10. See Olive Banks's *Becoming a Feminist* for a brief discussion on Owenite socialism and feminism. For a more extensive discussion, see Barbara Taylor, *Eve and the New Jerusalem: Socialism and Feminism in the Nineteenth Century* (London: Virago, 1983).

Chapter 8

1. For example, see: David Mitchell, *The Fighting Pankhursts* (London: Jonathan Cape, 1967); Dawn Morgan, *Suffragists and Liberals. The Politics of Woman Suffrage in England* (Oxford: Blackwell, 1975); Olive Banks, *Becoming a Feminist*; Sheila Rowbotham, *Women, Resistance and Revolution*; Susan Kent, *Sex and Suffrage in Britain 1860–1914* (Princeton, N.J.: Princeton University Press, 1987); and Patricia W. Romero, *E. Sylvia Pankhurst: Portrait of a Radical* (New Haven, Conn.: Yale University Press, 1987.)

2. Showalter, *A Literature of Their Own*, 224. Also see Susan Gibson's unpublished dissertation (see Bibliography) for a discussion of joy in the women's suffrage movement.

3. Gibson observes that most suffrage plots don't include sexual love with the fulfillment of other feminist goals. Banks observes though that historically most women were married, although a large minority was single. Perhaps these plots reveal the married woman's desire to be single again?

4. Gibson observes that many suffragist novels seem to be, near their end, seized with loathing for the action they've set in motion, so they create victims. It's as if the joy that characterizes the movement has to be contained at the end. In *The Convert*, Gibson observes, Vida at the end says, "I'm hurt," while the plot says, "I've conquered." Gibson also observes that perhaps both love and work couldn't yet be imagined for women.

Wendy Mulford ("Socialist-feminist Criticism: A Case Study, Women's Suffrage and Literature, 1906–14," in Peter Widdowson, ed., *Re-Reading English*, London: Methuen, 1982, 179–92) observes a split in the novel between the public plot, which she describes as using a documentary approach, and the personal plot, which relies upon the conventions of romance and melodrama.

Robins's having Vida have an abortion is odd since only one of the leading suffragists Banks studied reported having one. Robins, it appears, uses Vida's abortion to make her appear more odd to her reader, more notorious, and so may be yet another way in which she subtly marginalizes Vida for the reader, if not also making her the object of prurient interest.

5. See Lovat Dickson (*H. G. Wells: His Turbulent Life and Times*, New York: Atheneum, 1969) for a discussion of the publication history and reception of *Ann Veronica.*

6. The biographical circumstances surrounding the writing and publication of *Ann Veronica* also invite such a reading of the novel's conservative project. Wells, then married, was in the middle of being forced to break off a passionate affair with a younger woman, Amber Reeves, who bore him a daughter.

7. Dickson notes that the raid Wells sketches in the novel was based on a real historical event. The protestors raided the House of Commons, in their boldest move to date. Perhaps one explanation for Wells's thin description is his assumption that his readers would be already familiar with the details.

Bibliography

Primary Works

Birrell, Olive. *Love in a Mist*. London: Smith, Elder & Co., 1900.

Clapperton, Jane Hume. *Margaret Dunmore or, A Socialist Home*. London: Swan Sonnenschein, Lowrey & Co., 1888.

Conrad, Joseph. *The Secret Agent*. New York: Doubleday, 1953 (first published 1907).

Dix, Gertrude. *The Image Breakers*. New York: Frederick A. Stokes, 1900.

Gissing, George. *Demos: A Story of English Socialism*. London: Harvester, 1982 (first published 1886).

Harkness, Margaret Elise. *A City Girl*. London: Vizetelly, 1887.

______. *Imperial Credit*. London: Adelaide, 1899.

______. *In Darkest London*. London: William Reeves, 1891.

______. *George Eastmont: Wanderer*. London: Burns & Oates Ltd., 1905.

______. *A Manchester Shirtmaker*. London: Authors' Cooperative Publishing Co., 1890.

______. *Out of Work*. London: Swan Sonnenschein & Co., 1888.

Howell, Constance. *A More Excellent Way*. London: Swan Sonnenschein & Co., 1888.

James, Henry. "The Art of Fiction." *The Portable Henry James*, ed. Morton Dauwen Zabel. New York: Penguin, 1951.

______. *The Princess Casamassima.* New York: Penguin, 1977 (first published 1886).

Morris, William. *Political Writings of William Morris,* ed. A. L Morton. New York: International, 1973.

______. *Three Works by William Morris.* New York: International, 1968 (*News from Nowhere* first published 1888).

Robins, Elizabeth. *The Convert.* Old Westbury, N.Y.: The Feminist Press, 1980 (first published 1907).

Shaw, George Bernard. *An Unsocial Socialist.* New York: Brentano's, 1904.

______. *The Intelligent Woman's Guide to Socialism and Capitalism.* New York: Brentano's, 1928.

Wells, H. G. *Ann Veronica: A Modern Love Story.* New York: Harper & Brothers, 1909.

Woolf, Virginia. *Night and Day.* London: Hogarth, 1977 (first published 1919).

______. *A Room of One's Own.* New York: Harcourt, Brace & World, 1927.

Principal Secondary Works

Althusser, Louis. *For Marx.* New York: Vintage, 1969.

Armstrong, Nancy. *Desire and Domestic Fiction: A Political History of the Novel.* New York: Oxford University Press, 1987.

Bakhtin, Mikhail. *The Dialogic Imagination.* Austin, Tx.: University of Texas Press, 1981.

Banks, Olive. *Becoming a Feminist: The Social Origins of "First Wave" Feminism.* Athens, Ga.: The University of Georgia Press, 1986.

Batchelor, John. *H. G. Wells.* Cambridge: Cambridge University Press, 1985.

Belsey, Catherine. *Critical Practice.* London: Methuen, 1980.

Bentley, Eric. *Bernard Shaw.* New York: W. W. Norton, 1976.

Bodenheimer, Rosemarie. *The Politics of Story in Victorian Social Fiction.* Ithaca, N.Y.: Cornell University Press, 1988.

Boumelha, Penny. *Thomas Hardy and Women: Sexual Ideology and Narrative Form.* London: Harvester, 1982.

Costa, Richard Hauer. *H. G. Wells*. New York: Twayne, 1967.

Cunningham, Gail. *The New Woman and the Victorian Novel*. London: Macmillan, 1978.

Dietrich, R. F. *Portrait of the Artist as a Young Superman*. Gainesville, Fla.: University of Florida Press, 1969.

DuPlessis, Rachel. *Writing Beyond the Ending*. Bloomington, Ind.: Indiana University Press, 1985.

Eagleton, Terry. *Criticism and Ideology*. London: New Left Books, 1976.

Edel, Leon. *Henry James: 1882–1885, The Middle Years*. Philadelphia: Lippincott, 1962.

______, ed. *Henry James and H. G. Wells*. London: Rupert Hart-Davis, 1959.

First, Ruth and Ann Scott. *Olive Schreiner*. New York: Schocken, 1980.

Gallagher, Catherine. *The Industrial Reformation of English Fiction: Social Discourse and Narrative Form, 1832–1867*. Chicago: University of Chicago Press, 1985.

Gibson, Susan. "Love and the Vote: Fiction of the Suffrage Movement in Edwardian England." Unpublished PhD dissertation, University of Massachusetts, 1974.

Goode, John. *George Gissing: Ideology and Fiction*. New York: Barnes & Noble, 1978.

Hobsbawm, Eric J. *Industry and Empire.* London: Penguin, 1968.

Jacobson, Marcia. *Henry James and the Mass Market*. University, Ala.: The University of Alabama Press, 1983.

Jameson, Fredric. *The Political Unconscious*. Ithaca, N.Y.: Cornell University Press, 1981.

Jones, Gareth Stedman. *Outcast London*. London: Penguin, 1971.

Kapp, Yvonne. *Eleanor Marx 2*. New York: Pantheon, 1976.

Keating, P. J. *The Working Classes in Victorian Fiction*. New York: Barnes & Noble, 1971.

Klaus, H. Gustav, ed. *The Rise of Socialist Fiction 1880–1914*. Sussex: Harvester, 1987.

Letters of Olive Schreiner 1876–1920, ed. S. C. Cronwright-Schreiner. Boston: Little Brown, 1924.

Lodge, David. *Language of Fiction*. London: Routledge & Kegan Paul, 1966.

Loewenstein, Fritz E. *The History of a Famous Novel*. London: Folcroft Library Edition, 1973.

Lukács, Georg. *History and Class Consciousness*. Cambridge, Mass.: MIT Press, 1968.

Macherey, Pierre. *A Theory of Literary Production*. Geoffrey Wall (trans.). London: Routledge & Kegan Paul, 1978.

MacKenzie, Norman and Jeanne MacKenzie. *H. G. Wells: A Biography*. New York: Simon & Schuster, 1973.

Marxist-Feminist Literature Collective. "Women's Writing: *Jane Eyre, Shirley, Villette, Aurora Leigh*." *Ideology and Consciousness*, vol. 1, no. 3, Spring, 1978, 27–48.

Massé, Michelle. "Dark Idolatry of Self: Narcissism and the *Bildungsroman* from Goethe through Woolf." Unpublished PhD dissertation, Brown University, 1981.

Moi, Toril. *Sexual/Textual Politics*. London: Methuen, 1985.

Nettels, Elsa. *James and Conrad*. Athens, Ga.: The University of Georgia Press, 1977.

Nord, Deborah Epstein. *The Apprenticeship of Beatrice Webb*. Amherst, Mass.: The University of Massachusetts Press, 1985.

Pierson, Stanley. *Marxism and the Origins of British Socialism: The Struggle for a New Consciousness*. Ithaca, N.Y.: Cornell University Press, 1973.

Roberts, David. *Paternalism in Early Victorian England*. New Brunswick, N.J.: Rutgers University Press, 1979.

Rowbotham, Sheila. *Hidden from History: 300 Years of Women's Oppression and the Fight Against It*. London: Pluto, 1973.

______. *Women, Resistance and Revolution*. New York: Vintage, 1972.

Showalter, Elaine. *A Literature of Their Own*. Princeton, N.J.: Princeton University Press, 1977.

______. *Sexual Anarchy: Gender and Culture at the Fin de Siècle*. New York: Penguin, 1990.

Sporn, Paul. "Gissing's *Demos*: Late Victorian Values and the Displacement of Conjugal Love." *Studies in the Novel*, Fall, 1969, 334–46.

Suvin, Darko. *Metamorphoses of Science Fiction*. New Haven, Conn.: Yale University Press, 1979.

Thompson, Edward P. *William Morris: Romantic to Revolutionary*. London: Merlin, 1955, 1977.

Trilling, Lionel. *The Liberal Imagination*. Garden City, N.Y.: Doubleday, 1950.

Urlaub, Werner G. *Der Spätviktorianische Sozialroman von 1880 bis 1890.* Bonn: Bouvier Verlag Herbert Grundmann, 1977.

Williams, Raymond. *The English Novel from Dickens to Lawrence*. London: Chatto & Windus, 1973.

Woodcock, George. *Anarchism*. Cleveland, Oh.: Meridian, 1962.

Yeats, William Butler. *Autobiography*. New York: Macmillan, 1965.

Index